Studies in Oriental Culture   Number 13
Mei Yao-ch'en and the Development of Early Sung Poetry

Imaginary portrait of Mei Yao-ch'en by Kanō Tanyū, 1641. To the right of the poet is inscribed his name, and above, the text of his poem, *Gold Mountain Temple* (WLC, 8/8a-b). Calligraphy by Ishikawa Jōzan. Copy of damaged original. Shisendō Temple, Kyoto, Japan. (Photograph courtesy Ishikawa Takudō, Chief Priest, Shisendō Temple.)

Mei Yao-ch'en and the Development of Early Sung Poetry

JONATHAN CHAVES

Columbia University Press
New York and London
1976

The Andrew W. Mellon Foundation, through a special grant, has assisted the Press in publishing this volume.

Library of Congress Cataloging in Publication Data

Chaves, Jonathan, 1943–
    Mei Yao-ch'en and the development of early Sung poetry.

    (Studies in Oriental culture; no. 13)
    Bibliography: p.
    Includes index.
    1. Mei, Yao-ch'en, 1002–1060.   2. Chinese poetry—Sung dynasty, 960–1279—History and criticism.   I. Title.   II. Series.
PL2687.M4Z6   895.1'1'4   75-40299
ISBN 0-231-03965-4

For My Mother and Father

PREFACE

For various reasons, Western students of Chinese poetry have tended to devote their attention to a handful of poets. Faced with a huge corpus of unfamiliar material, they have thought it best to limit themselves to the study of those figures who, the Chinese have assured us, are their greatest writers. But this approach, however appropriate in the early years of sinology, no longer appears to be necessary, or even desirable. For one thing, a greater familiarity with the *shih-hua* literature is bringing about the realization that the Chinese themselves often disagreed about the relative merits of individual poets. Still more important is the obvious fact that we are not Chinese living in the T'ang or Sung dynasty. It would hardly be surprising if we discovered that our preferences among the Chinese poets were not always identical with those of the ancient Chinese. Thus, we should feel free to resurrect lesser-known poets whose work seems to have a particular appeal for us today.

Mei Yao-ch'en is one such poet. Although never without his staunch defenders, Mei was attacked by many traditional critics, and was never generally considered to be one of the more important poets. Because Mei is little known even among educated Chinese, a first monograph on him must touch on nearly every aspect of his life and work. The present thesis attempts to do this within the following framework:

Chapter One, *Life,* is a brief sketch of Mei's life, illustrated with poems by Mei.

Chapter Two, *Background,* is an account of developments in Sung poetry prior to Mei.

Chapter Three, *Response,* describes the response of Mei, Ou-yang Hsiu, and their friend Shih Chieh to the influence of the poetic styles dealt with in Chapter II, and identifies the poets to whom Mei turned for inspiration.

Chapter Four, *Theory,* is largely devoted to a discussion of *p'ing-tan,* a key concept for Mei.

Chapter Five, *Practice,* is essentially an anthology of poems by Mei, with notes and commentary. Emphasis is placed on the importance of realism in Mei's most characteristic work.

Particular attention has been given to the translations, as a poet cannot survive in another language unless the translations of his poems are themselves poems.

ACKNOWLEDGMENTS

I AM INDEBTED to the scholars of the Department of East Asian Languages and Cultures at Columbia University who have taught me and encouraged me to pursue the study of Chinese literature. In particular, I should like to mention Professors C. T. Hsia, Burton Watson, William Theodore deBary, Hans Bielenstein, and Donald Keene. Thanks are also due to Mr. Kakehi Fumio of the Research Institute for Humanistic Studies, Kyoto University, whose writings on Mei Yao-ch'en have been invaluable and with whom I had several enlightening conversations on Mei while I was in Japan.

CONTENTS

Mei Yao-ch'en and the Development of Early Sung Poetry

Chapter One

LIFE

THE PERIOD in which Mei Yao-ch'en (*tzu* Sheng-yü; 1002–1060) lived, corresponding to the last twenty years of the reign of Emperor Chen-tsung (r. 997–1022) and to almost the entire reign of Emperor Jen-tsung (r. 1022–1063), is usually described as a time of peace. But the fact that the reign-title (*nien-hao*) was changed no less than nine times while Jen-tsung was on the throne would seem to indicate that all was not well in eleventh-century China. Mei Yao-ch'en's closest friend, the great Ou-yang Hsiu (1007–1072), wrote a brief essay on the reasons for these changes of the reign-title [1] in the course of which reference is made to two enemy states in the north—the Khitan Liao and the Tangut Hsi Hsia—and to famines which at their worst caused the deaths of "eight out of every ten people."

Although an uneasy peace had been negotiated with the Liao in 1004, the Hsi Hsia quickly took their place as a belligerent northern power whose incursions across the border were a constant annoyance. In 1032, the Hsi Hsia leader Chao Yüan-hao proclaimed himself the "Prince of the Hsi Hsia State," and in 1038 promoted himself to the supreme position of "August Emperor of the Great Hsia." This move initiated a series of successful invasions by the Hsi Hsia armies which were only brought to an end by the humiliating treaty of 1044, according to which China had to pay annual tribute to the Tangut state. The poems Mei Yao-ch'en wrote during this period bear eloquent testimony to the hardships endured by the common people when the government drafted local militia to supplement the inadequate army forces, and when the people were compelled to supply the troops with huge amounts of grain which they desperately needed themselves. As if this were not enough, in 1040, at the height of the Hsi Hsia invasions, the province of Honan was struck by floods and swept by a great wind storm. Mei Yao-ch'en, who at this time was Magistrate of Hsiang-ch'eng subprefecture in the center of Honan, wrote poems on all these events. Few "peaceful" periods in history have been so fraught with anxiety and suffering.

The best contemporary source for Mei Yao-ch'en's life is the *Grave Inscription for Mei Sheng-yü—with preface* which was composed by Ou-yang Hsiu.[2] Here we learn that Mei "was a native of Hsüan-ch'eng subprefecture in Hsüan-chou prefecture." Hsüan-ch'eng, in southeastern Anhui, had once been known as Wan-ling, hence Mei's *hao* of Wan-ling Hsien-sheng. The *Nien-p'u* compiled by Chang Shih-tseng in 1336 adds this detail:[3] "His family lived between the Twin Streams of Wan-ling, where the topography is even and level." The *Grave Inscription* says further of the Mei family of Hsüan-ch'eng: "Sheng-yü's great-grandfather was named Yüan [or Ch'ao, according to the text given in the appendix to WLC[4]], and his grandfather was named Mo. Neither of them held official position. [According to Ou-yang's grave inscription for Mei Hsün, however, Mei Mo had been posthumously awarded the title of Vice-Minister of Justice.[5]] His father was named Jang, and held the position of Under-secretary of the Heir Apparent in the Right Secretariat, from which he resigned. He was posthumously awarded the title of Office Chief of the Bureau of Regional Defense." The position temporarily held by Mei Jang, Under-secretary of the Heir Apparent in the Right Secretariat, was a low one (rank 7B) with little prestige.

The *Grave Inscription* continues with a curious statement: "Sheng-yü's mothers were the Lady of Hsien-yu subprefecture, née Shu, and the Lady of Ch'ing-ho subprefecture, née Chang." Hsia Ching-kuan, correcting an error in the 1336 *Nien-p'u*, has interpreted this to mean that the former lady was Mei's father's legitimate wife, and the latter, Mei's actual mother, was a concubine.[6]

Although Mei Jang (959–1049) held a low official position of little importance, his younger brother Mei Hsün (964–1041) rose through the ranks of the bureaucracy to attain the exalted position of Han-lin Academician. As the *Grave Inscription* says, "The family had always been poetically gifted, but only achieved prominence in the world of officialdom with his [Mei Yao-ch'en's] uncle Hsün, and in poetry with Sheng-yü himself." It was Mei Hsün who tried unsuccessfully to convince his elder brother Jang, Mei Yao-ch'en's father, to enter official life. He used his influence to have Jang appointed Undersecretary of the Heir Apparent in the Right Secretariat, but Jang resigned without ever serving.[7] In his grave inscription for Mei Hsün, Ou-yang Hsiu says that he "loved learning and was a man of culture; he especially liked to write poetry." Like Mei Yao-ch'en, Mei Hsün was interested in military affairs. Early in 1002, when the Hsi Hsia troops invaded Ling-chou in Kansu, he volunteered to act as the emperor's envoy to a potential ally. The emperor was impressed, but was reluctant to send Mei Hsün to an embattled region. Mei nevertheless insisted: "If we can keep Ling-chou alive and stop the troops from the west, small matter if we lose one Mei Hsün!" The emperor thereupon agreed to send Mei, but before he reached his destination, Ling-chou had surrendered to the Hsi Hsia troops.

Mei Hsün was also known for his love of fine incense. Ou-yang Hsiu relates that "by nature, he loved to burn incense. While he was working in the office, he would get up every morning and burn two censers before leaving for work. Over these he would spread the sleeves of his official robe, and then pinch the sleeves together. When he had reached the office and settled in his place, he would suddenly open the sleeves. A rich fragrance was thus released, which floated out and filled the entire room."[8]

At an early age, Mei Yao-ch'en left home and traveled in the company of his uncle. The *Nien-p'u* entry for 1016,[9] when Mei was fourteen years old, records this fact, and also notes that Mei "took the *chin-shih* examinations several times." But Mei was not successful, and he was forced to embark on his official career through the "hereditary prerogative" (*yin*) of his uncle. This practice has been described by E. A. Kracke as "unquestionably harmful to the morale of the service as a whole." [10] Already in the eleventh century it was "regarded critically" by such outstanding statesmen as Fan Chung-yen (989–1052) and Ssu-ma Kuang (1019–1086). Like most *yin* nominees, Mei was initially granted the title Sacrificer in the Imperial Temple.

It was probably in 1027, when Mei was twenty-five, that he met the famous poet Lin Pu (967–1028). The significance of this event for Mei's development as a poet will be discussed in the following chapter. In the preceding years, Mei had undoubtedly been pursuing the traditional studies of a young scholar, and mastering the exacting art of Chinese poetry. Lin Pu was the most important man of letters young Mei had met to date, and the meeting made a considerable impression on him.

It was also in 1027 that Mei married the nineteen-year-old daughter of Hsieh T'ao (960/61–1034). By this marriage, Mei was associating himself with one of the most distinguished families of the day. Mei's new brother-in-law, Hsieh Chiang (*tzu* Hsi-shen; 995–1039) was to become a close friend, as were Hsieh's two sons, Hsieh Ching-ch'u (*tzu* Shih-hou; 1020–1084), and Hsieh Ching-wen (*tzu* Shih-chih). All four of the Hsiehs are given biographical accounts in the *Sung shih*, and they were related by marriage to many of the distinguished men of letters of the Northern Sung. Hsieh Chiang's daughter was the wife of Wang An-li, the brother of Wang An-shih (1021–1086). Ching-ch'u's wife was the sister-in-law of Ou-yang Hsiu. Ching-ch'u was also known as a poet, and Huang T'ing-chien (1045–1105) is said to have praised one of his couplets as not being inferior to those of Tu Fu.[11] But perhaps Huang was merely being polite: his wife was Ching-ch'u's daughter. Huang was proud of this connection with Mei Yao-ch'en. In a colophon to one of Mei's poems,[12] he wrote, "Mei Sheng-yü was related to my wife's family."

In 1030, the year in which Ou-yang Hsiu earned his *chin-shih* degree, Mei was appointed to his first real official post, Registrar of

T'ung-ch'eng subprefecture in west-central Anhui, west and south of the Yangtze River. This was the first of a long series of local posts which Mei was to hold. In the following year, 1031, at the age of twenty-nine, Mei became Registrar of Honan City (i.e., Loyang), and thus began one of the most important periods of his life. The Official Left in Charge of the City at this time was Ch'ien Wei-yen (977–1034), one of the chief contributors to the influential Hsi-k'un poetry anthology. Also serving under him, besides Mei himself, were Yin Shu (1001–1047), one of the most influential masters of "ancient style prose," and Ou-yang Hsiu, whom Mei now met for the first time. Mei's brother-in-law Hsieh Chiang was also an important member of the circle. Ou-yang wrote a series of poems in 1031 entitled *Seven Poems on the Seven Friends*.[13] Aside from Ou-yang himself, Mei, and Yin Shu, the group included Chang Ju-shih (*tzu* Yao-fu; 997–1033);[14] Yang Tzu-ts'ung; Chang T'ai-su; and Wang Yüan. In the poem on Mei Yao-ch'en, the earliest reference to Mei in his works, Ou-yang emphasized Mei's poetic talent, which was already considerable: "He uses fragrant plants metaphorically, like the author of the *Li Sao*; / He knows birds and animals, like the poets of the *Odes*." The first half of this couplet alludes to Mei's having been born in the Ch'u region, a fact already noted earlier in the poem. The second line is based on Confucius's famous statement on the uses of the *Book of Odes* (in Waley's translation): "The Master said, Little ones, why is it that none of you study the *Songs*? . . . They will widen your acquaintance with the names of birds, beasts, plants and trees."[15] Already, if only playfully, Ou-yang was associating Mei with the orthodox Confucian tradition of poetry. Next, the influence that Mei's poetry was exerting at even this early date is hyperbolically described by Ou-yang: "Everyone in the city is chanting his poems [literally, "pressing their noses," so as to produce the desired nasal tone while chanting poetry]; / They wish to emulate him, but cannot attain his level."

Mei Yao-ch'en's earliest surviving poetry dates from this period. Many of these early poems describe excursions which Mei took with his friends to the scenic spots around Loyang. A long ancient-style poem quoted in the *Nien-p'u* entry for 1031 [16] was written on

the occasion of one such trip, along the I River between the cliffs of
Dragon Gate, famous for their magnificent caves adorned with
Buddhist sculptures:

ON AN AUTUMN DAY, I TRAVELED TO DRAGON GATE AND FRAGRANT
MOUNTAIN WITH HSI-SHEN [Hsieh Chiang] AND HIS BROTHER(S).
IN THE EVENING WE BOATED ON THE I RIVER. AFTER DRINKING WINE
AND CHANTING POEMS FOR A LONG TIME, EACH OF US COMPOSED AN
ANCIENT-STYLE POEM TO EXPRESS FULLY THE PLEASURE OF THE OCCASION.

The setting sun is beautiful on the stream;
We linger here in our solitary boat.
Beating time on the gunwales, we draw near the mountain pass;
Singing brightly, leave the ferry-head behind.
The rapids are too shallow to navigate;
Pull in the oars, drift with the middle flow!
Cups in hand, we face the greenery;
River birds freely bob and float.
We rinse our feet, rippling the reflected hills,
Pluck water-chestnut round the fragrant isles.
The thousand caves stand silent in evening mist;
The two banks are autumnal with red trees.
A brook trickles thin among the rocks;
A tower seems to tremble beyond the waves.
By the river, limpid as a washed mirror,
A myriad images fill our eyes.
K'ang-lo finds sufficient pleasure here;
Hui-lien also wanders with him now.
Selecting scenes, leaving nothing out,
We wield our poets' brushes without pause.
We are like Yüan-ming in our drunkenness,
Though not Tzu-yu, whose inspiration had an end.
Returning by the quiet fishing weirs,
Walking, we watch the night-fires in the dark.
Dew flowers have begun to drip,
How sad the soughing of the night wind.
If we did not linger past the city curfew
Who would say we loved these nearby hills?

The allusions in lines sixteen and seventeen, and twenty-one and
twenty-two, suggest that already at this time Mei's thoughts often
turned to the Six Dynasties period and its great poets and scholars.
Hsieh Hui-lien (397–433) was the younger cousin of Hsieh Ling-yün

("K'ang-lo," 385–433), and was himself an excellent poet. T'ao Ch'ien ("Yüan-ming," 365–427), introduced here for the first time in Mei's works, was always to be one of his favorite poets. Wang Hui-chih ("Tzu-yu," d. 388), son of the great calligrapher Wang Hsi-chih (321–379), is best known for having returned from a visit to a friend without actually meeting him because his "inspiration came to an end." [17]

During the months Mei spent with his friends in Lo-yang, his "inspiration" seems never to have "come to an end." One of the most frequently visited sites was Mt. Sung to the east of the city, one of the five sacred peaks of China. Mei wrote a series of twelve poems describing one trip to the mountain: *Twelve Poems on Travelling to Mt. Sung with Yung-shu* [Ou-yang Hsiu] *and* [Yang] *Tzu-ts'ung*.[18] One of these, *The Rock of the Three Tipplers*, captures particularly well the untrammeled freedom Mei and his friends experienced during these excursions:

Come together for a trip beyond the world
Three friends drink wine on the immortals' altar rock.
Raised fingers brush against the vaulted sky,
Cool breezes blow along our arms.
All forgotten, the troubles of this dusty life;
Laughing proudly, we're happy here.

Ou-yang Hsiu also wrote a series of twelve identically titled poems.[19] His poem on *The Rock of the Three Tipplers* is accompanied by a prose note that further clarifies the circumstances under which the poem was written:

The Rock of the Three Tipplers is on the Altar of the Eight Immortals. To the south it commands a view of huge cliffs and winding peaks. Green mists and white clouds lie thick below. Here in other-worldly pleasure we drank wine together, sitting on the rock and leaning unsteadily in our intoxication. Mei Sheng-yü wrote the characters "Three Tipplers" on the rock, and the three of us also inscribed our names and had them engraved.

Brushing rock we climb the ancient altar,
Hearts expanded, drink together here.
Clouds and vapors accompany our drunken joy;
Suddenly we have risen above a thousand peaks.

After sitting long, we sober up again
As pine trees start to murmur in the setting sun.

But the happy days at Loyang were not to last long. In 1032, Mei's brother-in-law Hsieh Chiang was appointed Vice-Prefect of Honan City, and because of a stricture against relatives working in the same government office, it became necessary for Mei to leave. His new post was to be Registrar of Ho-yang, a subprefecture to the north-east of Loyang on the north bank of the Yellow River. In the seventh month of the year, Ou-yang Hsiu and some of the other friends held a farewell party for Mei, which Mei describes in a long prose preface to the poems that were written on that occasion: [20]

> When I was about to travel north to Ho-yang, my friend Ou-yang Yung-shu and two or three other gentlemen collected cups and platters and tried to find a beautiful spot where we could enjoy to the fullest a day of pleasure to celebrate my departure. They were able to obtain the use of the Monastery of Universal Light, and there, in the bamboo grove, we strained our wine. Young and old sat around in a circle. Formal banquet etiquette was suspended, and yet no one lost his composure or got out of hand. In harmony we sang together, and our joy seemed to transcend the skies. When our spirits were heightened by the wine, Yung-shu said, "Today's happiness need not yield to that of the ancients. Inspired by a lovely scene, far from the dust of the world, we have spoken of the things in our hearts. But, while the affair has been a success in this respect, we have not yet produced any poems. Let paper be brought forth and the outstanding lines of the great poets of the past written down. These we will place in the center, and each of us will select a line, using each of its words as a rhyme in his own poem. In this way we shall record the excellence of this gathering." At this, all of us said, "Yung-shu's words are correct! If we do not do as he says, future gentlemen will consider us to be no more than mad lovers of wine and meat." In a moment all the poems were completed. We then took our wine cups, reached the height of inebriation, and departed. The next day, the poems were put in order, and I was asked to write this preface.

Shortly after taking up his new position in Ho-yang, Mei had to return to Loyang on official business. At that time, Ou-yang Hsiu wrote a long prose piece entitled, *Preface on Seeing Off Registrar Mei on His Return to Ho-yang*.[21] Ou-yang compares Mei, "hidden in a low official position" in Ho-yang, with a treasure buried in the mountains or in the ocean. But like the treasure, Mei is easily dis-

tinguishable from the vulgar masses by his "exalted will and purity
of conduct." The preface goes on to describe the development of
their friendship:

> I used to wander with him in the region of Mt. Sung and the Lo River.
> Whenever we came upon precipitous peaks or sunken valleys, deep
> woods or ancient temples, we would chant poems together among them.
> At first, we simply enjoyed being together. But with the passage of time,
> a deeper joy seemed to pervade our relationship, until we felt that we
> would never grow weary of each other's company.

Ou-yang was as impressed by Mei's poetry as he was by his personality. Just before Mei left for Ho-yang, Ou-yang asked him for a
draft copy of his poems, and to these he added a long colophon.[22]
The result was the first edition of Mei's poetry. A large portion of
the colophon is devoted to an extended discussion of music. The
point is made that, while it is possible to speak about the technical
aspects of music, even an accomplished musician cannot explain in
words the emotional effect that music has on the listener. The colophon then continues:

> Poetry can be said to be the descendant of music. Su and Li [Su Wu,
> c. 143–60 B.C.; and Li Ling, d. 74 B.C.] of the Han dynasty, and Ts'ao
> and Liu [Ts'ao Chih, 192–232; and Liu Chen, d. 217] of the Wei dynasty
> mastered the method of "correcting the origin." But the poets of the
> (Liu) Sung and Ch'i dynasties and after only mastered the ephemeral
> and superficial aspects of poetry. In the T'ang dynasty, there were such
> poets as Tzu-ang [Ch'en Tzu-ang, 661–702], Li and Tu [Li Po, 701–762;
> and Tu Fu, 712–770], Shen and Sung [Shen Ch'üan-chi'i, d. c.713; and
> Sung Chih-wen, d. c.713], and Wang Wei (700–759). Some of them mas-
> tered a tone which was pure and ancient, bland and calm; others mas-
> tered a measure which was stately and harmonious, exalted and expan-
> sive. And such poets as Meng Chiao (751–814) and Chia Tao
> (c.793–c.865) also mastered a spirit which was grievous and sad, de-
> pressed and withdrawn. After this, there were occasional poets of merit,
> but none was a true master.

In this passage, Ou-yang introduces a view of poetic history
which, with few changes, both he and Mei were to hold throughout
their lives. The orthodox tradition of poetry began with the *Book of
Odes*: the expression "correcting the origin" appears in the *Great
Preface* to the Mao edition of the *Odes*, attributed to Wei Hung

(c.25), where it is said that "The Chou-nan and Shao-nan are the Way for correcting the origin." Su Wu and Li Ling, traditionally considered to have been the originators of the classic five-character metre, carried on this tradition in the Western Han dynasty, as did Ts'ao Chih, and the "Seven Masters of the Chien-an Period," including Liu Chen. In the course of the Six Dynasties, poetry declined, but a revival took place in the early T'ang dynasty at the hands of Ch'en Tzu-ang, Shen Ch'üan-ch'i and Sung Chih-wen. The renaissance reached its peak with Li Po, Tu Fu, and Wang Wei. So far, Ou-yang's ideas are essentially conventional, but he had some original views as well. The phrase "pure and ancient, bland and calm" anticipates the term "even and bland" which Mei Yao-ch'en was going to make his chief criterion of poetic style. Although, as will be shown in a later chapter, there was precedent for describing poetry as "bland," the word was not regularly used in such a context. Nor were Meng Chiao and Chia Tao ordinarily mentioned side by side with such luminaries as Su Wu, Li Ling, Ts'ao Chih, Li Po, Tu Fu, and Wang Wei. And Ou-yang even included Mei Yao-ch'en in this exalted company:

> In modern times, Sheng-yü has also mastered the Way of poetry. His style is based on human emotion, and he is particularly good at depicting natural scenes and creatures. His poems are brilliant and beautiful, refined and correct. They display a hundred different aspects, expansive like spring or bleak like autumn. Reading them, one is by turns happy and sad. One is overjoyed by them, until before one knows it, one is nearly moving one's arms and legs in a rhythmic dance. Truly, he has mastered the art to a profound degree! Is it not precisely because such poetry moves people deeply that I say it shares a common ancestry with music?

Ou-yang, only twenty-five at the time, looked upon his thirty-year-old friend as a teacher of poetry:

> I asked Sheng-yü about poetry. He was able to instruct me and give me pointers on such matters as the proper placement of tones, and defects of diction. But when it came to the mastery of poetry in the heart, there was nothing he could tell me.

Ou-yang was not alone in recognizing Mei's talent as a poet. Ch'ien Wei-yen "particularly admired and appreciated him," ac-

cording to Mei's biography in the *Sung shih*. And, according to the
Grave Inscription, "when he was in Honan [i.e., Loyang], Wang
Wen-k'ang Kung [Wang Shu (963–1034)] saw his writings and ex-
claimed. 'For two hundred years there have not been such works as
these!' " Shen Yüeh (441–513) is reported to have made a similar
comment on the poetry of Hsieh T'iao (464–499).[23]

A recent student of Ou-yang Hsiu has written that "the years at
Loyang turned out to be the most enjoyable of his life. Study and
writing seemed to blend well for him with women, wine, and
song." [24] The same author also states that Ou-yang "perfected his
ability" to write in "the traditional poetic forms," "stimulated by
Mei Yao-ch'en, perhaps the best poet of the time." In a letter sent to
Mei some time after Mei had gone to Ho-yang,[25] Ou-yang already
expressed his nostalgia for the days the friends had spent together:

> Now you are no longer with me. When I remember those days, and try
> to recall the things we did, although not even a year has passed, it all
> seems like a dream. Ho-yang is actually quite near, but it seems as if
> you are thousands of miles away. . . . Since you left, I have written no
> poems, nor have I "echoed" any of the poems you were good enough to
> send me.

Nostalgic references to the "Loyang days" abound in Ou-yang's
later poetry. In a long poem to Mei Yao-ch'en written in 1039,[26] for
example, Ou-yang recalls, "I remember when I first knew you; I
was young, you were at the peak of manhood . . . Our circle of
friends flourished in Loyang. We shared the wine cups and platters
of prime ministers. . . . I was ashamed to be a member of such an
élite literary group, but you were certainly the leader of our poets."

Ten years later, in a poem to another member of the circle, Sun
Tsu-te,[27] Ou-yang writes, "Our Loyang society flourished incompa-
rably in those years; the old men of Loyang boast of it to this day.
But now many of us have died, and the few who survive are lamen-
table in their old age, with decaying teeth and fading hair." A note
to the poem informs us that in addition to Sun, Ou-yang, Mei, and
Chang Ju-shih, the group also included the famous poet Chang
Hsien (990–1078), who was to remain a close friend of Mei's.

Mei Yao-ch'en, too, looked upon the days spent with Ou-yang
Hsiu in Loyang as the happiest period of his life. One of the poems

acknowledged by Ou-yang in the letter quoted earlier is described as "the poem about the dream." This almost certainly refers to a poem which is still preserved in the second *chüan* of Mei's collected works,[28] in which Mei expresses his nostalgia for the period which had just come to an end:

ONE AUTUMN EVENING AT HO-YANG I DREAMED THAT YUNG-SHU AND I TRAV-ELED TOGETHER TO MT. SUNG. WE ESCAPED THE RAIN AT SUMMIT MONASTERY AND COMPOSED SOME VERSES. WHEN I AWOKE I COULD STILL REMEMBER THEM. SOON AFTER, A MESSENGER ARRIVED FROM LOYANG AND TOLD ME THAT YUNG-SHU AND THE OTHER GENTLEMEN HAD ACCOMPANIED HSI-SHEN IN SACRIFICING TO THE MOUNTAIN. I WAS MOVED BY THIS TO WRITE A SHORT POEM.

Asleep at night below the northern casement
With you in dream I sought the green mountains.
Happy together, just as in the past,
Those splendid times became the living present:
Hidden forest, calm in rain and wind;
Ancient temple, deep in clouds and mist.
   (These two lines came to me in my dream)
Putting on my morning clothes, moved to sad reflection,
I joyed again to hear the messenger's news.

The *Nien-p'u* entry for 1032 [29] explains that in the ninth month (Mei had gone to Ho-yang two months earlier), Hsieh Chiang (Hsi-shen) received an imperial commission to offer incense to Mt. Sung. He was accompanied on this occasion by Ou-yang Hsiu, Yang Tzu-ts'ung, Yin Shu, and Wang Yüan. Hsieh sent Mei a long letter in which he described in detail the sights of the mountain. Mei then turned the letter into a hundred-line poem [30] by selecting its salient points, thus demonstrating, as he was often to do in the future, his virtuosity at writing poetry based on material which most poets would have considered to be intractable. Hsieh, duly impressed, wrote a second letter in which he praised Mei's poetic talent: "The likes of us can never hope to enter these realms." [31]

In 1033, Mei was appointed Magistrate of Te-hsing subprefecture in northeastern Chianghsi, east of Lake Po-yang. On his way to Te-hsing, Mei paid a visit to his parents at Hsüan-ch'eng. Ou-yang Hsiu wrote a letter to Mei at this time in which he encouraged him to see the bright side of his trip south: [32]

When you were with me in Loyang, you often said that you wanted to return south to serve your parents at home. Now you will be able to fulfill this desire. As your friend, I feel as if I shared your good fortune. And your place of appointment lies in the region between the Yangtze and Che Rivers, where the mountains and streams are lush and beautiful. What images for the poetry of K'ang-lo [Hsieh Ling-yün]! Who will be able to match you?

The year 1034 brought the deaths of Ch'ien Wei-yen and Mei's father-in-law, Hsieh T'ao. Mei had reached Te-hsing, and was performing his official duties there. In a letter to Mei,[33] Ou-yang, now in the capital, Pien-ching, wrote:

You have always loved the south. Now that you actually live there, are you happy? I occasionally get letters from you, but they are extremely brief and I cannot tell from them what your feelings are. I am also surprised to find that you have not written any poetry for such a long time. I have wondered whether your inspiration has suddenly gone dry.

Chang Shih-tseng quotes this passage in the *Nien-p'u* entry for 1034, and then notes, "If we examine Mei's poetry collection, we find that there are indeed no poems from the Te-hsing period. This is why Ou-yang was surprised." [34]

Mei was transferred to a new post in 1035, this time to become Magistrate of Chien-te subprefecture in southwestern Anhui, just east of the Yangtze River. Mei had a wall constructed around his new office, as the local officials had been taxing the people exorbitantly on the pretext that the hedge which then surrounded the office building was in need of continual repairs. (A poem which he wrote about the new wall will be discussed in chapter 5.) The poems which date from this period suggest that Mei had a number of good friends at Chien-te, and was not entirely unhappy. Here is an example in five-character regulated verse: [35]

ON THE DAY OF THE WINTER SACRIFICE I WENT OUT HUNTING AND VISITED A
TEMPLE ON PLUM MOUNTAIN

My friends and I, three men on horseback,
Gallop by the side of a lonely fort.
Chasing deer, we come to a country temple,
Rest our horses and sit on folding chairs.

The hawks remind me of Chih-tun, who loved them;
My friends recall wild days in Pa-shang.
We return in the approaching twilight,
The stream aglitter with reflected hearth fires.

Hsia Ching-kuan assigns this poem to the Chien-te period, and
suggests that Plum Mountain was in the Chien-te region. He also
quotes a passage from the *Chien-k'ang shih-lu* by the T'ang writer
Hsü Sung which clarifies the allusion in line five: "Chih-tun [a
famous Buddhist monk, 314–366] liked to keep hawks and horses,
but he never sported with the hawks, and never rode the horses.
When someone asked him the reason for this, he replied, 'I love
them for their noble spirit.' " The sixth line of the poem refers to a
place in the area of the T'ang capital Ch'ang-an which was popular
for hunting.

Mei remained at his post in Chien-te throughout 1036. In this
year, he heard news from the capital which must have upset him
considerably. Fan Chung-yen, who at this time held the position of
Scholar Attending to Imperial Edicts in the T'ien-chang Pavilion,
had repeatedly attacked the Prime Minister, Lü I-chien (978–1043)
in his memorials. He was consequently demoted to the office of
Prefect of Jao-chou prefecture on Lake Po-yang in northeastern
Chiangsi, a punishment amounting to exile. When the censor Kao
Jo-no (997–1055) failed to protest this move, Ou-yang Hsiu sent him
a letter taking him to task for his negligence. But Kao used this letter to have Ou-yang exiled to I-ling subprefecture in western
Hupei. Yin Shu and Yü Ching (1000–1064) also publicly supported
Fan, and were sent into exile as well. Mei wrote poems about the
banishment of Ou-yang and Yin. The first of these is translated
here: [36]

ON HEARING THAT OU-YANG HSIU HAS BEEN EXILED TO I-LING
When we both lived in the western capital
You often expressed indignation at the times.
Now you have incurred your sovereign's wrath
By frankly exposing the wrong done to a censor.
You are exiled to the land of the southern barbarians,
There to encounter heavy fog and rain.
The Three Gorges and Yellow Ox are near:
Try not to listen to the apes' mournful cry.

Ou-yang's place of exile was near the Three Gorges of the Yangtze River, and the treacherous Yellow Ox Gorge which is sometimes counted as one of the three. The "mournful cry" of the apes along the gorges was famous for its ability to inspire homesickness in the traveler. The fourth line of the poem refers obliquely to Fan Chung-yen as a "censor," even though Fan did not in fact hold this office. Perhaps Mei means that Fan was functioning as a censor when he criticized Lü I-chien. It is also possible that Mei intends a slight rebuke to Fan for overstepping his position. (An edict issued shortly after these events warned all officials against "overstepping their official positions." [37]) Although Mei could admire the courage it must have taken for Fan to act as he did, he also realized the dangers of the political factionalism to which Fan's action inevitably gave rise. Mei expressed this opinion metaphorically in a number of poems sent to Fan, most notably in his poem, *On Hearing Some Guests at the Home of Fan Jao-chou* [Fan Chung-yen] *Speak of Eating the River-Pig Fish* (fully discussed in chapter 5), written in 1037. At that time, Mei had an opportunity to meet Fan at Ch'ih-chou prefecture on the southern bank of the Yangtze in Anhui. (Fan was on his way to Chen-chiang, where he had been transferred.) The two men got along well, and Fan invited Mei to accompany him on an excursion to Mt. Lu. But their disagreement on the issue of political factionalism was ultimately to lead to the breaking off of friendly relations. This entire sequence of events, and the poems Mei sent to Fan, have been fully discussed in an article by James T. C. Liu,[38] and will therefore not be dealt with in detail here.

In the spring of 1038, the year in which Chao Yüan-hao proclaimed himself August Emperor of the Great Hsia, Mei left his post in Chien-te and set out for the capital, arriving there in the summer. In Pien-ching, Mei again sat for the *chin-shih* examinations, but, to the surprise of his friends, failed to pass. Ou-yang Hsiu wrote a letter to Hsieh Chiang [39] in which he expressed his disappointment:

> The names of the successful examination candidates have been posted, but Sheng-yü's is not to be found among them. Imagine how upset I am! . . . While the fact that Sheng-yü has failed to achieve this empty fame

does not mean he is any less a gifted scholar, it is a pity that of all our old friends, he will have to hold the lowest official position . . . If this is the way they administer the examinations, how will they ever find outstanding men? And can we really admire those who *did* pass?

While in the capital, Mei submitted to the court a poem entitled *A Eulogy of the Wise Virtue of the Dynasty on the Occasion of the Triennial Ancestral Sacrifice*.[40] The poem is typical of this genre, composed entirely in four-character lines modeled on those of the *Book of Odes*, and filled with patriotic hyperbole describing the pomp of the sacrifice. Perhaps as a kind of consolation prize for failing the examinations, Mei was granted an imperial edict of praise for this poem. The edict, the text of which was composed by Ou-yang Hsiu, is preserved in Mei's collection,[41] and reads in part:

> It is hereby proclaimed that the poem on the triennial sacrifice submitted by Mei Yao-ch'en describes the event in question in every particular. His learning is superior and refined; his conduct is virtuous and pure. He is famous for his poetry, and all acknowledge his talent. How much more so, now that he has sung the achievements and virtues of our ancestors, and related the sounds and forms of the ritual. His poem should be set to the music of red-stringed zithers, and performed in the pure temple.

In 1039, Mei received still another local appointment. This time he was to be Magistrate of Hsiang-ch'eng subprefecture on the northern bank of the Ju River in central Honan. He only reached his post in the ninth month, after having spent about ten days with Ou-yang Hsiu in the fifth month. (Ou-yang was now stationed at Ch'ien-te subprefecture to the northwest of Hsiang-yang subprefecture in Hupei.) Mei was traveling together with Hsieh Chiang, who was on his way to his new post in Teng-chou prefecture in southwestern Honan. But in the eleventh month, Hsieh, who had just reached Teng-chou, died. Ou-yang Hsiu visited Mei again at this time, and Mei rode out to welcome him beyond the city walls. The two friends mourned together for Hsieh Chiang. Later Ou-yang sent Mei a letter urging him not to spend too much money on Hsieh's funeral: "It would be no help to Hsieh, and might cause you hardship." [42] Sometime thereafter, Mei left his post at Hsiang-ch'eng, and went to Teng-chou to direct Hsieh's funeral.[43]

In 1039 the newly proclaimed emperor of the Hsi Hsia dynasty, Chao Yüan-hao, began a large-scale invasion of China. Inspired, perhaps, by this event, Mei annotated the military classic, *Sun Tzu*.[44] In a poem written at this time, *Echoing Mr. Li's Poem on Reading My Annotations to Sun Tzu—following his rhymes*,[45] Mei explains that he is a Confucian scholar, and is thus concerned with the annotation of old texts. But while most of these have been adequately dealt with, few writers have turned their attention to military texts. In annotations of this kind, terseness of expression is an important aim: "In wielding my brush, I strove for precise analysis; / I was weary of the prolixity of my predecessors." Mei also insists that his interest in writing annotations to the *Sun Tzu* is essentially literary rather than military; but in another poem written slightly later, *Parting from Yung-shu and Tzu-li* [Lu Ching, a mutual friend of Ou-yang's and Mei's] *at a Farewell Drinking Party*,[46] Mei complains, "We discuss what's wrong with the army, but what good does it do? Everyone says we Confucian scholars know nothing about such things!" Kakehi is certainly correct in saying that Mei annotated the *Sun Tzu* in the hope that he might thereby influence government military policy.[47]

Ou-yang Hsiu did not see the new *Sun Tzu* until 1040, the year following its composition. In a letter to Mei,[48] Ou-yang wrote, "I thirst day and night for a glimpse of your annotated *Sun Tzu*. You have already formally submitted the work. Would you be so kind as to let me see it, too?" Once the book was in his hands, Ou-yang wrote a long colophon to it.[49] In this essay he discusses the relative merits of annotated editions of the Sun Tzu by earlier writers, among them, rather unexpectedly, the T'ang poet Tu Mu (803–852). He comes to the conclusion that "although there have been many annotators of the work (a statement which contradicts Mei's poem), few have hit the mark." Ou-yang goes on to praise the new edition, saying that in the future, Mei's opinions will often prevail over those of the earlier annotators: "He is every inch a Confucian scholar."

Ou-yang was not the only scholar to be impressed by Mei's new work. In 1040, the influential thinker and teacher, Hu Yüan (993–1059), submitted a *Memorial Proposing the Establishment of a*

Military Academy,[50] in which he suggested that Mei Yao-ch'en, whose expertise in military matters had been demonstrated in his annotations to the *Sun Tzu,* and a number of other men be appointed as the faculty of a new military school. The student body would consist of two or three hundred sons of military officials. The proposal met with opposition, however, and was not implemented.

In 1040, the Hsi Hsia invasions were at their height, and the government was forced to draft local militia at the rate of one out of every three able-bodied men. The poems Mei wrote on these events, most notably *The Farmer's Words* and *The Poor Girl of the Ju River Bank* (both discussed in chapter 5) are themselves valuable documents for studying the effects of the Hsi Hsia wars on common men and women. Intensifying the hardships which the people had to endure was a series of floods that swept Honan. One of the rivers that flooded at this time was the Ju, and Mei, who was then Magistrate of Hsiang-ch'eng on the northern bank of the river, had to take charge of the work of sealing the city gates against the flood waters. Mei describes this experience, and the ravages of the flood, in two poems,[51] one of which contains an appropriate reference to the *Autumn Floods* chapter of *Chuang Tzu:*

WATCHING THE FLOOD

> In autumn, during the seventh month of the year Keng-ch'en [1040], the Ju River flooded and overflowed its banks. I personally led the district officials in sealing the gates of the outer city wall with earth. The residents, realizing that danger was near at hand, all built huts in the tree-tops. Anxious and sadly sighing, I wrote this poem.

The autumn floods swell beyond the dikes;
Plains and suburbs, lost in water everywhere.
Our isolated city is sealed with earthen walls;
In the tallest trees, nesting folk appear.
My ears are tired of the bullfrogs' piercing sound.
Bubbles rise in rows where raindrops strike.
The cows cannot be seen from one bank to the other— [52]
Who will sweep away these rainbows and clouds?

AFTER THE GREAT FLOOD THERE WERE OVER A THOUSAND
RUINED COTTAGES. I WROTE A POEM TO BLAME MYSELF.

Though my district is not lacking in morality
Our city walls have been buried in the flood.

Do I dare to speak of a natural disaster?
I must feel ashamed of my bad administration.
The waves have receded, leaving ten thousand broken tiles;
Driftwood hangs stranded in a thousand trees.[53]
Alone here, beset by a hundred woes,
I long to retire to a cloud-filled valley.

The last line of the second poem, "I long to retire to a cloud-filled valley," echoes the final couplet of *The Farmers' Words*; "Rather should I sing *The Homecoming*, / And gather firewood in some secluded valley." In the frustration of not being able to do anything about the barbarian invasions, or about the floods which somehow seemed to be a visitation to punish him for his "bad administration," Mei wondered, as had many Chinese scholar-officials before him in similar circumstances, whether he should follow the example of T'ao Ch'ien, and retire from government service altogether.

Shortly after the floods, Mei did in fact leave his post at Hsiang-ch'eng, and travel to Teng-chou to bury Hsieh Chiang, as we have seen. In the sixth month of the following year (1041), another of Mei's relatives, Mei Hsün, died at Hsü-chou prefecture in central Honan, to the northeast of Hsiang-ch'eng. In this year, Mei was appointed Supervisor of Hu-chou Salt and Commercial Taxes and assigned to Wu-hsing subprefecture, just south of Great Lake in northern Chekiang. He reached Wu-hsing in the third month of 1042, and there followed two relatively uneventful years at his new post. Mei's closest friend during this period was Hu Su (995–1067), the prefect of Hu-chou, and on his death the subject of a grave inscription by Ou-yang Hsiu.[54]

In retrospect, the months spent at Wu-hsing must have seemed an idyll, the calm before the storm. Mei left his post there in the fifth month of 1044, and, after a brief visit to Hsüan-ch'eng, set out for the capital. The events which occurred during the following journey are recorded in detail in a poem written after Mei reached the capital,[55] as well as in several poems of reminiscence, written years later.[56] On the seventh day of the seventh month (August 2, 1044), Mei reached a place called San-kou in Kao-yu subprefecture, on the Grand Canal north of Yang-chou. There his wife suddenly died. Later that month, his baby son also died. "There were no sacks of gold to purchase coffins," Mei wrote, "I had to depend on my friends for the funeral expenses." Having arranged for a temporary gravesite for his wife, Mei resumed his journey, arriving in the capital in the eighth month.

The unusual degree of intimacy that existed between Mei and his wife is revealed in the many poems that he wrote on her death, and in the grave inscription which Ou-yang Hsiu wrote for her at Mei's request.[57] The poems will be discussed in chapter 5. The inscription is translated here: [58]

In the autumn of the fourth year of the *Ch'ing-li* period [1044], my friend Mei Sheng-yü of Wan-ling arrived from Wu-hsing. He showed me some poems he had written lamenting the death of his wife, and said sadly, "My wife, née Hsieh, has passed away." He then asked if I would write a grave inscription for her funeral. At that time I was too busy to meet his request.

In the course of the following year, I received seven or eight letters from him, none of which failed to make some mention of his wife's grave inscription. He wrote,

"My wife was the daughter of the late Chief Counsellor of the Heir Apparent, [Hsieh], T'ao, and the younger sister of Hsi-shen. Both these men, father and son, were famous in their time, and indeed, their ancestors have been prominent for generations. Miss Hsieh was thus born into an illustrious family. At the age of twenty [i.e., nineteen], she was married to me, and now has died after seventeen years of marriage. On the evening of her death, the garments in which her corpse was dressed were the very ones in which she had been married. Such was the degree of our poverty! But she always accepted it without complaint. In managing the household, she maintained perfect order. The eating and drinking utensils, for example, could hardly have been called luxurious, but they were always attractive and in the best of taste. Most of her clothes were old, but these she washed and sewed regularly so that they were clean and never tattered. The official residences we had to live in were mean places indeed, but she always kept the courtyard and rooms immaculately clean, so that they presented a fresh and dignified appearance. In her daily conduct, speech and deportment, she was without exception composed and calm.

"For a long time now I have been frustrated in my worldly ambitions. And yet when I went out, I was fortunate enough to enjoy the company of worthy gentlemen and high officials; and when I came home, I saw how content my wife was, and forgot my anxieties. Thus, if I did not let such matters as wealth or poverty, nobility or low station weigh on my mind, it was because I was helped by my wife.

"Often, while I was speaking with some scholar-official, she would listen secretly from behind a door or a screen. After only a few moments of this, she would be able to hold forth at length on the man's attainments, and to discuss in logical sequence the vicissitudes of contemporary affairs. While I was in office in Wu-hsing, I would sometimes come home drunk. On such occasions, she would always ask, 'With whom have you been drinking so happily tonight?' If the man I named was a worthy gentleman, she would be pleased. But if he was not, she would sigh and say, 'Your friends are all worthies of our time. How can you lower yourself like this? Relationships must be based on the Way. Thus there will be very few men deserving of your friendship. Could you really enjoy yourself drinking with such a fellow as this?'

"This year there was a great drought in the south. She looked up at the sky, saw the locusts flying there, and said with a sigh, 'The troops from the west [i.e., the Hsi Hsia] have still not dispersed. The country is enduring tremendous hardships. Robbers and rebels have been rampaging between the Huai and Yangtze Rivers. And now we have a drought and locusts as well. Under such conditions, I will consider myself lucky to be buried by you as your wife.' These are only a few of the many ways in which she demonstrated her willingness to live a life of poverty without complaining, and showed her innate intelligence and sense of morality.

"Alas! During her life she had to endure the poverty I imposed upon her. And now that she is dead, I haven't the means to give her a handsome burial. I feel now that the only way to make manifest her undying virtues is through literature. During her life, she knew that literature was of great value. If you were to write her grave inscription, her spirit would be consoled, and my own grief mitigated. It is for these reasons that I am so importunate in making my request."

This being the case, how could I help but write the inscription?

The lady lived to the age of thirty-seven [i.e., thirty-six; her dates are thus 1008–1044]. Because of her husband's official position, she was enfeoffed as the Lady of Nan-yang subprefecture. She gave birth to two sons and a daughter. Her death occurred on the seventh day of the seventh month of the year at Kao-yu. The Mei family have traditionally buried their dead at Wan-ling, but as Mei Yao-ch'en is too poor, he has not been able to send her body there. At a certain time, she was therefore buried at a certain place in Jun-chou prefecture [Chen-chiang in Chiangsu, across the Yangtze from Yang-chou].

The inscription reads:

A tall cliff by a deep valley
Overlooking the plains of Ching-k'ou [Chen-chiang]:
The mountains are green, the waters deep,
The earth is thick and firm.
This is an auspicious burial site,
And so the geomancer approved.
Here her bones and flesh may turn to dust.
But her spirit will surely rise to heaven.
What need is there to bury her back home?
Is it only there that she can be at peace?

According to Ou-yang's text, Mei's first wife "gave birth to two sons and a daughter." The grave inscription for Mei himself has this to say on the matter of his children: "He had five sons: Tseng, Ch'ih, T'ung, Kuei-erh, and one who died as an infant. He had two daughters." Hsia Ching-kuan has stated that the two sons to whom Mei's first wife is said to have given birth were Tseng and Shih-shih, the baby who "died as an infant" less than a month after his mother's death, and that Mei's second wife, née Tiao, gave birth to Ch'ih, T'ung, and Kuei-erh.[59] But the *Nien-p'u* states that the two sons of Mei's first wife were Tseng and Ch'ih, and quotes a gazetteer to the effect that his second wife only gave birth to T'ung and Kuei-erh.[60] The source of what appears to be Hsia's error is probably Ou-yang's statement that the first wife had only two sons. Ou-yang must have meant that she only had two sons who grew to become adults, and he therefore omitted Shih-shih from the final reckoning of her progeny, as does the *Nien-p'u*.

As for Mei's daughters, the elder of these would have been the daughter referred to in the grave inscription for his first wife. Of her, Ou-yang writes, "The elder has married the Sacrificer in the Imperial Temple, Hsüeh T'ung." The younger daughter would thus have been the child of Mei's second wife. When Ou-yang wrote Mei's grave inscription, she was "still a child." Again, Ou-yang omits a third daughter, Ch'eng-ch'eng, who was born to Mei's second wife in the tenth month of 1047, but died about five months later.

In the sixth month of 1045, Mei was appointed Signatory Regional Supervisor of Chung-wu Military Prefecture, a post which took him to Hsü-chou in central Honan. Several of Mei's friends and relatives gave a farewell party for him. In the preface to a poem Mei wrote on this occasion,[61] he relates that he was entertained at the "Wang family garden" on the twenty-first day of the sixth month of the year *i-yu* (August 6, 1045) as he was about to leave for Hsü-chou. Among those present were Hsü Yen, the father of the wife of Mei's nephew-in-law Hsieh Ching-ch'u (whose absence from the party is regretted in the fourth couplet of the poem), and Mei's friends Sung Chung-tao, younger brother of the better known Sung Min-ch'iu (1019–1079), and P'ei Yü (d. 1067). Also present were members of the Tiao family:

Retiring by nature, I have few friends;
The ones I have are great men of the realm.
This morning, who has come to see me off?
—My relatives, carrying jars of wine.
Among the companions of my declining years
There are only Hsü and Sung and P'ei.
Master Hsieh alone is missing,
Still not back from his journey home.
We find a famous garden by the river bank,
Moor our boats and linger.
Lovely lotuses greet us with smiles,
Their vermilion cheeks reflected in the stream.
The southern yard is filled with trellised grapes:
Ten thousand clustered nipples bursting from the vine.
All the flowers are tiny jewels;
Reds and purples bow to each other.
In the past, we may have come together
But who cared then if the flowers were blooming or falling?
Done with wine, we go our different ways,
The brilliant sun sinking in the west.
—Now we are separated by city walls;
Facing north, I gaze toward Windy Tower.

Windy Tower, located in the southeast part of K'ai-feng subprefecture, is used here as a synecdoche for the capital which Mei is leaving.

Shortly after beginning his journey to Hsü-chou, Mei learned that Ou-yang Hsiu had lost a daughter. Ou-yang's own poem on his daughter's death is one of his most powerful works.[62] Mei Yao-ch'en, whose personal tragedies of the previous year were still fresh in his memory, was quick to console Ou-yang in a poem of his own: [63]

Last year I lost my wife and son;
You learned of my sorrow and bowed your head.
Now I hear that you have lost your daughter;
Memories press me as I sit by a lonely bank:
How you loved this girl,
So charming when she played below your knees!
She must have been clever as she grew,
Aping her mother, smearing on shadow and rouge.
All your love is in your tears,
Falling in the autumn rain, blown in the wind,
Blown north in the wind, dampening my sleeves:
Only a friend shares happiness and grief.
Long life and early death have always been a mystery;
Heaven is high and hidden; who can control it?
Let the Way take its course and relief will come,
Especially with such a fine son before your eyes!

The last line of this poem may refer to the birth of Ou-yang's son I, which occurred in 1045.

More unhappy news was to follow. In the eighth month of the year, Ou-yang was exiled to Ch'u-chou prefecture in eastern-central Anhui, where he was to remain until early in 1048 when he became Prefect of Yang-chou.

In 1046, after a brief trip to Ju-chou prefecture on the Ju River in Honan to meet Wang Su (1007–1073), Mei returned to the capital. Here he was urged by his friends and relatives to remarry, because his "sons and daughter were still young." [64] Mei agreed, and married the daughter of Tiao Wei. Tiao's brother, Tiao Chan (971–1049) was the father of Hsü Yen's wife. As Hsü Yen was in turn the father of Hsieh Ching-ch'u's wife, Mei was actually marrying a distant relative of his first wife. Tiao Chan's son, Tiao Yüeh was another of Mei's good friends.

On his way back to Hsü-chou, Mei made a long detour and paid a visit to the ex-Prime Minister, Yen Shu (991–1055), now Prefect of Ying-chou in northwest Anhui. The friendship which developed between the two men was to have important consequences for Mei two years later. Mei continued to hold his Hsü-chou office until the

ninth month of the following year (1047), when he again returned to
the capital. It was there, in the tenth month, that his baby daughter
Ch'eng-ch'eng was born, only to die early in 1048.

Mei was deeply affected by his daughter's death, and in addition
to a series of three poems which will be discussed later, wrote *A
Tomb Inscription in Brick for My Little Daughter Ch'eng-ch'eng*.[65]
From this we learn the date of her birth. Mei complains that while
birds, animals, and even ants live for at least a year, his daughter
did not. She was physically perfect: eyes, ears, nose, eyebrows,
mouth, hands and feet were all perfectly formed. As she could not
yet speak, she had not transgressed in speech; as she could not yet
walk, she had never walked in dangerous places; as she drank only
milk, she had not violated any dietary prohibitions. And yet she
died young. All things, Mei concludes, must occur through chance;
nothing is definitely fated. His daughter's soul may disperse in the
great void, or perhaps be reborn in another body. But her physical
substance will surely turn to earth. Even the rich, the noble, and the
long-lived cannot avoid this end.

During this period, two of Mei's best friends built new villas in
their places of exile. In 1046, Ou-yang Hsiu, at the age of forty *sui*,
took the nom-de-plume of Drunken Old Man. Sometime thereafter
he built his Pavilion of the Drunken Old Man in Ch'u-chou, and
wrote his famous *Record of the Pavilion of the Drunken Old Man*.[66]
Mei was impressed by the brilliant use of rhetorical questions in
this prose piece, and introduced the technique into his poem, *Sent
to be Inscribed on the Pavilion of the Drunken Old Man in Ch'u-chou*,[67]
probably written late in 1047:

The stream at the mouth of Lang-yeh valley
Forks in its flow, reflects the mountain colors.
The Prefect loves the clearness of the stream,
And often comes there to sit and drink wine.
When he is drunk, his hat-strings dangle in the water.
When he is drunk, he chants poems and forgets his grief.
Then at sunset the Prefect returns
And is visited by crowds of rustic scholars.
Only the mountain birds remain
To accompany with their singing the wind in the pines.
May I ask why a hut has been built in this place?

Here it is that the Prefect roams and rests.
May I ask what is meant by "when he is drunk"?
Such are the Prefect's feelings in leisure.
And may I ask what is carved in the stone?
A record of the place by the Prefect himself!
If this is the way he wishes to live
I certainly won't rebuke him in my poem!

The Southern Sung critic Ko Li-fang (d. 1164) was a great admirer of this poem.[68] After quoting lines seven through sixteen, he comments, "This poem is based entirely on the style of the *Record of the Pavilion of the Drunken Old Man* by Ou the eighth [Ou-yang Hsiu]. I feel that the landscape of Ch'u-chou has been made even more radiant by Ou-yang's prose piece, and that this prose piece has been made even more significant by Mei's imitation of it."

Also dating from 1047 is Mei's poem *Sent to be Inscribed On the Ts'ang-lang Pavilion of Su Tzu-mei.*[69] Su Shun-ch'in (1008–1048) was, together with Mei and Ou-yang, one of the three greatest poets of the period. A friendship had developed among the three men over the years. In 1044, Ou-yang worte a long poem praising Su and Mei as poets, and describing what he considered to be the characteristics of their respective styles.[70] In brief, Ou-yang felt that Su's poetry was heroic and untrammeled, while Mei's concealed an inner richness of meaning beneath a surface which was "clean and succinct," "dry and hard" (Watson), and disconcertingly difficult to penetrate. Ou-yang compared his two poet-friends with a pair of phoenixes, "most auspicious of the hundred birds." Shortly after the death of Mei in 1060 (Su had died in 1048), Ou-yang wrote another poem entitled *Memories of the Two Gentlemen,*[71] in which he lamented that the "phoenixes will not sing again. Ever since the two gentlemen, Su and Mei, died, heaven and earth have been desolate; the thunder has ceased to sound . . . Although it is spring, the ten thousand trees do not put forth buds." In the same poem, Ou-yang praises the literary talents of the two poets. They are compared with Li Po and Tu Fu, who also "startled the world, like unicorns or phoenixes."

The first poems sent by Mei to Su date from 1044.[72] Two of the poems which Su sent to Mei in response to these also survive.[73]

One of Mei's poems, *Seeing Off Su Tzu-mei*,[74] is of particular interest, as it refers to Su's exile to Su-chou as a result of one of the most notorious political scandals of the time. In accordance with an old custom, Su and a number of other officials who were sympathetic to the reforms advocated by Fan Chung-yen, including Wang I-jou, sold some old paper money to buy wine and other things, and held a party in the office building of the Memorial Acceptance Bureau as an offering to the gods. In the course of this party, Wang I-jou sang an impromptu song which included the lines, "Drunk, we lie on the North Star, ordering around the emperor and the Buddha; / The Duke of Chou and Confucius we command as our slaves." Wang's indiscretion offered the enemies of Fan Chung-yen a perfect opportunity to attack Fan. A certain Li Ting, a maternal nephew of Yen Shu, had attempted to gain admittance to Su's party on the basis of his uncle's admiration for Mei Yao-ch'en's poetry. When Su refused to invite Li to the party, Li became extremely resentful. He managed to find out about Wang's song, and put this damaging information into the hands of the enemies of Fan Chung-yen. They lost no time in communicating the information to the emperor, and, as they were later able to congratulate themselves, "caught them all with one net." Su, Wang, and all the other participants were banished. Su lost his official position, and was exiled to Su-chou as a mere commoner.[75]

Mei Yao-ch'en was understandably irritated that his name had been dragged into this affair by Li Ting, and he expressed his opinion of Li in a number of poems. One of these, *Random Feelings*,[76] written shortly after the actual event, refers directly to the party: "The host had invited ten guests, all to eat from a cauldron of delicacies. But one guest was not allowed to eat, so he upset the cauldron, harming everyone else." And, although Mei's feelings about Fan Chung-yen's political activities were ambiguous, he clearly expressed his sympathy for Su Shun-ch'in in his seeing-off poem. The poem is loosely based on the *Summons to the Soul*, the *Great Summons*, and the *Summons to a Recluse*, all included in the *Ch'u Tz'u* anthology. As in these poems, the subject (here Su Shun-ch'in) is warned of the dangers he will have to face in the southeast, including the wind-swept waves of the sea, frightful creatures, noxious vapors and the like. Su is then exhorted to return to the northwest, i.e., to the capital, where he can partake of various delicacies. Mei admits that some of the mountains in the south are magnificent, but feels that one cannot spend too much time simply sight-seeing. He hopes that Su will heed his words, and not remain in the south for too long.

But Su was, in fact, to remain in Su-chou, where he arrived in the fourth month of 1045, until his death at the age of forty in 1048. In the eleventh month of that year, he was finally reinstated as an official and appointed Prefect of Hu-chou, but he died only a month later.[77]

When he came to Su-chou, Su knew that his chances of returning to the capital in the near future were slim. He therefore purchased some unused land and built the Ts'ang-lang Pavilion. This name is somewhat misleading; later pictures of the "pavilion" show that it was in fact an extensive villa, with magnificent gardens and winding verandahs.[78] Mei must have realized that the "recluse" he had summoned was most unlikely to return, and in his poem *Sent to be Inscribed on the Ts'ang-lang Pavilion of Su Tzu-mei*, he admitted that Su's new life was perhaps not so bad after all. After describing the amenities of the villa, including the delicacies which were served there, Mei continues, "Formerly, when you first left the capital, I exhorted you not to 'be confused about the ford' [i.e., remain in Su-chou]. I said that one ought not to live in the four directions, that things are pure only in the central region. But now you are enjoying your residence out there, and you are, I must admit, far from the dusty world."

In 1048, the year of Su's death, Mei's own fortunes were finally taking a turn for the better. Early in the year, he was appointed Professor of the Directorate of Education, and was awarded the scarlet robe and silver fish which officials in the fifth and fourth ranks were allowed to wear. The system of official robes and insignia which had originated in the T'ang dynasty continued to be used in the Sung. The fish was originally a fish-shaped tally on which were carved the position and name of the bearer. In the Sung, the tally itself disappeared, and was replaced by the tally-pouch in which it used to be kept, embroidered with a silver or gold fish.

This would hang down in back from the belt of the ceremonial robe. The gold fish was presented to officials of the highest ranks, who wore the purple robe, while the silver fish was presented to officials of the fifth and fourth ranks, who wore the scarlet robe. Mei, finally allowed to wear these prestigious insignia at the age of forty-six, realized that had he passed the examinations, he would have been able to wear them years ago. (He may have reflected that when his uncle, Mei Hsün, was awarded the scarlet robe and silver fish in 1000, he was only thirty-six, ten years younger than Mei.[79]) The irony of the situation is expressed in his poem,[80]

I AM GRANTED THE SCARLET ROBE AND THE FISH

Forty-seven years have stumbled by
And at last the fish hangs at my waist.
But though I should be proud of this madder gown
My hair is thinning and my teeth are loose.
My children are unused to such splendor
And scramble around pulling at my skirts.
I had never known the outer court's pomp
And am shamed by my lord's beneficence.

Similar sentiments had already been expressed by Po Chü-i (772–846) in a poem sent to his friend Yüan Chen (779–831), *On First Wearing the Scarlet Robe—playfully sent to Yüan the Ninth:* [81]

Untalented, I have only reached high rank late in life;
Already I am deteriorating, racked by illness.
Who would have thought that my hair would turn grey
In the year when I first wore the scarlet robe?

Po "first wore the scarlet robe" in 821, when he was forty-nine.

Mei wanted to share his newly received honor with his parents, and in accordance with the usual custom, he and his wife set out for Hsüan-ch'eng to visit them. Mei's trip took him down the Grand Canal, past Kao-yu, where he recalled his first wife's death four years ago, and Yang-chou, where he visited Ou-yang Hsiu. Shortly after his arrival at Hsüan-ch'eng, Mei set out again for Ch'en-chou prefecture in eastern-central Honan where, at the invitation of Yen Shu, the then Prefect, he became Signatory Regional Supervisor of Chen-an Military Prefecture. On his way to Ch'en-chou, Mei was able to pay a second visit to Ou-yang Hsiu at Yang-chou.

Mei took up his new position in the tenth month of 1048, but in the first month of the following year, his father Mei Jang died at the age of ninety, and Mei was obliged to return to Hsüan-ch'eng for the traditional three-year (calendrical) period of mourning. At Mei's request, Ou-yang wrote a grave inscription for his father.[82] Mei remained in mourning until early in 1051. In the fifth month of this year, he returned to the capital. The months at Hsüan-ch'eng passed uneventfully, except for a flood in the fifth month of 1049, about which Mei wrote a poem.

Upon his return to the capital in 1051, Mei was granted the honor of taking the special "decree examinations." According to the grave inscription, "Great officials repeatedly presented him for service in the institutes and archives.[83] Once he was summoned to take the examinations, and presented with a *chin-shih* degree, but aside from this he was not appointed to the institutes and archives." Mei was nevertheless awarded the honorific title, Professor of Imperial Sacrifices.

Kracke has written of the decree examinations that they "were intended to find men qualified for specially difficult work and afford them a means of rising rapidly to a place of responsibility. Since the purpose was to discover new talent, higher officials were not permitted to take them." [84] It is strange that despite his success in the examinations, Mei was in fact not given an important position. Kracke also states that after 1029 the examinations were given in the Imperial Archives, and that prior to that they had been held in the Bureau of Academicians. But according to the *Hsü tzu-chih t'ung-chien ch'ang-pien* by Li Tao (1115–1184), Mei was summoned to take the examinations in the Bureau of Academicians.[85] The same source dates the presentation of Mei's degree precisely to the day *keng-shen* of the ninth month of the third year of the Huang-yu period (October 20, 1051).

An embellished and partly erroneous account of these events is found in the *Shao-shih wen-chien lu* by Shao Po (c. 1122): [86]

> During the *Chia-yu* period (1056–1063), various officials at the court repeatedly presented the Professor of the Directorate of Education, Mei Yao-ch'en, for service in the institutes and archives. Emperor Jen-tsung said, "Is that the man who was able to write the couplet, 'One glimpse

of the celestial visage and the ten thousand people are happy; / As we withdraw down the palace avenues, we still hear music in the distance?' '' When the emperor was residing in the Ching-ling palace, Yao-ch'en had written a poem which was somehow transmitted to the inner court. His Majesty liked these two lines, and therefore summoned Yao-ch'en to take the examinations. He was placed in the first class, but still was not appointed to the institutes and archives.

The fact that Shao Po dates these events to the *Chia-yu* period makes it necessary to doubt the veracity of the entire passage. It is true, however, that Mei was beginning to earn a reputation as a poet within the imperial precincts. Writing after Mei's death, Ou-yang Hsiu relates this anecdote: [87]

> The wife of the Assistant Court Commissioner of Military Affairs, Wang Ch'ou, was the daughter of Mei Ting-ch'en [the eldest son of Mei Yao-ch'en's uncle, Mei Hsün]. When Wang was first appointed to his post, his wife went to the Tzu-shou Palace to pay her respects to the Empress Dowager. The Empress Dowager asked the lady about her family, and she replied, "I am the daughter of Mei Ting-ch'en." The Empress Dowager smiled and said, "Is he a relative of Mei Sheng-yü?" It was then realized for the first time that Sheng-yü's name had reached the inner court.
>
> When Sheng-yü was still alive, he was extremely poor. Once I visited him, and he served me a superb wine which one rarely encounters in common homes. When I asked how he had gotten it, he told me that an imperial relative who loved learning had had it sent to him. I have also heard that a certain imperial relative purchased the text of one of Mei's poems for several thousand cash. Such was his fame at that time!

In spite of his newly earned degree, in 1052 Mei was appointed to the relatively unimportant post of Inspector of the Yung-chi Granaries. These granaries were located along the Yung-chi canal in the northern part of the capital. Mei was indignant: "I am not a sparrow or a rat! What am I doing here in this huge granary?" [88] In a long poem to Sung Chung-tao which survives only in the fragmentary Sung edition of Mei's works,[89] after protesting that Sung's talents have not been recognized, Mei goes on to lament his own lot: "I too have met with unfair treatment. When I go out in the morning, I don't even have time to wash! Here I am, slaving away in this obscure granary, fooling around with pints and litres!" In another poem which only survives in the Sung edition,[90] Mei complains, "I'm over fifty years old now, and yet I'm still a minor subofficial. Alas, covered with grime and dust, I run around at my tasks."

The ignominy of Mei's official position was, however, mitigated by his continuing friendships with some of the most distinguished scholars of the day. Mei was seeing a good deal of Liu Ch'ang (1019–1068), one of the first of the Sung antiquarians, and an outstanding collector. Another friend was Ts'ai Hsiang (1012–1067), one of the greatest calligraphers of the Sung dynasty. Chiang Hsiu-fu (1005–1060), an important minor poet, was also a member of this circle. As all three men were particularly interested in art and antiquities, Mei spent many pleasurable hours with them inspecting collections of painting and calligraphy.

In 1053, Mei's mother died, and he returned to Hsüan-ch'eng to mourn for her. There is some confusion as to which of the two mothers named in Ou-yang's grave inscription is involved. Chang Shih-tseng, the author of the *Nien-p'u*, came to the conclusion that the lady Chang was Mei's stepmother, and that it was her death that occurred in 1053.[91] The lady Shu, Mei's real mother, had died before Mei became Registrar of Honan in 1031, that is, before the period of his earliest extant poems, so that there is no mention of her death in Mei's poetry. Hsia Ching-kuan,[92] as we have seen, corrects this error and establishes the fact that Shu, who was in fact Mei's official mother only, died in 1053, and that Mei's real mother, the concubine Chang, was still alive at the time of his death in 1060.

Although Shu was not Mei's real mother, he felt a good deal of affection for her, and wrote two powerful poems on her death. In the first of these, *Held Up at Ning-ling by Wind and Rain—sent to my friends in the capital*,[93] Mei relates how, during a recent visit to his mother, he found her on the point of death. She begged him not to impose on his friends by asking them for a large loan to pay for her funeral. He should not be ashamed of his poverty, she said; only a simple coffin would do. She had no illusions about the state of her health, and warned Mei not to entertain false hopes for her recovery. After her death, Mei did receive contributions toward the funeral expenses from his friends Liu Ch'ang and Li T'ing-lao. P'ei Yü composed the text of her grave inscription, and it was written in seal calligraphy by a certain Yang Yüan-ming.

The second of Mei's poems on the death of his official mother is entitled *Moved by the New Frost*.[94] "Though her coffin is only three inches of dirt away," he writes, "I feel we are separated by ten thousand miles." Mei recalls how his mother sewed clothes for him to protect him from the cold, and cooked for him so that he would not be hungry. Now that she is dead, he cannot bear to put on his robe or swallow his food. These are, of course, conventional sentiments, but Mei expresses them with a simplicity of diction and starkness of imagery that are extremely forceful, and suggest that he was indeed quite close to his official mother.

Mei's friendship with Ou-yang Hsiu continued to be a major source of consolation during this period. Ou-yang had just completed his New History of the Five Dynasties, and he wrote about it to Mei: [95]

> In my leisure I haven't been doing any writing, but I have put the *History of the Five Dynasties* in order. There are seventy-four chapters in all. I have not presumed to let many people know about this work, but I would very much like you, my elder brother, to have a look at it. . . . This is a book which one cannot allow the vulgar to see, but which one must show to a scholar.

The year 1054 and the spring and summer of 1055 were spent uneventfully at Hsüan-ch'eng, as Mei fulfilled the required period of mourning. In the autumn of 1055, he was able to leave for the capital. Early in 1056, during his trip to the capital, he stopped at Ssu-chou prefecture between the Pien and Huai Rivers in northeastern Anhui to visit the Prefect, Chu Piao-ch'en. When he finally reached Pien-ching, Mei was recommended by a group of over ten scholars, led by Ou-yang Hsiu and Chao Kai (996 or 998–1083) for the position of Auxiliary Lecturer of the Directorate of Education. (In 1044, Chao Kai had courageously protested against the banishment of those involved in the Su Shun-ch'in scandal.) The text of the memorial they submitted is quoted by Chang Shih-tseng,[96] and reads in part:

> In vain are we numbered in the ranks of officials; in fact we have not aided the rule of our sage emperor. Although we have known of scholars, we have not presented them. We are thus guilty of "hiding worthy men."
> We humbly perceive that the Professor of Imperial Sacrifices, Mei Yao-

ch'en, is pure of nature and correct in conduct. He joys in the Way and holds to the proper measure. His literary scholarship is superior, and his classical scholarship is enlightened. He is particularly gifted at poetry, and has mastered the orthodox tradition of the *Kuo Feng* and the *Ya*. Although famous in his time, he has not been able to rise in the hierachy through his own efforts.

We note that the staff of the Directorate of Education is lacking two auxiliary lecturers. Yao-ch'en meets the requirements for this position both in his age and in his personal qualifications. We hope he will be appointed Auxiliary Lecturer to help make up the full complement of staff. . . . He will be able to lecture on the classics, and teach the students of the Directorate, singing the wise influence of our dynasty in the schools. Thus he will assist in the splendid educational program of the court.

As a result of the efforts of Ou-yang Hsiu and Chao Kai, Mei was indeed appointed to the staff of the Directorate of Education as an auxiliary lecturer. He was now in the capital to stay, and his home was visited by many of Pien-ching's most distinguished officials. A poem probably dating from 1056 [97] describes one such visit, and the effect it had on the neighbors in the poor area where Mei's poverty still obliged him to live:

THE TWO HAN-LIN ACADEMICIANS OU-YANG YUNG-SHU AND WANG YÜAN-SHU [WANG SHU (997–1057)] AND THE TWO DRAFTING OFFICIALS HAN TZU-HUA [HAN CHIANG (1011/12–1087/88)] AND WU CHANG-WEN [WU K'UEI (1011–1067)] TOGETHER VISITED MY HUMBLE HOME, BUT AS I WAS OUT AT THE TIME, I DID NOT GET TO SEE THEM. THE SEVENTH DAY OF THE TWELFTH MONTH.

My gate is woven of withered bamboo,
No room for carriage or horseman to pass.
And what is worse, like Professor Cheng,
I have no sitting-rugs to offer my guests.
The end of winter, seventh day of the month,
Noble visitors came with jade-bridled steeds.
Their outriders looked splendid in the little alley;
My boy servant was ordered to bring out seats.
The visitors inquired where I had gone;
They all left greetings inscribed on the wall.
My foolish boy has no idea who they were:
Brass insignia, he says, reflected off the floor.
Since I have been honored by distinguished officials,
I regret that I didn't personally sweep up.
The stars again circle high in orbit;

What hope is there that the unicorns will return?
The next-door neighbors huddle together,
Look at each other and sigh to themselves:
"Who would have thought that this gaunt old man
Could attract to his home such important guests?"
Never before have my humble paths
Known the glory of this visit today.

Cheng Ch'ien (d. c.761), to whom the second couplet of this poem refers, was a particularly appropriate figure for Mei to choose. Both men held academic positions (Cheng was Professor of the School of Literature), and both were poor. In a poem sent to Cheng,[98] Tu Fu wrote,

Famous for your talent for thirty years
You still have no sitting-rugs to give your cold guests!

Mei must have recognized here a paradigm of his own case, and he thus based his couplet on Tu Fu's.

In the spring of 1057, Ou-yang Hsiu was one of the officials in charge of the *Chin-shih* examinations. At his behest, Mei was appointed Assistant Examiner. Mei's task, according to an entry in the *Sung hui-yao*,[99] was to correct the examination papers. Writing ten years later, Ou-yang described how the examiners passed the days when they were locked in the examination halls: [100]

> In the second year of the *Chia-yu* period (1057), Han Tzu-hua [Han Chiang], Academician of the Tuan-ming Hall, Wang Yü-yü [Wang Kuei (1019–1085)], Elder Han-lin Academician, Fan Ching-jen [Fan Chen (1007/8–1087/88)], Han-lin Reader-in-waiting, Mei Kung-i [Mei Chih], Academician of the Lung-t'u Pavilion, and myself all held the position of Doctoral Examination Administrator in the Ministry of Rites. Mei Sheng-yü was appointed Assistant Examiner. The six of us were locked into the examination halls for a total of fifty days. During this period we exchanged poetry in both the ancient and regulated styles, producing over one hundred seventy poems. These we put together into a book of three chapters. . . .
>
> Sheng-yü had been a "poet-friend" of mine since the *T'ien-sheng* period (1023–1031). I once sent him a poem on flat-peaches in which I jokingly compared myself and him with Han Yü and Meng Chiao. Thus, during the examinations, Mei sent me a poem in which he said, "Again we enjoy testing the talents of world-famous scholars, / Better than Tung-yeh [Meng Chiao], better than Han [Han Yü]! [101] . . .

The six examiners got along famously, and we would spend the entire day together. Each of us composed long poems with difficult rhymes, which were then answered by the others. Our scribes grew weary from writing them down; boy messengers dashed back and forth. Some of the poems were humorous and mocking, couched in satiric terms. When these were exchanged and rebutted, the entire company would often [102] burst out laughing. We all felt that this was a great event of the times, something that had never been done before.

A number of the poems exchanged by Mei and Ou-yang during these examinations are recorded in their collected works. One of these, Mei's *Don't Climb the Tower!*,[103] became particularly famous, according to a passage in the *Ts'ai K'uan-fu shih-hua*,[104] a work of the first half of the twelfth century which survives only in fragments:

> The *chin-shih* examinations used to be given in the eastern chamber of the "southern department."[105] A magnificent tower was situated nearby in the Ministry of Justice. . . . Often, on the night of the first full moon of the year, the examiners would stealthily climb the tower to view the splendid lanterns along the imperial avenues. . . .
>
> In the *Chia-yu* period, Ou-yang Wen-chung Kung was in charge of the examinations. Mei Sheng-yü wrote the poem *Don't Climb the Tower!* and all the other examiners wrote poems in response. From then on, this became a great tradition in the examination halls of the Ministry of Rites.

Here is Mei's poem:

Don't climb the tower!
Your legs may be strong but you'll strain your eyes.
Horses and oxen are everywhere down there,
Horses proud in saddle and bridle, oxen pulling carriages.
Song and music sound ceaselessly from open pavilions;
Ladies in red sleeve-bands dance to a hundred hourglass drums.
First they perform the *Liu-yao,* then the *Liang-chou;* [106]
Curtained booths line the roads, filled with lovely girls.
Burly servants sport new clothes and rakishly curled mustaches;
They shout and swagger with jeweled whips, protected by noble masters.
Vying in charm and beauty, the girls steal glances at the boys;
Who is flirting with them now, wine-befuddled in the cold?
—My body stays here, propped against a pillar, though my heart's outside:
To see such a splendid festival and not be able to go!

The white-walled office is sunk in silence, the green curtains are still;
I'm chilly under my blue silk blanket as winds go whistling by.
If these are the feelings that come to me,
Why insist on gazing from the tower?

Ou-yang Hsiu's poem "echoing" this one [107] is accompanied by a note explaining, again, that the poems were written on the night of the first full moon (i.e., the night of the lantern festival) while the examiners were supposed to be locked in the examination halls.

Further material on the examinations of 1057 can be gleaned from the *Shih-lin shih-hua* by Yeh Meng-te (1077–1148): [108]

> In the *Chih-ho* and *Chia-yu* periods (1054–1063), candidates in the examination halls wrote in a style which prized novelty and obscurity, and could hardly be read in coherent sentences. Ou-yang Wen-chung Kung devoted his energies to the reform of this decadent practice. When he became an examiner, he rejected all writings which smacked of excessive polishing. At that time, Fan Ching-jen, Wang Yü-yü, Mei Kung-i and others were his colleagues, and Mei Sheng-yü was Assistant Examiner. Before the examinations actually began, these men exchanged a great many poems. Ou-yang's couplet, "Without a sound, the brave soldiers bite down on their gags; / Brushes move on paper with the rustle of spring silkworms munching leaves," was particularly fine. Sheng-yü's couplet, "Ten thousand ants are drunk with battle on the long spring day; / Five stars glitter, deep in the hall at night," [109] was also praised by the other examiners. But when the names of the successful candidates were posted, scholars who were ordinarily highly thought of, like Liu Hui (1030–1065), were not included. These men were naturally resentful, and it was not long before everybody was complaining that the examiners had done nothing but exchange poems, and so did not have the time to read the examination papers carefully. They were also indignant at the "scandalous lines" the examiners had written, "in which they compared themselves to five stars, and us to silkworms and ants!" From this time on, examiners never dared to write poems. [110] This continued to be the case for some thirty years, through the end of the *Yüan feng* period (1078–1085). In the beginning of the *Yüan-yu* period (1086–1093), the tradition was revived, but with nothing like the splendor of the old days.

Despite the complaints of Liu Hui and friends, the results of the 1057 examinations were most impressive. As Yeh Meng-te writes,

> But in these examinations, Su Tzu-chan [Su Shih (1037–1101)] was ranked second highest, and Tzu-yu [Su Ch'e (1039–1112)], Su Shih's

younger brother, and Tseng Tzu-ku [Tseng Kung (1019–1083)] were also
among the successful candidates. It can hardly be claimed that the examiners failed to discover worthy men!

These are, of course, the names of three of the most important figures in Northern Sung literature.

In the *Nien-p'u*, Chang Shih-tseng, quoting from Su Shih's grave
inscription by Su Ch'e, relates how Mei and Ou-yang became interested in him: [111] "At that time, Mei came upon Su Tzu-chan's *Essay
on "Punishments and Rewards as the Ultimate Expression of Loyalty
and Generosity,"* [112] and liked it very much. He immediately
showed it to Ou-yang, who was greatly pleased and wanted to put
Su above all the other candidates." But it was finally decided to
rank him second. In his *Letter to the Auxiliary Lecturer Mei*, [113] Su
describes his feelings on this occasion:

> I had thought that at a time when scholars were concerned only with
> parallelism and tonal regulations in literature, and with seeking the
> emolument of an official position, I would have no chance at all to make
> the acquaintance of such men as you [i.e., Mei and Ou-yang]. Thus I
> lived in the capital for over a year, without getting so much as a peek at
> your gate. In the spring of the present year, scholars from all over the
> country gathered in the Ministry of Rites. You and Mr. Ou-yang were in
> charge of the examinations. To my amazement, I found that I had been
> given the second highest rank. Upon inquiry, I discovered that you had
> liked my writing, considering it to have the spirit of Mencius, and that
> Mr. Ou-yang too had felt it was above the average vulgar literature of
> our times.

Su goes on to praise Mei:

> Your fame fills the land, but your official position is no higher than
> the fifth rank. And yet your facial expression is warm and never angry.
> Your writing is broad and generous, honest and simple, and never re-
> sentful. Thus you must be able to find your joy in the Way. I hope to
> learn about this from you.

Mei showed this letter to Ou-yang Hsiu, and Ou-yang wrote in
response, "As I read Su Shih's letter, before I knew it I was actually
perspiring! How wonderful! We old men will have to step off the
road and allow him to move ahead." [114]

Something of the intimacy that must have developed among the young Su Shih and the two elder men who were his examiners is suggested by this anecdote from Ou-yang Hsiu's *Liu-i shih-hua:* [115]

> The scholar Su Tzu-chan is a native of Shu (Szechwan). Once, at Yü-ching prefecture (north of Ch'ang-ning subprefecture in Szechwan), he bought a bow-cover of native cloth from a barbarian of the southwest. Woven into the cloth was the text of Mei Sheng-yü's poem, *Spring Snow.* [116] This poem is not one of the best in Sheng-yü's collection, but when it was somehow transmitted to the barbarian tribes, they prized it to this extent! Tzu-chan, knowing that I was a particularly good friend of Sheng-yü's, gave me the bow-cover. I also happened to have in my family collection a zither which had been carved by Lei Hui in the third year of the *Pao-li* period (827), that is, some two hundred and fifty years ago. The sound of the instrument is clear and resonant, like striking a bell or musical stone. I used the bow-case given to me by Su as a cover for this zither. The two objects are indeed among my greatest treasures.

Su Shih was to remember Mei Yao-ch'en years after Mei's death. In 1092, in a colophon to a poem by Mei written in Mei's own hand,[117] Su wrote.

> Mei was tall and had bushy eyebrows, large ears, and red cheeks. He could drink over a hundred cups of wine, and still sit bolt upright in a dignified position. Such was the man in his cups! Although I was much younger than Mei, I was lucky enough to be able to associate with him. As I look at this poem of his, written in his own hand, I feel as if I see him again, clapping his hands, smiling and talking.

Su's statement that Mei had large ears is corroborated by a poem in which Mei describes a drinking party at which he and his friends took turns at mocking each other.[118] On this occasion, Mei was dubbed "Big Ears."

Mei was important to Su Shih not only as one of his examiners who first called the attention of Ou-yang Hsiu to his writing, but also as a poet. The great Southern Sung poet Lu Yu (1125–1210), in his *Preface to Mei Sheng-yü's Auxiliary Collection* (dated 1203),[119] wrote, "The Han-lin Academician Su [Su Shih] admired few of the ancients. The only poets whose poems he echoed, following their rhymes, were T'ao Yüan-ming and Mei Yao-ch'en." Unfortunately, most of Su's poems "echoing" originals by Mei appear to be lost. As the Ch'ing scholar Wang Shih-chen (1634–1711) wrote, commenting on this passage, "This means that Su Tung-p'o also wrote

poems echoing Mei's, but none of them are to be found in present
editions of Su's works, nor does anyone seem to know anything
about this matter." Wang appears to have overlooked a poem by Su
entitled *Tree Mountain*, the preface to which relates how Mei Yao-
ch'en had written a poem on a landscape garden owned by Su's father some thirty years ago. Su gives Mei's poem, then one of his
own, following Mei's rhymes.[120]

After the examinations in which Su Shih and Tseng Kung earned
their degrees, Mei wrote a poem called *Seeing Off Tseng Tzu-ku and
Su Shih*,[121] dated 1057 in the *Nien-p'u*.[122] Mei points out that Ch'u,
where Tseng was born (he was a native of Nan-feng subprefecture
in Chiang-hsi), had produced the great Sao poets Ch'ü Yüan
(343–c.290 B.C.) and Sung Yü (c.290–c.223 B.C.), while Su Shih's native Szechwan had produced the Han dynasty poets Ssu-ma
Hsiang-ju (c.179–117 B.C.) and Wang Pao (d. 61 B.C.). The two men,
Mei is sure, will carry on these great traditions: "Now you two
gentlemen are returning home; your fame will surely startle the
vulgar!" Subsequent developments were, of course, to prove Mei
right.

Mei was also among the first to recognize the talents of a third future luminary of Sung literature, Wang An-shih. In 1057, when
Wang was on the point of leaving for his new post as Prefect of
Ch'ang-chou ("P'i-ling" and "Wu" in the poem) in Chiang-su, Mei
wrote the poem, *Seeing Off Wang Chieh-fu* [Wang An-shih]—*on his
Departure to Become Prefect of P'i-ling*.[123] As the poem is of considerable interest in the light of future developmemts in Wang's career,
it will be translated here in its entirety:

The buffaloes of Wu are afraid of heat;
The farmers of Wu fear dried-out fields.
There are trees,
         but their shade wouldn't shelter a calf;
There is water,
         but too little to nourish the grain.
Who thinks of tilling the fields in spring?
They only know the pressure of autumn taxes.
The Prefect hounds the magistrates,
Beard bristling with anger in the audience chamber.
The magistrates oppress the village heads,

Whipping and clubbing them below the hall.
They do not embody the emperor's humanity;
They have no compassion for the folk who run away.
I wonder if any government men
Ever break out of this dreary pattern!
Now you have asked for a local position,
I rejoice that the people will soon revive.
One often sees officials of "two thousand piculs"
As they make preparations to leave the capital:
Saddle-cloths of silk with embroidered hems,
Silver bridles plated with gold;
Soldiers and officials surging forward in the rear,
Swords and whips looking splendid in the vanguard.
But you aren't like this at all;
Your horse has a leather bridle and mud-guards black with dirt.
Proceeding slowly, you inquire about local customs;
Full of humility, you ride an old nag.
Popular opinion never fails to reach you,
Significant points are heeded, trivialities ignored.
Has it ever been your purpose to differ from the mob?
Yet you never follow the world's fashions.
I hear that you have mastered the *Odes:*
Maybe the poem on the sweet pear-tree will apply to you too.

Wang's personal frugality, his interest in reforming local government, and his willingness to listen to the grievances of the people are all depicted here. The last line refers to the ode *Sweet Pear-Tree*,[124] which was believed to have been composed by villagers who wished to praise the enlightened policies of the Duke of Shao.

Mei was also impressed by Wang's writings. He had written a poem entitled *On Reading the Record of the Meng Pavilion by Wang Chieh-fu* several years earlier (probably in 1050 or 1051),[125] and in 1059, the year before his death, Mei echoed Wang's famous *Ballads of Ming-fei,* as did Ou-yang Hsiu, Liu Ch'ang, and Ssu-ma Kuang.[126]

After his arrival in Ch'ang-chou, Wang corresponded with Mei. Mei answered one of his letters in verse, *On Receiving Wang Chieh-fu's Letter from Ch'ang-chou.*[127] Kakehi has deduced from this poem that Wang studied the *Book of Odes* under Mei.[128] In the poem, Mei writes, "You urgently ask about my little commentary on the *Odes;* I have just finished the section on the ode *Fibre Shoes*[129] in the *Kuo*

Feng." This refers to Mei's *A Short Commentary on the Mao Edition of the Odes* in twenty chapters (mentioned in his SS biography), which is no longer extant. Mei goes on to excuse himself for not sending Wang a copy of the work; he will certainly do so in the future.

Like Su Shih, Wang greatly admired Mei as a poet. According to a passage in the fragmentary *Hsi-ch'ing shih-hua* by Ts'ai T'ao (d. 1126),[130] "Once, at a literary gathering, Wang Chieh-fu, Ou-yang Yung-shu, and Mei Sheng-yü all wrote poems on the theme, *A Painting of Tigers*." In the preface to Mei's poetry by Lu Yu which has already been quoted,[131] Lu tells us that Wang considered his own poem to be inferior to Mei's *On a Painting of Tigers by Pao Ting*.[132] Among the poems in which Wang echoes originals by Mei is a series of fifteen on various farm tools.[133]

In the year after the examinations in which Su Shih, Su Ch'e, and Tseng Kung earned their degrees, Ou-yang Hsiu wrote a letter to Han Ch'i (1008–1075), one of the chief statesmen of the day, asking him to recommend Mei for a position in the prestigious "institutes and archives": [134]

> I have noted that the Auxiliary Lecturer of the Directorate of Education, Mr. Mei, is famous for his writing and his personal conduct. I need hardly say that such fame as Mei's will have met with your approval; in fact, I have known this to be the case for some time now. It is the opinion of scholar-officials of both the inner and outer courts that you should recommend Mei for a position in the institutes and archives. If Mei were able to begin his new career under your aegis, this would be one splendid affair. Your presenting him would be a second splendid affair. And if the court were able to benefit from your recommendation, this would be a third splendid affair. Would I risk preventing three splendid affairs by failing to write a single letter? Therefore I have written this one.

But nothing seems to have come of Ou-yang's suggestion.

Another disappointment occurred when Han Chiang proposed that Mei Yao-ch'en be commissioned to compose a new liturgy for the triennial ancestral sacrifice which the emperor was to perform in the imperial temple. Again, nothing happened. According to the *Table of Historians Who Compiled the* [New] *T'ang History* by Ch'ien Ta-hsin (1728–1804),[135] however, in the twelfth month of 1059,

"Yao-ch'en . . . submitted his *Poem on the Triennial Ancestral Sacrifice* and was granted an imperial edict of praise," as he had been for a similar work in 1038. In addition, "he was promoted to the position of Auxiliary Secretary of the Ministry of Justice," on the strength, it is implied, of his poem. But this takes us too far into the future.

Mei was learning to live with his failure to rise appreciably in the official hierarchy. Already in 1057, in one of the poems written to Ou-yang Hsiu during the examinations,[136] Mei had asserted,

The only things I desire in life
Are poetry and wine.
A single day without them and I feel depressed;
Fame and nobility never cross my mind.
The storage jars are empty, the pots cold, but I don't frown;
My wife and children, hungry and cold, are furious with me.
I only want to write and drink, at odds with the world;
There is nothing else that I care to know about.

And in another poem, probably written some two years later,[137] Mei elaborated on this theme: "You have said that I have a natural love for wine, and have also said that I am addicted to poetry. Indeed, if I don't drink for a single day, I feel depressed, and if I don't write for a single day, I feel as if I've accomplished nothing. Wine can relieve my depression, and make me forget riches and high station. In poetry, I want to lead our group, flaunting drums and banners." Yokoyama Iseo takes this last statement to refer to Mei's desire to protest the Hsi Hsia invasions in his poetry, but with the conclusion of a treaty between the Chinese and the Hsi Hsia emperor, Chao Yüan-hao, in 1048, these invasions had ceased to represent a serious threat to Chinese security. It is more likely that Mei is here asserting a desire to devote his energies to the literary, rather than the political, battlefield.

Mei's continuing friendship with Ou-yang Hsiu was another consolation to the aging poet. Ou-yang Hsiu was rising in the hierarchy, and in 1058 was appointed Provisional Prefect of K'ai-feng Prefecture. A visit from the newly promoted Ou-yang is described in

THE HAN-LIN ACADEMICIAN YUNG-SHU PAYS A VISIT [138]

My home is in the eastern quarter,
A hidden neighborhood where carriages rarely pass.
Suddenly the Prefect is announced;
My servants scatter like startled birds.
He enters the door, takes a seat and laughs,
Full cheeks bright with the glow of health.
He asks if I have been eating well:
Making do as always with parched barley and gruel.
He asks if my poetry is coming along:
Still entangled in the dreary old round!
Goosefoot and purslane grow in my garden,
Hardly proper fodder for his thoroughbred horses.
My bottles are empty of thick wine or clear,
So I can't give his people a good drink.
But I'm glad that affairs are less pressing today
And he could pay me a visit, leaving the world behind.
It's not because of pride that I never go out,
But I've had enough nervous bustle.

Still another consolation was the birth of a third son to Mei's wife in 1058, Kuei-erh. In accordance with custom, the baby was ceremonially bathed three days after his birth. Ou-yang Hsiu contributed a poem entitled *The Baby-Washing Song*,[139] explaining in a prose note, "The other day I sent Sheng-yü some wine which helped in the baby-washing. I also wrote this short song for a laugh and have presented it to him." Mei replied to this poem with his *Echoing Yung-shu's Baby-Washing Song—following his rhymes*,[140] in which he alludes to one of the poets of the Han Yü circle, Lu T'ung (d. 835). In a poem *Sent to Lu T'ung*,[141] written in 811, Han had said, "Last year you had a son and named him T'ien-ting" ("One More Boy"). Lu himself wrote a poem entitled *To T'ien-ting*,[142] in which he spoke of himself as an old man whose hair was turning white. The reference to Lu in Mei's poem is particularly appropriate in that Mei and Ou-yang were profoundly interested in the poets of the Han Yü circle. This will be taken up further in chapter 3.

According to the *Grave Inscription*, Mei "once presented his work entitled *T'ang tsai [chi]* in twenty-six chapters,[143] which corrects many of the errors and omissions in the old *T'ang History*. Because of this, he was invited to participate in the compilation of the

[New] T'ang History. The *History* was completed, but he died, aged fifty-nine, before it could be presented." Work on the *New T'ang History* had actually been progressing since its compilation was first ordered in 1045, but Ou-yang Hsiu had only entered the ranks of the compilers in 1054, and now Mei was appointed in 1059.[144] Mei received the news of this honor with typical irony. In his poem, *Following the Rhymes of Wang Ching-i's Poem Congratulating Me on my Appointment to the Committee of Historians*,[145] he wrote, "For nearly fifteen long years they've been researching and discussing, continually refining their work. And now they insist on dragging me in! But I've always been a specialist in the classics!" Mei's wife was also aware of the irony of his new appointment. As Ou-yang wrote several years later,[146]

> Mei Sheng-yü was famous as a poet for thirty years, and yet was never appointed to a position in the institutes. In his old age, he did partici-pate in the compilation of the *[New] T'ang History*, but he died before the work was completed and presented. All of the scholar-officials la-mented his ill luck.
> When Mei was first invited to participate in the compilation of the history, he spoke to his wife about the matter, saying, "My compiling a history is like a monkey crawling into a cloth bag!" To this she replied, "What difference is there between your holding any official position at all, and a catfish climbing a bamboo pole?" All who heard of this consid-ered it to be an excellent reply.

In his *Ch'un-ming sung-chao lu*,[147] Sung Min-ch'iu notes that "in the sixth month of the fifth year of the *Chia-yu* period (1060), the *[New] T'ang History* was completed, but Sheng-yü had died more than a month earlier." Mei's eldest son, Mei Tseng, was appointed to an official position in honor of his father's work on the history.

Earlier in 1059, Mei had received his final official title, Auxiliary Secretary of the Ministry of Justice. An entry in Ou-yang's *Liu-i shih-hua*[148] relates how Liu Ch'ang poked fun at Mei for holding this relatively unimportant position:

> Cheng Ku (d. c.896) was famous as a poet toward the end of the T'ang dynasty. His collected poems are entitled *The Cloud Terrace Edition*, but this book is commonly called *The Poems of Auxiliary Cheng* after his of-ficial position. The poems are extremely interesting and contain many fine lines, although their style is not very exalted. Because they are easy

to understand, people often use them to teach poetry to young children. When I was a child, I also recited them. But recently the collection has not been too popular.

In his later years, Mei Sheng-yü also attained the official position of Auxiliary Secretary of the Ministry of Justice. One day, at a drinking party at my house, Liu Yüan-fu [Liu Ch'ang] poked fun at him, saying, "Sheng-yü's official career will certainly go no further than this." All present were amazed at this statement, but Yüan-fu explained, "Formerly there was 'Auxiliary Cheng.' Now there is Auxiliary Mei!" Sheng-yü became quite dejected at this. Shortly thereafter, he died of an illness. I wrote a preface to his collected poetry, which I called *The Wan-ling Collection*. But people today only refer to it as *The Poems of Auxiliary Mei*. Thus a mere joke has actually come true. What a shame!

Ou-yang's *Grave Inscription for Mei Sheng-yü* opens with a description of the circumstances under which Mei died:

In the fifth year of the *Chia-yu* period (1060), there was a great epidemic in the capital. On the day *i-hai* of the fourth month (May 20, 1060), Sheng-yü became ill and took to bed in the Pien-yang area of the city's eastern quarter. The next day, so many worthy officials of the court went to inquire about his illness that the cries of their escorts continuously filled the streets. People who were marketing in the eastern quarter had to stop: those who were traveling could not move. They all looked at each other with startled expressions and said, "What great man is living in the neighborhood? He attracts so many visitors!"

On the day *kuei-wei* (May 28, 1060), after a period of eight days as an invalid, Sheng-yü died. The worthy officials who then came to offer their condolences were even more numerous than before. Those who had been particularly intimate friends of his came together and consulted about future events [i.e., the burial, etc.]. From the Grand Councillors down, they all consoled his family by contributing toward the funeral expenses. On the day *chia-shen* of the sixth month (July 27, 1060), his son Tseng returned south with his coffin. He was buried the following year on the day *ting-ch'ou* (of the first) month (January 16, 1061), at Shuang-kuei Mountain in Yang-ch'eng-chen in Hsüan-chou.[149]

Some further details are provided by Liu Ch'ang in his Text on Sacrificing to Mei Sheng-yü,[150] which also refers to the death of Chiang Hsiu-fu. Chiang had died on the eighteenth day of the fourth month (May 20, 1060), only eight days before Mei:

Recently, Lin-chi [Chiang Hsiu-fu]'s illness became critical. You called on him, and then withdrew and paid me a visit. Facing each other, we

sighed and lamented. At that time, I noticed that your face was an unusual color, and, taking it upon myself to pronounce a diagnosis, I ad-
vised you to see a doctor. You agreed with me, but you were still uncertain what to do. The next day there was a Great Feast, and people came
from all four directions to offer congratulations. Toasts were drunk to the
emperor's long life; military officials were also present. With the
hundred officials all hurrying to attend, wouldn't it be selfish to stay in
bed at home? So you too were presented with food before the emperor,
fearful that he had been overly generous. It was after this that your
illness really became serious; you lay prostrate in bed, and couldn't get
up. The incompetent doctors were solicitous for your life, but they confused the outside and the inside. You were dehydrated within and dry
without: it was as if you were all consumed by fire. Your condition
became critical and you were beyond help. It all happened so fast!
Morning and evening meant the difference between life and death. I was
shocked and grieved: my cries of sorrow seemed unending. Who would
have thought that within ten days,[151] two such worthy scholars would
have submitted to this illness!

. . . In your literary works, you show your faithfulness to your
friends, and you are praised for this as well as for filial piety in your native province. Yet in your official position you never rose above the
average, and you did not live to an advanced age. When matters come to
such a pass, it is not unfair?

The "unusual color" Liu Ch'ang noticed in Mei's face may also be
referred to in a relevant passage from the *Wen Kung hsü-shih-hua* by
Ssu-ma Kuang: [152]

> At the time of Mei Sheng-yü's death, Sung Hsüan, [*tzu*] Chih-ts'ai,
> Han Tsung-yen, [*tzu*] Ch'in-sheng, Shen Kou, [*tzu*] Wen-t'ung, and my-
> self were all working in the Ministry of Finance, Together we lamented
> Sheng-yü's death. Chih-ts'ai [153] said, "I saw Sheng-yü recently, and his
> face was particularly glistening and lustrous. At the time I took this to be
> a sign of imminent prosperity; little did I know that it was really inaus-
> picious!" It happened that Ch'in-sheng's face was also glistening and
> lustrous. Wen-t'ung pointed to it and said, "Ch'in-sheng is next!" We
> all reprimanded him for this crude joke. A few days later, Ch'in-sheng
> was stricken with illness, and died. I said to Wen-t'ung, "Although you
> did not actually put a curse on his head, it can be said that you killed
> him with a jest."

Mei Yao-ch'en's death was lamented by nearly all the great literati
of the day. Ou-yang Hsiu and Liu Ch'ang, of course, wrote poems
of mourning. Ou-yang's colleague Sung Ch'i (998–1061), who

shared with him the task of compiling the *New T'ang History*, wrote a poem in which he mourned the deaths of Mei and Liu Hsi-sou (1017–1060), a friend of Mei's who also participated in the compilation of the *History*. [154] The poem is entitled, *The Obituary Notices of Mei Sheng-yü and Liu Chung-keng, Scholars in the Office for the Compilation of the History, Have Arrived in Succession, and I Am Moved to Tears.*

Wang An-shih wrote a long poem of lamentation [155] in which he pointed out that neither Li Po nor Tu Fu had attained high official position. But like them, Mei will achieve fame through his poetry: "The tiger and leopard may die, but their patterned skins remain forever." Ssu-ma Kuang wrote two *chüeh-chü* poems on Mei's death, [156] one of which suggests the importance of Mei's poetry for the great generation of poets that was to follow: "What are Sheng-yü's poems to me? A treasure worth more than a thousand coins or pearls, to be handed down to my sons and grandsons!"

Unfortunately, the only account of Mei which attempts to describe his characteristic personality traits is Ou-yang's *Grave Inscription for Mei Sheng-yü*. Ou-yang writes:

> As a person, Sheng-yü was humane, generous, good-natured, and easygoing. He was never intractable in his relations with others. When he desired to satirize or mock because of the angry feelings to which his poverty and sorrow gave rise, he did so in poetry. But this was for his own pleasure, and not out of resentment or hatred. Thus he can be considered a Superior Man.

To this can be added Mei's unusual devotion to the craft of poetry, a point made in several sources. Here, for example, is an anecdote related by Sun Sheng, a member of the "*Yüan-yu* clique," [157] in which Mei's way of working is described: [158]

> Once I was traveling by boat with Tu T'ing-chih [159] and Mei Sheng-yü. We were sailing upstream on the Pien River. I noticed that Sheng-yü was writing poems at the rate of one a day; no one could keep up with him. So I decided to spy on him and find out how he did it. I found that whether lying in bed or eating, or traveling about to see the sights, he would never for a moment stop chanting lines and ruminating. At times he would abruptly withdraw from a party, grab a brush, and jot some-

thing down on a little piece of paper. This he would put in a bamboo container. As we were traveling in the same boat, I was able to examine the container secretly. It turned out to contain poetic phrases, half a couplet or even a single character. He had put in whatever he felt might be useful in some future poem. One of Sheng-yü's poems contains the lines, "In writing poetry, no matter whether past or present, / It is only achieving the 'even and bland' that is difficult." [160] This was one of the couplets I saw in the bamboo container.

Mei's commitment as a poet was probably his most admired quality. Su Shih, the greatest poet of the next generation, held him up as an example in a letter to Ch'en Ch'uan-tao: [161]

I have realized that it is best to practice by writing a poem a day. Even a man with great talent cannot achieve mastery in this art if he does not practice. This is the way Mei Sheng-yü used to work.

Chapter Two
BACKGROUND

IN HIS FAMOUS *Ts'ang-lang shih-hua*, written about 1200, Yen Yü gives short shrift indeed to early Sung poetry:[1]

> At the beginning of the present dynasty, poets still slavishly copied the T'ang masters. Wang Huang-chou [Wang Yü-ch'eng (954–1001)] emulated Po Lo-t'ien [Po Chü-i]; Yang Wen Kung [Yang I (974–1020)] and Liu Chung-shan [Liu Yün (c.1016)] emulated Li Shang-yin (?812–858); Sheng Wen-su [Sheng Tu (d.1041)] emulated Wei Su-chou [Wei Ying-wu (736–c.790)]; Ou-yang Kung [Ou-yang Hsiu] emulated the ancient-style poetry of Han T'ui-chih [Han Yü (768–824]; Mei Sheng-yü emulated the "even and bland" passages in the T'ang poets. It was only with Tung-p'o [Su Shih] and Shan-ku [Huang T'ing-chien] that Sung poets expressed their own ideas in poetry, and the styles of the T'ang poets were transformed.

Later, in his chronological periodization of poetic styles, Yen emphasizes his disdain for early Sung poetry by skipping directly from the "Late T'ang Style" (referring here to poetry written toward the end of the T'ang dynasty only) to the "Style of the present dynasty," a general term for Sung poetry, and then to the "Style of the *Yüan-yu* period (1086–1094)," a term referring to the poetry of Su Shih, Huang T'ing-chien, and their followers, among them Ch'en Shih-tao (1053–1102).[2] Finally, in his breakdown of styles by individual poets, Yen finds it possible to skip directly from the relatively unimportant late T'ang poet Tu Hsün-ho (846–904) to Su

Shih. The only hint in this section that some poetry might have been written in the century and a half separating Tu Hsün-ho and Su Shih is the mention of a "Hsi-k'un Style." This is described as the style of Li Shang-yin, Wen T'ing-yün (fl. mid-ninth century), and Yang I and Liu Yün of the Sung dynasty.[3]

A somewhat more sympathetic account of early Sung poetry is given by the critic Fang Hui (1227–1306). In a prose essay sent to a friend, Fang develops what must have been the most detailed analysis of early Sung poetry available at that time:[4]

> The practice of emulating late T'ang poetry did not begin with the Four Lings.[5] When the Sung swept away the outmoded practices of the Five Dynasties, there arose the Po [Po Chü-i], the K'un [Hsi-k'un], and the Late T'ang styles in poetry.
>
> The Po Style included Li Wen-cheng [Li Fang (925–996)], the Grand Political Counsellor Hsü and his brother [Hsü Hsüan (916–991) and Hsü K'ai (920–974)], Wang Yüan-chih [Wang Yü-ch'eng], and Wang Han-mou.[6]
>
> As for the K'un style, it included the *Hsi-k'un* [*ch'ou-ch'ang*] *chi* of Yang [I] and Liu [Yün] which has been transmitted through the generations, as well as the two Sungs [Sung Hsiang (996–1066) and his younger brother Sung Ch'i], Chang Kuai-ya [Chang Yung (946–1015)], Ch'ien Hsi Kung [Ch'ien Wei-yen], and Ting Ya-chou [Ting Wei (962–1033)].
>
> In the Late T'ang style, the Nine Monks [Hsi-chou, Pao-hsien, Wen-chao, Hsing-chao, Chien-chang, Wei-feng, Hui-ch'ung, Yü-chao, Huai-ku] are most characteristic, while several tens of other poets, such as K'ou Lai Kung [K'ou Chun (961–1014)], Lu San-chiao,[7] Lin Ho-ching [Lin Pu], Wei Chung-hsien and his son [Wei Yeh (960–1018) and Wei Hsien (980–1063)], P'an Hsiao-yao [P'an Lang (c. 1000)], all wrote poetry of considerable richness, full of spirit and extremely forceful.

Fang goes on to speak highly of Ou-yang Hsiu, Su Shun-ch'in, and Mei Yao-ch'en. These poets, he tells us, turned back the tide of Late T'ang poetry. (Fang's further remarks will be quoted in the following chapter.)

Fang Hui's analysis of early Sung poetry has proved to be quite useful, and is followed by the modern writer on Sung poetry, Liang K'un, with only slight changes. In the present treatment of the subject, the poets of the Late T'ang, Po Chü-i, and Hsi-k'un schools will be dealt with in that order. There will also be a brief discussion of Chia Tao, who provided the main inspiration for the Late T'ang style.

1 THE LATE T'ANG STYLE

Chu Tung-jun has commented on the vagueness of the term "Late T'ang," and has attempted to elucidate what it meant for different critics.[8] He takes the Ming critic Kao Ping to task for giving the term so broad a meaning that it encompasses Han Yü, Liu Tsung-yüan (773–819), Chang Chi (c.765–c.830), Wang Chien (c.751–c.835), Yüan Chen, Po Chü-i, Li Ho (791–817), Lu T'ung, Meng Chiao, and Chia Tao (c.793–c.865). On the other hand, he feels that Fang Hui, in the passage quoted above, and the Ming critic Yang Shen, in a passage to be quoted shortly, use the term in too narrow a sense, failing to include several important poets who lived in the later years of the T'ang dynasty. Chu Tung-jun thus considers the term to be primarily chronological, rather than stylistic. It is nevertheless convenient, for the purposes of the present study, to use the term "Late T'ang" in much the same way as Fang Hui does, that is, refer-ring to a certain type of intimate landscape poetry written by Chia Tao and his followers in the late T'ang period, and also practiced by a number of important early Sung poets.

This interpretation of "Late T'ang poetry" is enunciated in various Sung sources. Typical is a passage in the *Ts'ai K'uan-fu shih-hua:*[9] "On the whole, they [i.e., poets of this school] based their style on such poets as Chia Tao and called it the 'Chia Tao style.' They took nothing at all from Li [Po] and Tu [Fu]." In fact, the pas-sage goes on to say, they made fun of what they conceived to be the shortcomings of these two great poets.

A more detailed discussion of Late T'ang poetry is found in the *Sheng-an shih-hua,* a work by the Ming scholar Yang Shen (1488–1559).[10] Yang attributes to the scholar Chang Chi (933–996) the idea that there were actually two Late T'ang schools. One derived from Chia Tao, and included such poets as Yao Ho (c.831), Fang Kan (c.860) and the Nine Monks already named in the Fang Hui passage quoted earlier. The other school derived from Chang

Chi (c.765–c.830), and included such poets as Ssu-k'ung T'u (837–908) and Hsiang Ssu (c.836). Both schools, Yang says, wrote nothing but five-character regulated verse. "They also hated to use allusions, which they called 'conjuring up ghosts,' but only sought the actual scenes before their eyes, and then thought about them intensely. This is what is meant by the couplet 'While writing a line of five-character verse / I twist off several hairs of my beard.' " [11] Reference to Chang Chi's preface to the collected poetry of Hsiang Ssu [12] reveals that Chang was only responsible for the concept of a school of poetry derived from Chang Chi (c.765–c.830). He does not even mention Chia Tao. Yang Shen must be given the credit for elaborating a theory of two late T'ang schools. Also Yang's is the evaluation of the schools which follows: "I laugh at this; what a narrow conception of the Way of poetry! . . . These followers of Chang Chi and Chia Tao were truly lice living in a pair of trousers."

Chia Tao, by all accounts the poet who exerted the greatest influence on the Late T'ang school, appears to have been one of the better minor poets of his time, with a real gift for the depiction of charming natural scenes. The subtlety and intimacy of his style are apparent, for example in

SEEING OFF T'ANG HUAN ON HIS RETURN TO
THE FU RIVER VILLA [13]

Your door faces the Peak of the Hirsute Lady;
Your hair is still uncombed when the sun is high.
The ground is swept where it's shadowed by mountains;
Characters are written on dew-streaked leaves.
Monks search for herbs down the pine-sheltered path;
Cranes peer at fish in the sandy stream.
An entire river of beautiful landscapes:
All that's missing is a house for me!

The third couplet of this five-character regulated verse poem is typical of the precisely balanced, sensitively observed scenes that came to be considered characteristic of Late T'ang poetry. The contrast between Buddhist monks and birds of some kind (cranes in the present case) is typical. Later poets who adopted this style produced couplet after couplet of elegant description, the carefully chosen elements always perfectly parallel. Although a similar kind of

intimate landscape poetry had been written earlier by such poets as
Wang Wei and Meng Hao-jan (689–740), these men did not devote
themselves as exclusively to this mode of expression as did Chia
and his followers. The emphasis on well-wrought couplets in this
kind of poetry led Ssu-k'ung T'u to criticize Chia Tao for writing
impressive lines at the expense of the poem as a whole. [14] This may
stand as the final judgment on a style which produced many superb
couplets, but few if any great poems.

The term "Late T'ang" in the present context refers both to that
poetry of the late T'ang period which was inspired chiefly by Chia
Tao's style, and to the poetry of the early Sung period which carried
on this tradition. It is in the second sense that Fang Hui uses the
term in his analysis of early Sung poetry. From the perspective of
the twentieth century, some of the poets Fang names as representatives of the school seem insignificant. But four at least have maintained their reputations as important early Sung poets: P'an Lang,
Wei Yeh, K'ou Chun, and Lin Pu. Two of these—P'an Lang and Lin
Pu—will be discussed at greater length.

P'an Lang makes the source of his poetic style quite clear in

REMEMBERING CHIA LANG-HSIEN
[CHIA TAO] [15]

How mysterious the Way of the *Feng* and *Ya!*
I remember Lang-hsien's exalted chantings.
Most men reach their end within a century
But he should live on for a thousand years.
His bones have been buried in Shu, to the west,
But his soul has probably flown north to Yen.
I do not know who, between heaven and earth,
Will read the lines he has left behind.

In this poem, P'an goes so far as to associate Chia Tao with the
tradition of the *Book of Odes* itself, referring to two divisions of the
Odes—the *Kuo Feng* and the (greater and lesser) *Ya*—in the first line.
The third couplet probably means that although Chia died in exile
at Ch'ang-chiang subprefecture in Szechwan, his spirit has returned to Fan-yang subprefecture in Hopei, where he was born.
The poem ends with a rhetorical question: P'an wonders if anyone
in these degenerate times reads Chia Tao's poetry any more. Or he

may imply that he, P'an Lang, is the one who still reads Chia, and carries on his style.

One way in which P'an resembles Chia is that he, too, apparently took great pains with the diction of his verse. In a poem inscribed at the end of a volume of his own work, he says, "One volume of verse! Twenty years in the writing; / I've forgotten to eat during the day or sleep at night." [16] Again, while describing his leisurely life of retirement, he tells us, "I'm always pleased when my poems turn out flawless; / Never saddened if my family's poverty grows worse." [17] And in still another poem,[18] P'an speaks of his hair turning white with the effort of composition.

As might be expected, P'an wrote many poems of landscape description in the Chia Tao manner. Here is an example:[19]

WRITTEN ON LAKE VIEW TOWER

Standing all day on Lake View Tower,
Too lazy to think of going home,
I listen to the river flow off toward the Milky Way
And watch the clouds pass an isolated peak.
A lonely boat is pulled up on the bank;
A bird stands facing me in perfect calm.
—I turn my head, the double gates are closed;
Bullfrogs are croaking in the sunset.

Of the early Sung poets who wrote in the Late T'ang manner, Lin Pu (967–1028) is the most important for the study of Mei Yao-ch'en. Mei actually visited Lin at his retreat near West Lake. The meeting probably took place shortly before Lin's death, when Mei was still a young man in his twenties, as a poem by Mei which almost certainly dates from 1047 refers to the visit as having taken place some twenty years ago.[20] Mei also wrote a series of three *chüeh-chü*, dated 1047 in his *Nien-p'u*,[21] entitled *Facing the Snow I Remember Visiting Lin Pu Years Ago at West Lake Near Ch'ien-t'ang*. These poems all indicate that Mei enjoyed the natural beauty of West Lake and the surrounding mountains in the snow, and that he admired Lin's life of quiet seclusion. Poems were apparently exchanged between the two men, but since Mei's earliest surviving poetry was written around 1030, any poems he might have written on that oc-

casion have been lost. Lin's collection, however, still includes a
poem called

ECHOING A POEM BY MEI SHENG-YÜ WRITTEN WHEN HE VISITED ME
IN THE SNOW WITH THE MONK HSÜ-PO [22]

You've come to enjoy the lake's lovely snowscape
Bringing with you a monk like Tao-lin.
Morning smoke suggests a distant village;
Swollen Spring waters leave scars on the bank.
My home is secluded, beyond the three paths.
I live quietly here and practice the Five Beasts.
—As your boat returns, there's feeling to spare:
How can you be compared with the visitor from Shan-yin?

Lin uses no less than four allusions here, although allusion was
frowned upon by most poets of the Late T'ang school. The "Tao-
lin" of the second line is Chih-tun (314–366), one of China's great
Buddhist monks. The use of his name is intended as a compliment
to Hsü-po. The "three paths" of the fifth line refer to the retreat of
Chiang Hsü, a Han scholar who went into retirement when Wang
Mang usurped the throne. Chiang is said to have had three paths
leading to his house, and these came to represent the life of the
scholar-recluse in later literature, most notably in T'ao Ch'ien's
famous poem, *The Homecoming*.[23] Neatly parallel with this line, in
good Late T'ang fashion, is a reference to the Five Beasts exercise
attributed to the Han physician Hua T'o.[24] This exercise imitated
the movements of various creatures: tiger, deer, bear, monkey, and
bird. Finally, the last couplet recalls the well known story of Wang
Hui-chih's visit to Tai K'uei, already referred to in the first chapter.
As the visit took place while Wang was living at Shan-yin, the
place-name "Shan-yin" is used in the poem. Although Wang returned withou seeing Tai, because his "feeling came to an end,"
there is still feeling to spare after Mei and Lin part.

Some of Lin's other poems are more typical of Late T'ang ideals
than the one on Mei's visit. Here is an example, in five-character
regulated verse: [25]

AN AUTUMN DAY—LEISURELY BOATING ON WEST LAKE

The water's breath mingles with reflected mountains;
Autumn has come to the vast sky.

I joy to see temples hidden deep in the forest,
Regret the broken silence when my boat moves from the shore.
Sparse reeds are snapping, though it isn't cold yet;
A rainbow's fragment arches in the setting sun.
Which way now to my little hut?
The fishermen's songs bring thoughts of home.

An Autumn Day . . . is a full-fledged Late T'ang poem, free of allusions of any kind and replete with landscape imagery. The central couplets display Lin's mastery of parallelism, an aspect of his poetry which is frequently praised by later critics. The northern Sung scholar Hsü I (c. 1111), for example, states that "the parallelism in Ho-ching's poetry is lucid and precise." [26]

Mei Yao-ch'en was sufficiently impressed by Lin's work to write a preface to his collected poetry when asked to do so by Lin's grandnephew Ta-nien. This preface,[27] dated in accordance with July 1, 1053, is of interest not only for the information it provides on Lin Pu, and Mei's attitude toward him, but also as a rare document of Mei's ideas on poetry. It will therefore be translated in full:

PREFACE TO THE COLLECTED POEMS OF
MR. LIN HO-CHING

In the *T'ien-sheng* period (1023–1031) I heard that on West Lake in Hai-ning there lived a Mr. Lin of noble fame. He was like a waterfall cascading down a towering peak: attractive in a distant view, and still sweeter and purer in its fresh spray upon close approach, so that one never grows tired of it.

At that time I happened to be going to Kuei-chi, and so I paid him a visit in the snow. In his discussion of the Way, he praised Confucius and Mencius. In his discourse on recent prose, he praised Han [Yü] and [Han's follower,] Li [Kuan (766–794)]. When he was in harmony with things, enjoying his feelings, he would write poems which were even and bland, profound and beautiful. Reading them made one forget the hundred affairs. His words achieved the ultimate in calm and correctness, and did not stress satire and protest. Thus I realized that his taste was comprehensive and detached, and that he was simply expressing his happiness through poetry.

Already in the *Hsien-p'ing* and *Ching-te* periods (993–1007), Mr. Lin was quite famous. It happened that when the emperor was engaged in performing the *feng-shen* sacrifice, he did not get to summon Mr. Lin to become an official. He was therefore never employed in public service.

Whenever nobles or great officials came to meet him, they found him compatible in conversation and worthy of respect; they would linger on, reluctant to leave.

When Mr. Lin had grown old, the court did not want to force him into service, but an official would be sent to convey greetings to him for the seasons of the year. Upon his death, he was posthumously entitled "Mr. Ho-ching."

In his youth, Mr. Lin was sickly; he never married or had children. His grandnephew Ta-nien was able to collect some of his poems, and he has asked me to write this preface to them.

Mr. Lin's personal name was Pu; his *tzu* was Chün-fu. He lived to the age of sixty-one. His poems were more highly prized by the men of his time than jewels and jade, but Mr. Lin himself never valued them. He would throw his poems away upon completing them, so that only one or two out of every hundred survives. Alas and alack!

 —written on the thirteenth day of the sixth month of the fifth year of the *Huang-yu* period (July 1, 1053)

The significance of this preface for Mei's poetic theory will be discussed in a subsequent chapter. Here it may be noted that Mei apparently engaged in discussions on poetry with Lin. As Lin, like Mei himself, never wrote a systematic exposition of his ideas on poetry, it is difficult to say precisely what they were. A couplet from Lin's poem, *On Reading the Collected Poems of Wang Huang-chou* [Wang Yü-ch'eng] [28] is of considerable interest in this respect:

It was Tutor Po [Po Chü-i]
 who was free and untrammeled
  in the T'ang dynasty;
It is Huang-chou who ranges freely
 over our Sung dynasty.

Elsewhere, Lin uses the term "demon of poetry" in conjunction with the phrase "cannot be subdued," an association which occurs in a line by Po Chü-i: [29] "It is only the poetry demon that I haven't been able to subdue." These examples suggest that Lin Pu was also interested in the tradition that led from Po Chü-i to Wang Yü-ch'eng. This is not entirely unexpected, as Po's use of simple, easily comprehensible diction, and the tone of intimacy which often informs his poetry, are points of similarity with the Late T'ang poets.

2 THE PO CHÜ-I STYLE

Wang Yü-ch'eng (954–1001) is by far the most important of the poets assigned by Fang Hui to the Po Chü-i school. Wang was being compared with Po already in the Northern Sung dynasty,[30] and, as might be expected, references to Po are found throughout Wang's collection.[31] Wang even speaks of burning as offerings to Po and Yüan Chen a group of poems he had written after some of their works.[32]

But it appears from other passages that Wang was equally interested in Tu Fu.[33] For example, he praises the poetry of Ting Wei by comparing it with that of Tu Fu.[34] Once when his eldest son objected that two of his lines were very similar to lines from a Tu Fu poem, Wang replied (in Burton Watson's version), "I am one who follows after Lo-t'ien [Po Chü-i]; / I wonder if I dare take Tzu-mei [Tu Fu] as my predecessor?" [35]

Elsewhere he expands his repertoire of T'ang poets still further: "Li Po, Wang Wei, and Tu Fu: / Crazy with poetry, wild with wine, they shook the universe." [36] Later in the same poem, Li Ho appears in a dream.

The chief characteristics of Po Chü-i's poetry seem to be social concern (in the *New Yüeh-fu* poems especially), the leisurely depiction of everyday experience, and simplicity of diction. Taking the last point first, Wang once composed a series of poems describing local agricultural practices. In a long preface, he asserts that "their [the poems'] diction is low, so that the mountain farmers can easily understand them." [37] In general, the diction of Wang's ancient-style poems, which are his most important works, is relaxed and lucid, often approaching colloquial speech in its directness.

The depiction of everyday experience is also a feature of Wang's poetry, the set of poems on agriculture just mentioned being an example.

But most significant is the social commentary expressed in Wang's poems. There can be little doubt that Po Chü-i's protest poetry and Tu Fu's poetry of social comment are the primary influences here. As poetry of social comment was to play an important role in the work of Mei Yao-ch'en, it is difficult to over-emphasize the significance of Wang's achievement in this mode.

Some of Wang's best poems bring together all the features just detailed. *Facing the Snow* [38] is a particularly good example:

The year draws to a close in the emperor's city;
My humble gate stays shut all day.
Excused from paying court,
No work to do at the institute,
I lie and read late into the night,
Often waking when the sun is high.
I wake: cold in my skin and bones;
Outside the window jeweled petals fall.
I pull my clothes on, go out for a look:
Floating, dancing, they fill heaven and earth.
Dare I complain that I live in poverty?
Rather rejoice at the prosperous year ahead!
Nothing's ever left from my monthly stipend,
But breakfast fires continue to burn.
Kindling and fodder aren't cut off,
Wine and meat are still in supply.
Cups of wine are offered to my parents,
A single pouring shared with my brothers.
Wife and children, neither hungry nor cold,
Sing together of the timely omen.

But think of the people north of the River
Pulling carts to supply the border towns;
Each cart heavy with its load of grain,
Roads stretching for hundreds of miles.
The skinny horses can't move in the cold,
The ice-locked wheels can't be budged.
Where do they camp when nightfall comes?
Amidst the loneliness of desolate slopes.
I also remember the border troops,
Carrying spears against barbarian horsemen.
They set their banners on fortress walls,
Watch from lookouts for signal beacons.
Powerful bows increase their strength,
But chilly armor cuts them to the bone.
Where will they be marching today?
Off in the vastness of an empty desert.

But then what sort of man am I,
Living in stolen security?
Surely a blight to the common people,
My censor's position a sinecure!
Without one word of frank remonstration,

How can I be an honest official?
Without a whisper of praise-and-blame,
What kind of historian do I make?
Not tilling even an acre of land,
Not holding even a single arrow,
Lacking a way to enrich the people
Or any proposal for frontier peace,
I can only write this song of the snow
Ashamed that my friends think so much of me.

As Ch'ien Chung-shu points out in his excellent notes to this poem, Wang held the positions of Right Completioner and Auxiliary Official of the Institute of History at the time of writing the poem. The Institute of History was one of the "three institutes" referred to in the fourth line of the original text, and was involved with the work of compiling the dynastic records. A "Right Completioner" was a kind of censor who was expected to criticize the government's faults. Wang feels that he has failed in both his official capacities at a time when the country is being subjected to the incursions of Khitan armies from the Liao state, and the people are suffering the hardships of war. He contrasts the plight of soldiers fighting on the border, whose "chilly armor cuts them to the bone," and of the people who must supply them with grain, with his own respectable poverty. Such details of his own everyday life as "kindling and fodder," "wine and meat," and "breakfast fires" are introduced. Wang also selects appropriate images to express the hardships suffered by the soldiers and the border folk: "skinny horses," "ice-locked wheels," "desolate slopes," "chilly armor," "empty desert." From the point of view of diction, the poem is easily comprehensible, achieving almost colloquial directness in such lines as "But then what sort of man am I, / Living in stolen security?" In all these respects, the poem recalls not only Po Chü-i, but such long poems by Tu Fu as *The Journey North* and *Traveling From the Capital to Feng-hsien Subprefecture—Five Hundred Words on My Feelings*.[39] Like these poems, the present one combines personal experience with social comment.

But Wang Yü-ch'eng's poem is not a mere imitation of T'ang models. In his social poems, Tu Fu tends to maintain a heightened tone (excepting occasional intimate descriptions of family life) which often rises to passionate intensity. The tone of Po's *New Yüeh-fu* poems is also quite intense, and historical allusions sometimes bring the poem to a ringing climax. But Wang's *Facing the Snow* is quieter and more intimate in tone. The realities of the situation are starkly presented, but instead of the expected righteous indignation, the poem concludes in a mood of frustrated resignation. The final lines are somewhat anticlimactic: "I can only write this song of the snow, / Ashamed that my friends think so much of me." In other words, the "aesthetic distance" between the poet and his materials has been lessened. We are moving closer to the real world. In this sense, Wang Yü-ch'eng foreshadows later tendencies in the tone of Sung poetry.

Another of Wang's outstanding poems is the *Song of the Crow Pecking at My Scarred Donkey*.[40] This extraordinary work was written in 992, the year after Wang had been exiled to Shang-chou prefecture in Shensi at the age of thirty-eight:

Old crow of Shang Mountain, you are cruel!
Beak longer than a spike, sharper than an arrow.
Go gather bugs or peck at eggs—
Why must you harm this poor scarred beast of mine?
Since I was exiled to Shang-yü last year
There has only been this one lame donkey to move my things.
We climbed the Ch'in Mountains and the Ch'an to get here;
He carried a hundred volumes for me on his back.
The ropes cut his skin to the spine: the scar reached his belly;
Now with half a year's healing he's nearly well again.
But yesterday the crow suddenly swooped down
And pecked through his wound to get the living flesh.
The donkey brayed, my servant cried out and the crow flew away!
Perched on the roof he preened his feathers and scraped his beak.
There was nothing my donkey and my servant could do
Without a crossbow to shoot or nets to spread.
But Shang Mountain has many birds of prey;
I'll ask our neighbor to lend me his autumn hawk:
With claws of iron and hooked talons
He'll snap the crow's neck and feed on his brain!
And this won't serve only to fill his empty gut;
No! It's revenge for my donkey's pain.

The violence of this poem, and the "lowness" of its subject matter, are most unexpected. The central image of a crow pecking at the scars of an animal probably derives its respectability from a brief occurrence in Tu Fu's *Song of the Skinny Horse:* [41] "At sunset crows keep pecking at his scars." Mei Yao-ch'en was also to make use of this image in *The Piebald Horse,*[42] a poem written in 1046: "Scarred birds swoop down to peck at him." But Wang certainly deserves the credit for developing an entire poem around this idea, which apparently happened to coincide with his personal experience while traveling to Shang-chou. Especially striking is the simple but powerful diction of the poem, which again approaches colloquial directness. The particle *liao* at the end of the last line helps reinforce the impression of intense anger. Although the emotion here is quite strong, it is the emotion of a small man living in the real world, rather than a suffering or passionate poet who is somehow larger than life.

Wang Yü-ch'eng was conscious of the need to create a revitalized poetics for the Sung dynasty. "After the *Hsien-t'ung* period (860–873)," he tells us in a poem, "literature fell apart and was no longer refined. Then it passed through the Five Dynasties (906–960), when the wielders of the brush wrote mostly in a romantic, pretty style."[43] He praises a poet's work by stating that "the poetry of the Imperial Sung has here returned to refinement and correctness."[44] In the preface to a poem on a mountain at his place of exile which had never before been used as a poetic subject, he asserts, "If I remain silent and do not write such a work, men of later generations who peruse my collection will say that there were no poets in the Sung dynasty!"[45] The breadth of vision revealed here, and the excellence of his own poems, entitle Wang to be called the father of Sung poetry. It is appropriate that two of the greatest Sung poets, Ou-yang Hsiu and Su Shih, should both have written poems in praise of Wang inspired by a portrait of him.[46]

3   THE HSI-K'UN STYLE

The Hsi-k'un style, the third of the three schools into which Fang Hui divides early Sung poetry, is so different from the style of Wang Yü-ch'eng that it comes as a surprise to learn that Wang knew and admired several of its practitioners. He sent poems to

Yang I, Li Tsung-o (964–1012), and Ting Wei,[47] all three of whom were to be contributors to the Hsi-k'un anthology. Wang was particularly impressed by Ting Wei, and compared his prose with that of Han Yü and Liu Tsung-yüan, and his poetry with that of Tu Fu. It should be remembered, however, that at Wang's death in 1001, Yang I, the editor of the anthology, was only twenty-seven years old, and had probably not yet formulated his ideas on poetic style. As Ch'ien Chung-shu has noted, Wang matured as a poet before the flourishing of the Hsi-k'un school.[48]

The preface to the *Hsi-k'un ch'ou-ch'ang chi* refers to the Ching-te period (1004–1007), and explains the title of the collection which, as James J. Y. Liu writes, "alludes to the tradition that ancient kings kept treasures of books on this mountain [i.e., the K'un-lun mountain]." [49] The poets represented in the work are Yang himself, Liu Yün, Ch'ien Wei-yen, Ting Wei, Li Tsung-o, and twelve others. The poetry emulates the style of Li Shang-yin, although the most recent student of Li finds that it is successful only in "achieving a superficial resemblance to some of his stylistic idiosyncracies but not in capturing the complexity and depth of his poetry." [50] The same writer complains that the "mannerisms and affectations" of the Hsi-k'un poets are sometimes attributed to Li as well.

Typical of the Hsi-k'un style are the poems called *Untitled (Wu-t'i)* in imitation of Li Shang-yin's frequent use of this term. Here is an example by Yang I: [51]

Blue mist rises from fragrant herbs in the bronze plate;
Incense sachets hang at the four corners of the round canopy.
Shen Yüeh, grieving, grows emaciated in vain;
Hsiang-ju's feelings are secret: Who can convey them for him?
The rain has passed at the golden pond; it still seems a dream.
Kingfisher sleeves turned back in the wind:
    perhaps it was a fairy.
—Every day she climbs the Ch'in tower, but cannot
    send him poems:
He rides to the east in a screened carriage, surrounded
    by a thousand horsemen.

Although there is a certain richness in the panoply of images presented in this poem, it is contrived and rather confusing. The paraphernalia of the room described at the beginning, and the Ch'in tower in the penultimate line are appropriate for a lady, but the second couplet would seem to indicate that the sorrowing lover is a man. Perhaps the lines mean that a girl is yearning for a lover who is compared with Shen Yüeh and Ssu-ma Hsiang-ju. But in that case he would hardly have ridden in a carriage surrounded by throngs of horsemen. Apparently Yang I was interested in little more than displaying his virtuosity. It is easy to see why later poets held poetry of this kind in such contempt.

In all fairness to the Hsi-k'un poets, however, it should be pointed out that not every poem in the collection conforms to the common stereotype of the "Hsi-k'un style." Yang I's poem, *On Hearing Someone Speak of the Old Residence at Chien-ch'i*,[52] for example, is a relatively personal poem with landscape imagery of a kind which is often closer to the Late T'ang mode discussed above than to typical Hsi-k'un poetry:

I hear him speak of my home,
    and remember the blue-green colors,
Waterfalls hanging from rocky cliffs,
    spraying the mountain gate . . .

Also unexpected is a poem on *The Old General* [53] by Liu Yün, which uses such images as "war-blood drying on his serpent spear," and "his old platform, deserted amidst white grass and yellow clouds."

Perusal of Yang I's personal collection further reveals the variety of poetic modes in which the most important Hsi-k'un poet was interested. One of his poems, a seven-character *chüeh-chü* consisting of two parallel couplets, is entitled *Reading the Histories—In Imitation of the Style of Po [Chü-i]*,[54] and despite the parallelism of the piece and the inclusion of two allusions, a certain looseness of texture and fluidity of syntax indicate that Yang understood Po's diction. Yang also demonstrates his mastery of the Late T'ang style in a series of ten poems on the sights of Chien-an. One of them, *Lang Mountain Monastery*,[55] is particularly fine:

Rolling mountains push toward the city;
A monastery stands on the highest peak.
Evening fog darkens the gold buddhas;

A waterfall moistens winding stone steps.
Empty valleys echo the voice of the bell;
The pagoda's shadow mingles with scruffy clouds.
A thousand horsemen sometimes visit here,
But I seek solitude, alone with my bramble cane.

Still more unexpected in the collected works of the chief Hsi-k'un poet are two poems of social comment. As Yoshikawa has pointed out, Yang "also wrote poems with such titles as *The Prisons are Full of Convicts*, or *Many of the People's Oxen are Dying of Plague*, which foreshadow the concern for political and social problems that was to become such a prominent mark of the poetry of the following period." [56] Here is the first of these poems:

Iron chains and silver cangues: crowds of prisoners.
Distinguished laws and humble proposals are continuously issued.
No more is heard of memorials to empty the prisons;
How ashamed I must feel before the man of "half a word!"
The pure Ying, land of Mr. Huang, is near;
Shao-po of the sweet pear-tree is our neighbor.
I long for those sages, but cannot follow their ways;
Are the people responsible for all these punishments?

Yang takes cognizance here of an important problem in contemporary society. But he has chosen to express himself in highly allusive terms. The "man of 'half a word' " is Tzu-yu, of whom Confucius is reported to have said, "Talk about deciding a law-suit with 'half a word'—Yu is the man for that." [57] "Mr. Huang" is Huang Pa of the Han dynasty, a virtuous official during whose administration of Ying-chou "there were no convicts in the prisons," as Yang informs us in a note. The following line refers to Shao-po near Chiang-tu in Chiangsu. A dam built here by Hsieh An (320–383) was named Shao-po Dike by the people, as they wished to compare Hsieh with the Duke of Shao, whose virtue is said to have been praised in the ode, *Sweet Pear-Tree*.

Thus, while Yang I does seem to have been interested in a broader range of themes and styles than the usual criticisms of the Hsi-k'un school would suggest, he tends to fall back on parallelism and allusiveness even in poetry of social comment. Liu Pin (1022–1088) reports that Yang disliked the poetry of Tu Fu, and even

called him "the village gentleman." [58] Yang's true tastes apparently
lay in "romantic, pretty" poetry after all.

Such, then, was the state of poetry in the early years of the Sung
dynasty before the generation of Ou-yang Hsiu and Mei Yao-ch'en.
It is possible to divide the poets into three schools, as Fang Hui was
to do, all of which derived from T'ang models. But these schools
were not as clearly distinguished from one another as might be
thought. "Late T'ang" poets like Wei Yeh and Lin Pu also admired
Po Chü-i. Yang I, leader of the Hsi-k'un school, also had some interest in Po. But Wang Yü-ch'eng, chief representative of the "Po
school," was at least equally influenced by Tu Fu. If any general-
ization can be made, it is that these poets were all conditioned by
later T'ang poetry, viz. the poetry of the so-called mid-T'ang and
late T'ang periods. It is partly for this reason that later critical opinion tended to dismiss early Sung poetry as a mere carryover of
T'ang styles. But it is important to note that anticipations of later
Sung developments were already appearing, especially in the ancient-style poetry of Wang Yü-ch'eng.

Chapter Three

RESPONSE

Mᴇɪ ʏᴀᴏ-ᴄʜ'ᴇɴ and Ou-yang Hsiu are often pictured by the Chinese critics as revolutionary figures who rejected the work of earlier Sung poets, and created a totally new style of their own. In fact, Mei and Ou-yang appear to have responded to their literary environment with a greater degree of subtlety than this view would suggest. They did feel that the Hsi-k'un and Late T'ang styles were limited, and that a more comprehensive poetic style was called for to express the mood of the still relatively young Sung dynasty. But Mei and Ou-yang were able to appreciate the merits of such early Sung poets as Lin Pu and Wang Yü-ch'eng. And, far from being revolutionaries, they turned to certain poets of the past for fresh inspiration. In this chapter, I will examine the opinions of Mei and Ou-yang with respect to early Sung poetry, and discuss the poets who exerted the most meaningful influence on Mei Yao-ch'en. These are the poets whose names occur in Mei's writings with the greatest frequency, or in the most significant contexts. The historical perspective is reversed—i.e., those poets who are closest in date to Mei are discussed first. It is not my intention to suggest that Mei was unique in his dependence on tradition; this was, of course, a characteristic of all Chinese poetry. But I do feel that it is impossible to understand any Chinese poet without first determining precisely which poets of the past were especially important to him.

Continuing his analysis of Sung poetry, Fang Hui writes, "Mr. Ou-yang then appeared and transformed poetry by means of the styles of Li T'ai-po and Han Ch'ang-li [Han Yü]. Su Tzu-mei [Su Shun-ch'in] vied with him, and it would be difficult to say which was superior. But Mei Sheng-yü was outstanding among poets of this [new] T'ang style. With this, the Late T'ang style withdrew." [1] Elsewhere, Fang elaborates slightly on this view: "The transformation of poetry of the Hsi-k'un style into poetry of the High T'ang began with the Auxiliary Secretary Mei Sheng-yü. At that time, the one who transformed the prose style of the Five Dynasties was Mr. Ou-yang. For this reason, they have been called 'Ou and Mei' through the generations." [2] It thus appears that Fang wished to draw a distinction between the Late T'ang style which flourished in the early Sung, and a superior style based on High T'ang poetry (apparently including Han Yü here) which was created by Ou-yang Hsiu, Su Shun-ch'in, and, especially, Mei Yao-ch'en.

A similar opinion had been expressed slightly earlier by Liu K'o-chuang (1187–1269): [3]

> Poets at the start of the present dynasty, such as P'an Lang and Wei Yeh, stuck slavishly to the Late T'ang style, and did not dare to step out on their own. Yang [I] and Liu [Yün] specialized even more and created the K'un style; this is why the actor made the joke about tearing off I-shan's [Li Shang-yin's] clothes. [4] The two masters Su [Shun-ch'in] and Mei [Yao-ch'en] then transformed it [i.e., poetry] into something even and bland, heroic and vigorous. But those who followed suit were still few.

As Liu's purpose in the passage from which this is quoted is to praise Huang T'ing-chien, his praise of Mei Yao-ch'en is qualified. But in another passage he waxes quite enthusiastic about Mei's position in the history of Sung poetry: [5]

> Mr. Ou [-yang]'s poetry is like that of Ch'ang-li [Han Yü]; it should not be discussed as poetry. It is Wan-ling [Mei Yao-ch'en] who is the mountain-opening patriarch [6] of the poetry of this dynasty. After Wan-ling appeared, the frivolous bawling of Sang and P'u [7] abated somewhat, and the pulse of the *Feng* and *Ya* was resumed. His [Mei's] achievement is not inferior to that of Ou[-yang Hsiu] and Yin [Shu].

In this passage, Liu states quite clearly his opinion that Mei's role in creating a Sung style of poetry that revived the orthodox tradition of the *Book of Odes* was as important as that of Ou-yang Hsiu and Yin Shu in revitalizing prose.[8] A comparable eminence is granted to Mei by Tseng Chi-li (c.1147) in his *T'ing-chai shih-hua:* [9]

> Tung-lai [Lü Pen-chung (c.1119)], in his *Preface on the Lineage of the Chiang-hsi School,* says that the ancient-style prose of the present dynasty began with Mu Po-chang [Mu Hsiu (979–1032)] and reached maturity with Mr. Ou-yang. This view is entirely correct. But how regrettable that in his discussion of poetry he does not mention Sheng-yü! Sheng-yü's contribution in poetry was like Mu Po-chang's in prose.

Mu Hsiu was one of the early admirers of Han Yü and Liu Tsung-yüan, and was considered to be among the most important early prose stylists of the Sung.[10] Liu K'o-chuang and Tseng Chi-li were thus agreed on Mei's importance as one of the founders of Sung poetry, but it is of some significance that Tseng had to remedy the omission of Mei's name from Lü Pen-chung's influential preface. Apparently opinion on the early development of Sung poetry was not unanimous.

One would expect that a circle of poets who took it upon themselves to reform poetic practice might have published some kind of manifesto. As it happened, neither Mei Yao-ch'en nor Ou-yang Hsiu produced such a document. But one of the important minor figures in the literary world at that time, Shih Chieh (1005–1045), did write an essay in three parts entitled *Discourse on Aberrations* [11] in which the expected antipathy toward Hsi-k'un poetry is expressed. As this essay is of considerable interest for the light which it throws on contemporary literary attitudes, it is worth examining in some detail.

The first part of the essay is concerned with defining the concept "aberration" as understood by Shih Chieh. An aberration is anything which runs counter to the Normal Way (*ch'ang-tao*) of heaven, earth, and man. The Normal Way of heaven is that the sun, the moon, and the stars are in place, and the four seasons follow each other in orderly sequence. Such phenomena as eclipses and comets are aberrations of heaven. It is the Normal Way of earth for mountains to be in position and rivers to flow in their courses. When mountains collapse or rivers dry up, these are aberrations. The Normal Way of man is defined in orthodox Confucian terms. When the four classes (scholars, farmers, artisans, merchants) wear the proper garments and caps, and follow morality, rites and music, and the Five Constant Virtues (humanity, righteousness, propriety, knowledge, faithfulness) as taught by China's great sages, then the Normal Way prevails. But the teachings of Buddhism and Taoism go against these traditions and are thus aberrations. Shih laments the influence of Buddhism and Taoism in China, and expresses the wish that a new Confucian champion will appear.

In the second section of the *Discourse*, Shih introduces his opinions on recent literary history. In partial translation, this section reads as follows:

> Formerly the Han-lin Academician Yang [I] wanted to become a model for the world in literature, but he was saddened that the world did not have complete faith in his Way. He therefore blinded the eyes of men . . . so that they could not see the Way of the Duke of Chou, Confucius, Mencius, Yang Hsiung, Wen-chung Tzu [Wang T'ung (584–617)], and Li-pu [Han Yü]. . . . Yang I, carrying prettiness to the ultimate degree, striking all possible postures, strung together wind and moon, and played around with flowers and plants. Excessive in his artfulness and extravagant in his loveliness, superficially beautiful and full of silken elegance, he carved up the classics of the Sage and destroyed the words of the Sage. He fragmented the Sage's meaning and corrupted the Sage's Way. . . . Is this not a great aberration?

Finally, in the third section of the *Discourse*, Shih is warned by a well-wisher that the followers of Buddhism, Taoism, and Yang I's school of poetry are so numerous that, however persuasive Shih's arguments may be, he is sure to get into trouble. Shih retorts that as a follower of the Confucian tradition he must defend that tradition against the corruptions of the "false and foolish, strange and boastful teachings" of Buddhism and Taoism, and the "excessively artful, superficial and false words" of Yang I. Shih says he is willing to risk danger and even death for these principles.

When the basic ideas of this essay are sifted from the pompous and repetitive rhetoric, Shih Chieh is seen to be associating Yang I with Buddhism and Taoism as one of a triumvirate of corrupters of the Confucian tradition. Han Yü is named as the last great representative of Confucianism, but Shih hopes that he himself may be able to lead a Confucian revival in his own time. The arguments against Buddhism closely resemble those used by Han Yü in his famous polemic *Yüan tao*,[12] a work for which Shih expresses great admiration elsewhere in his writings, even comparing Han to a doctor who cured the Way by "cutting out the root" of Buddhism and Taoism.[13]

It is not impossible that Shih's antipathy toward Yang I was in fact partially inspired by what appears to have been a close relationship between Yang and Buddhism. Yang was one of the officials charged with the printing and publishing of the *Ching-te ch'uan-teng lu*,[14] one of the most important Buddhist books of its time. Buddhist monks were among Yang's best friends, and he sent them poems filled with obscure Buddhist technical terms and references to the sutras.[15] But some of the phrases used in the *Discourse* to characterize Yang's poetry leave little doubt that Shih objected to it on primarily stylistic, aesthetic grounds. Yang "carries prettiness to the ultimate degree, strikes all possible postures, strings together wind and moon, and plays around with flowers and plants." (We will see later that Mei Yao-ch'en criticized Late T'ang poets for writing poetry consisting solely of descriptive landscape imagery.[16]) Yang is also "excessive in his artfulness and extravagant in his loveliness, superficially beautiful and full of silken elegance." It is thus Shih's remarkable idea that both the religious doctrine and the literary style prevalent in early Sung times were unorthodox in that they were non-Confucian.

A poem sent by Shih Chieh to a certain Chang Chi, *tzu* Yü-kung, expands on his view of literary history.[17] In partial prose paraphrase, the poem reads as follows:

> In the *Yüan-ho* period (806–820) of the T'ang dynasty, men of letters arose as numerous as bees. With heroic words, Li Ao (d. c.844) and Li Kuan (766–794) destroyed the treacherous and corrupt. The bitter poetry of Meng Chiao and Chang Chi moved heaven and earth. Holding to the Correct and not retreating, Tzu-hou [Liu Tsung-yüan] is considered supreme. Yüan [Chen] and Po [Chü-i], although theirs was a lesser Way, vied for fame without end. And the one who was able to command this cultural movement was Ch'ang-li, Master Han [Yü].

The poem then goes on to name some of the men in the early Sung literary world, when "men of letters were lined up like the teeth of a comb." Several relatively insignificant figures are given,

such as Sun Ho ("Han Kung") (961–1004) and his younger brother
Sun Chin (969–1017). But the important place given to Wang Yü-
ch'eng ("Huang-chou") is of interest, as is the qualified praise of
Ting Wei ("Wei-chih"), "a thoroughbred of literature, although he
is uneven." This qualification may refer to Ting's contribution to
the Hsi-k'un anthology. As the leader of this movement, and thus
Han Yü's successor in the early Sung, Liu K'ai (946–999) is named.
Liu, a passionate admirer of Han Yü and Liu Tsung-yüan, was,
together with Mu Hsiu, one of the first *ku-wen* prose stylists of the
Sung.[18] According to Ch'ien Chung-shu, the three surviving poems
in the present edition of Liu K'ai's collected works also show the influence of Han Yü.[19]

Following this account of early Sung letters, Shih Chieh's poem
goes on to lament the decline in literature which set in with the
death of Liu K'ai. But, says Shih, with the *Ching-yu* period
(1034–1037), the "great Confucians began to sing again," and men
of letters "stood up like rows of hemp." Shih asserts that he himself, "admiring the conduct of Han Yü and shouldering the ambition of Liu K'ai," wants to become the leader of the new literary
movement. Although the rest of the poem is given over to praise for
the Chang Chi of the title, and suggests that Chang might qualify
someday for this awesome position, Shih makes his true desire perfectly clear.

To what extent did Mei Yao-ch'en and Ou-yang Hsiu share Shih
Chieh's views? In his grave inscription for Shih, Ou-yang briefly
summarizes the argument of the *Discourse on Aberrations* without
further comment.[20] A poem by Ou-yang praises two pupils or associates of Shih for attacking Buddhism and Taoism.[21] In two poems
on reading the collected works of Shih, Ou-yang reveals considerable respect and affection for him, again referring to his spirited attack against Buddhism and Taoism, and expressing the idea that
immortality can be achieved through literature.[22] But in a letter to
Shih,[23] Ou-yang criticizes him rather forcefully (in the translation of
James T. C. Liu): "Your self-esteem seems too inordinate, your criticism of the current conditions too excessive. . . . As if you deliber-
ately set out to be different just for the sake of claiming superiority." Ou-yang also takes Shih to task for adopting a purposely

eccentric calligraphic style. To this Shih responded with a long, passionate letter [24] in which he asserts that he is alone in his time in not following Buddhism and Taoism, and Yang I's poetry; in this sense he is indeed different from anyone else. As for calligraphy, it is a trifling skill in which Shih admits he has little competence. He is interested in higher things, such as carrying on the Confucian tradition, and he is surprised that Ou-yang's understanding of him is so shallow. Of course, Ou-yang could not let this pass without a further rejoinder. In his reply,[25] he assures Shih that he had not meant to urge the study of calligraphy upon him, but one must, after all, write clearly enough so that one's writing is legible. Ou-yang objects again to Shih's arrogance in assuming that he is alone in eschewing Buddhism, Taoism, and superficial literature. It is of interest that Ou-yang refrains from naming Yang I in this corre-spondence.

Ou-yang's own attitude toward Hsi-k'un poetry appears to have been complex. Yang I's name appears frequently in Ou-yang's *Kuei t'ien lu*, almost always in contexts which, unexpectedly, indicate Ou-yang's admiration for him.[26] In one passage he is called "a true literary hero of his time." Ou-yang's clearest appraisal of the Hsi-k'un school appears in his *Liu-i shih-hua*,[27] a work of primary im-portance for understanding his and Mei Yao-ch'en's ideas about po-etry. Here he says,

> Yang Ta-nien [Yang I] exchanged poetry with several poets, including Ch'ien [Wei-yen] and Liu [Yün]. Ever since their Hsi-k'un anthology came out, men of the times have vied in imitating it, so that poetic style has been completely transformed. Gentlemen and elders have criticized this poetry for using so many allusions that the diction is obscure and hard to understand. But they fail to realize that this is a fault of the emulators of the style. For example, in Tzu-i's [Liu Yün's] poem, *New Cicada*, occur the lines,
> Wind blows on the jade tree;
> > the crow is first to fly away.
> Dew falls on the golden stem,
> > unperceived by the crane.[28]

Although these lines use allusions, does this prevent them from being beautiful? Again, Ta-nien [Yang I] wrote,
A lofty sail crosses the river
> by the willows at the official bridge;

Repeated drums startle into flight
　　　　the gulls at the seashore.[29]

This couplet does not use allusions, but is it not also beautiful? For these
are poets of heroic literary talent and broad learning, with more than
enough power in their brushes. Thus they are capable of achieving anything. They are not at all like those known as poets in the preceding
generation, who limited themselves to such trifling images as wind and
cloud, grass and trees, and were defeated by Hsü Tung.[30]

Another passage in *Liu-i shih-hua* [31] is also useful for determining
Ou-yang's attitude toward Hsi k'un poetry:

Ever since Yang [I] and Liu [Yün] exchanged poetry, and the Hsi-k'un
anthology became popular, younger scholars vied in imitating it. The
Feng and *Ya* were completely transformed; this was called the "K'un
style." From this time on, the poetry collections of all the T'ang worthies
practically went out of circulation.

The rest of this passage indicates that Po Chü-i and Tu Fu were
among the "T'ang worthies" Ou-yang had in mind.

After reading these passages, it is difficult to understand the
frequently expressed view that Ou-yang and Mei were implacable
enemies of Hsi-k'un poetry. The distinguished scholar Wang Fu-
chih (1619–1692), for example, even felt that Ou-yang was overly
zealous in his opposition to Yang I and the Hsi-k'un school,[32] a criticism which, as we have seen, Ou-yang himself applied to Shih
Chieh. Ou-yang's actual opinion appears to have been that the
chief contributors to the Hsi-k'un anthology, notably Yang I, Liu
Yün, and Ch'ien Wei-yen (for whom he expresses admiration elsewhere [33]), were fine poets, but that the characteristics of their style
degenerated into mannerisms in the hands of their less gifted followers.

The closing sentence of the passage translated earlier in which
Ou-yang quotes couplets by Yang I and Liu Yün refers to a group of
poets "who limited themselves to such trifling images as wind and
cloud, grass and trees, and were defeated by Hsü Tung
(c.972–c.1016)." Another passage from *Liu-i shih-hua* elucidates this
one, and gives some idea of Ou-yang's view of Late T'ang poetry: [34]

There were nine Buddhist monks in the present dynasty who were famous as poets in their time. Therefore their collected works were then known as *Poetry of the Nine Monks*. This work is no longer transmitted. When I was young, I often heard people praise one of them, called Hui-ch'ung, but I have forgotten the names of the other eight. I also recorded a few of their poems. One says,
Horses are set free on the surrendered land;
The battle is finished; hawks circle in the clouds.[35]

Another says,
Spring is born beyond Cassia Ridge;
My friend is west of Ocean Gate.[36]

Their outstanding lines are mostly of this kind. Now their collection has been lost, and few men today know what is meant by the "Nine monks." What a pity!

At that time there was a holder of the *chin-shih* degree, a certain Hsü Tung, who was good at literature. Indeed, he was a man of great spirit. He brought together these poet-monks, gave each of them a theme and a piece of paper, and asked that they each write a poem without using any of these words: "mountain," "flower," "grass," "snow," "frost," "star," "moon," or the names of beasts and birds and the like. At this, the monks all put aside their brushes.

It will be recalled that Fang Hui considered the Nine Monks to be the most representative poets of the Late T'ang school. Despite Ou-yang's comment that their collection was already lost, an anthology of one hundred thirty-four poems by the monks still survives today.[37] From this book the first couplet quoted by Ou-yang can be identified as the work of Yü-chao, and the second, that of Hsi-chou. Ou-yang's opinion of the monks' poetry is somewhat obscure. In the previously mentioned excerpt, the poets "who limited themselves to such trifling images as wind and cloud, grass and trees, and were defeated by Hsü Tung," in other words, the Nine Monks, are obviously held in contempt. The anecdote of their inability to write poems in which a handful of stipulated images would not appear also holds them up to ridicule. And yet Ou-yang quotes with approval two of their couplets, and laments the fact that their collection is not well known. A presumably earlier draft of the first part of this passage is even more enthusiastic in its praise for the monks.[38] After quoting the same two couplets, Ou-yang goes on to claim that "the men of letters of today could not achieve such fine lines."

Further light is thrown on Ou-yang's view of the Late T'ang style by this passage from *Liu-i shih-hua:* [39]

> In the later years of the T'ang dynasty, poets no longer wrote in the heroic, expansive manner of Li [Po] and Tu [Fu], but devoted themselves to surpassing each other in precision of expression. For example, Chou P'u (d. 878) was especially painstaking in thinking out a poem. Whenever he got an idea, he would cut and polish it to an extreme degree. For this reason, his contemporaries said of his poems that they were "forged for a month and refined for a season; before they are completed, people are already reciting them." Such was his fame at that time! And yet today his works are no longer transmitted. When I was young, it was still possible to see his collected poetry. Among his lines were,
>
> Bird calls scatter in the warm wind;
> Flowers' shadows are heavy in the noonday sun. [40]
>
> And again,
> The mountain birds are noisy as morning comes;
> Apricot blossoms are sparse
>   when the rains have passed. [41]

Wei T'ai (c. 1082), and Ch'en Shan (c. 1147) after him, have pointed out that the first of these two couplets really comes from the poem *Sorrow in the Spring Palace* by Tu Hsün-ho (846–904), [42] but as Tu was also a representative Late T'ang poet, the significance of the passage is not affected. Ou-yang thus seems to have felt that the poets of the Late T'ang style were definitely more restricted in their range than the great poets like Li Po and Tu Fu, but did produce some excellent lines that are worth knowing. In this respect, his balanced view of their work is similar to the opinion he held of the Hsi-k'un school.

Ou-yang's feelings about the Po Chü-i school are somewhat more difficult to ascertain. "During the reign of Jen-tsung (r. 1022–1063)," he tells us, "there were several high officials who were famous as poets and as a rule admired the style of Po Lo-t'ien. For this reason their diction is mostly of the easy type." [43] This is followed by an anecdote in which someone makes fun of a couplet in this style. In another passage, [44] Mei Yao-ch'en is quoted to the effect that "when lines in poetry make sense, but have diction which approaches shallowness and vulgarity, and is laughable, this is a defect." Mei goes on to ridicule two couplets which suffer from this fault.

On the other hand, elsewhere in *Liu-i shih-hua*,[45] Ch'en Ts'ung-i (c. 1004), whose "poetry was mostly similar to Po Lo-t'ien's," is said to have been "praised for his pure Confucianism and scholarship in ancient matters" at "a time when modish literature was in fashion." This is followed by a brief reference to the Hsi-k'un school, already translated, in which Ou-yang says that the poetic works of the "T'ang worthies" nearly went out of circulation because of the popularity of the Hsi-k'un style. It will also be recalled that Ou-yang wrote a poem in praise of Wang Yü-ch'eng, the chief representative of the Po Chü-i style.[46] Again, the overall impression is one of a sober, balanced view which takes cognizance of the excesses to which the style could lead, but also recognizes its good points.

Mei Yao-ch'en unfortunately did not write a *shih-hua* or similar critical text,[47] and we are dependent on occasional passages in his poetry, and a handful of quotations in *Liu-i shih-hua*, for his views on literary history and poetic theory. Nowhere in this material, to my knowledge, can specific references either to the Hsi-k'un school or to the Po Chü-i school be found. It can only be assumed that Mei more or less shared the views of his friend Ou-yang Hsiu on these matters. The preface to Lin Pu's poetry which was translated earlier, however, expresses Mei's profound admiration for one of the most important poets of the Late T'ang school, and in one of Mei's rare recorded statements of his concept of poetry (discussed in the following chapter), couplets in the Late T'ang style by Chia Tao, Yao Ho (c. 831), Yen Wei (c. 756; a precursor of the style?), and Wen T'ing-yün are quoted with approval as illustrations. In addition, Mei himself wrote a number of poems in this mode.

Although Mei was thus able to appreciate the beauty of the Late T'ang style, like Ou-yang Hsiu he felt that it was restricted in scope and inadequate for the purpose of revitalizing Sung poetry. This point of view is expressed quite clearly in a number of Mei's poems, all of which appear to date from 1045 or later. In a poem of 1045, for example,[48] he answers the criticism that he has devoted himself entirely to poetry to the exclusion of other forms of literature by describing the great seriousness with which he approaches the task of being a poet. He will not give up his effort until he has achieved poetry of the kind found in the two *Ya*'s of the *Book of Odes*. "How could I follow those few poets of the late T'ang," he writes, "who wore away their years trifling with natural images?" In another poem, written the following year,[49] this point of view is developed in somewhat greater detail. Mei begins by praising the poets of the *Book of Odes* who "were stimulated by some important matter which they would express through nature imagery." The *Feng* section of the *Odes* is important, because in it "those below influence those above." The *Ya* and *Sung* are held in esteem because they use "praise and blame," and also because they are good models for the attainment of literary skill. Mei next expresses his admiration for the *Li sao*, in which Ch'ü Yüan "lamented the frustration of his ambition," using plants and insects to show his contempt for the evil then rampant in the world. But in recent years, Mei continues, the Way of poetry has declined. Poets "describe the forms of mist and cloud, sing of the blues and reds of flowers." They use too many allusions in their poems, and are only concerned with achieving skill in parallelism. By writing such poetry, they win glory and profit. As a result, the men of the world say that their poetry is only comparable to such trifling arts as *wei-ch'i* (a Chinese board game resembling chess), and zither music.

In this poem, the argument of which closely follows that of Po Chü-i's famous letter to Yüan Chen,[50] Mei advocates poetry in which natural imagery serves an end beyond itself, and condemns poetry which merely stresses skill in the description of natural beauty and in poetic techniques such as parallelism and allusion. He is, in other words, calling for the revival of the orthodox Confucian tradition of poetry, originating in the *Book of Odes*, and the rejection of the kind of poetry which was being produced by both the Hsi-k'un and Late T'ang schools. To this extent, Mei can be said to have shared the literary views expressed in Shih Chieh's *Discourse on Aberrations* and in his poem to Chang Chi.

It will be recalled that Shih Chieh regarded the mid-T'ang period, centering on the Yüan-ho period (806–820), as a time when the Confucian tradition was revived in literature as well as in thought by Han Yü and his circle, including such poets as Meng Chiao and Chang Chi. Po Chü-i and Yüan Chen were also singled out by Shih. Mei Yao-ch'en and Ou-yang Hsiu, like Shih, looked to these men among others for inspiration in creating their new poetic style.

In a lengthy poem sent by Ou-yang Hsiu to Su Shun-ch'in in 1045, and reprinted in Mei's collection,[51] Ou-yang develops a comparison between himself and Han Yü on the one hand, and Mei Yao-ch'en and Meng Chiao on the other:

Hang and Meng in literature
Were two heroes, their powers evenly matched.
They amused each other with eccentricities,
Writing poetry that startled the T'ang. . . .
Meng was poor, entangled in suffering;
Han was rich and flourished greatly. . . .
One was vernal and sounded *kung;*
One was autumnal and sounded *shang.*
Though these were two different modes
They played together in ringing harmony.

But after their death, Ou-yang continues, Han and Meng were "left in obscurity for two hundred years. These supreme jewels were buried and gave off no light." There then follows a somewhat enigmatic couplet: "After Chiao's death, it was not Chia Tao, / But Sheng-yü who discovered his treasure-trove." A *chüeh-chü* poem by Han Yü entitled *Sent to Chia Tao* [52] helps to explain these lines. The poem may be paraphrased as follows: After Meng Chiao died and was buried at Pei-mang Mountain (a burial ground north of Loyang), the "wind and clouds" of fine poetry came to a temporary halt. But heaven, afraid that the literary tradition would be completely broken off, caused Chia Tao to be born in the world of men. In light of this poem, Ou-yang's lines can be taken to mean that Han Yü was wrong in considering Chia Tao to be the poet who carried on the tradition represented by Meng Chiao. It is only in Mei Yao-ch'en that Meng has found a worthy successor.

Mei responded to Ou-yang's poem with one of his own the first part of which may be paraphrased as follows: [53]

I have heard that T'ui-chih [Han Yü] and Tung-yeh [Meng Chiao] became friends when they were both still unknown. Although Meng's

poverty never abated while Han rose higher and higher, there was no
change in the two men's feelings for each other. Han was not haughty
nor did Meng experience any shame. They simply based their friendship
on moral right.

You and I are also like this; you need not yield before the ancients in
conduct.

In another poem, probably written in 1055 or 1056,[54] Mei praises
Han Yü for reforming literature, and compares his literary style
with the rumbling of thunder, the coiling of dragons and serpents,
the blowing of wind, and the crash of huge waves. "But after this,"
says Mei, "literature declined, and the lingering influence [of decadent literature] continued unchecked." Mei then reminisces about
the early period at Loyang when "three or four gentlemen of our
dynasty joined forces to express their righteous indignation." The
"gentlemen" included Hsieh Chiang, Ou-yang Hsiu, Yin Shu, and
Mei himself. "We revived the greatness of the *Yüan-ho* period.
What difficulty was there in completely transforming [literary
style]?"

Mei thus considered himself to be participating in a circle of
poets comparable to the men of letters who gathered around Han
Yü. This idea is developed further in other poems. In one,[55] for example, Mei points out that Han Yü accepted poets who wrote in
different styles. Meng Chiao, Lu T'ung, Chang Chi, and Chia Tao
each had his own style: "Some of them wrote many words of suffering; others devoted themselves to a heroic, untrammeled manner."
Ou-yang Hsiu, Mei intimates, wishes to emulate Han's catholicity
and to preside over a new literary circle. The same names appear in
still another poem.[56] Here Han Yü is said to have had universal ge-
nius. He swept away opposing views like so much dust. Chang Chi
and Lu T'ung vied in the "new and strange." Meng Chiao was
praised most of all for being "outstanding." In modern times, Ou-
yang Hsiu is like Han Yü, a vast ocean or a mighty mountain. Shih
Man-ch'ing (Shih Yen-nien, 994–1041) and Su Shun-ch'in are like
Lu T'ung and Chang Chi respectively. Mei himself is like Meng
Chiao.

The importance of Han Yü's influence on Ou-yang Hsiu's revival of *ku-wen* prose and Confucian ways of thinking is well known.[57] Indeed, the reverence for Han expressed by Liu K'ai and Mu Hsiu and the praise bestowed upon him by such early Sung literary figures as Wei Yeh and Wang Yü-ch'eng [58] suggest that Han was generally held in esteem during this period. But the frequency with which his name occurs in the works of Ou-yang and Mei indicates their special interest in him.

The two friends admired Han's poetry as well as his prose and thought. One of the entries in *Liu-i shih-hua* [59] refers to the fact that Han considered poetry a less important aspect of literature, but goes on to assert that his poetry "provides topics for discussion or laughter, joking or satire. It describes human emotions, and the forms of things. All of this he expresses through his poetry, exhausting the subtleties of each subject." Ou-yang goes on, in a rather technical passage, to praise Han's great skill at using difficult rhymes, and mixing rhyme-words of different types. In this, Ou-yang tells Mei, Han is like a good charioteer driving five horses through the streets, making them go in any direction he pleases. Mei was impressed by this argument, and refers to it in a poem probably dating from 1049; [60] "My friend [i.e., Ou-yang Hsiu] has said of Han's poetry / That it was unequalled in the past for difficult rhymes."

Other references to Han Yü as a poet can be found in Mei's works. In a poem on catalpa blossoms,[61] he writes,

I have heard that Han Li-pu
Once wrote a good poem about them.
He liked their shade, which no sunlight penetrated;
He sat in their shadow, either east or west.

The reference here is to Han Yü's poem, *The Catalpas in the Courtyard*,[62] in which Han describes how he sits to the east or west of the trees depending on the sun's position. The words *hsien-ch'uan* ("which no [sunlight] penetrated") in Mei's poem have been taken verbatim from the Han Yü original.

Mei's interest in Han's poetry appears to go back to his impressionable Loyang years. During that period, he wrote the first of his two poems specifically in imitation of Han Yü's style: [63]

WHILE LIVING SOUTH OF THE PALACE BRIDGE I HEARD A GHOSTLY
BIRD CRY AT NIGHT   —In the Manner of Ch'ang-li [Han Yü]

Midnight: darkening clouds hung low over the capital.
Suddenly I heard the groan of a carriage wheel.
I remembered a ghostly bird in the land of Ch'u
With nine heads like cancerous growths on a single body.
On moonless nights he flies above the towns
With stuttered cries and murmurs, as if seeking someone.
Children hide their heads, housewives douse the fires;
The gates are shut to keep in the dogs and chickens.
I asked why the folk of Ch'u were so terrified:
"This is the Ghostly Carriage, carrying ghosts abroad."
And what do they do, the ghosts of the Ghostly Carriage?
"Unravel your sinews and tie them to the carriage shafts!"
When I heard this I was incredulous;
In vain I wished to question the chief of gods.
Now the thing has come to central China, where all is correct:
How could he act here as he used to in the south?
Emperor of Heaven, if the wind can bring you my words,
Please banish this creature from our ninefold land!

Years later, in 1061, Ou-yang Hsiu also wrote a poem on *The Ghostly Carriage* [64] in which many similar images appear.

Mei's other poem after Han Yü is entitled *In Imitation of "The Shooting of the Horned Owl" by Han Li-pu.*[65] Han's poem[66] describes the horned owl as a bird of ill omen which musters together demons and evil creatures to aid it in its mischief. When the owl alights on the roof of the poet's house, the poet decides to go out and shoot it down. After the owl is killed, its young "wither away." The poem may well be an allegory of current political events. In Mei's poem too the owl perches on the roof of the poet's house and raises a brood of three or four owlets. At the bird's death, they are carried off by foxes and mice, and "the owl's faction is destroyed."

These two examples might tend to suggest that for Mei, Han Yü was simply a poet of the macabre and supernatural. But it is likely that Mei learned more than this from Han's poetry. The seemingly awkward, prose-like diction that is a chief characteristic of Han's style could not but exert some influence on a poet who was striving to transcend the nicely turned couplets produced by the Hsi-k'un and Late T'ang schools. That the poetry of Han Yü continued to interest Mei throughout his life is indicated by Mei's lengthy poem

on a copy of the stone drum texts sent to him by a friend.[67] Not
only is Han mentioned twice in the poem ("I would imitate Han:
not such a foolish idea!"), but the powerful diction is obviously
modeled on that of Han's masterpiece, *The Song of the Stone
Drums*,[68] a work written under similar circumstances (Han had just
received a rubbing of the texts from Chang Chi). Mei's poem, written in 1058 or later, inspired another on the same subject by his
friend Liu Ch'ang,[69] and was quoted at length by Ko Li-fang
(d. 1164) in a discussion of poems on the stone drums.[70]

Meng Chiao (751–814), the poet of the Han Yü circle with whom
Mei Yao-ch'en was compared both by himself and by Ou-yang
Hsiu, also was more to Mei than a mere name to be used as a literary allusion in his poems. For one thing, Mei saw a parallel between his own lack of material success and Meng's well-known
poverty:

Already an impoverished Meng Chiao
I've become a blind Chang Chi as well.[71]

Meng Chiao himself described the poverty that he, as a poet, had to
endure in one of twelve poems sent to a friend:[72]

To be a poet and suffer
Better to fly off into the empty sky. . . .
Begging as I go, with every step,
Wearing bits and pieces of clothes.
Of those who have made poetry their life,
From ancient times, few have grown fat.
I don't resent a poet's hungry old age
But I've moved you to weep tears of compassion.

Meng Chiao quite rapidly came to represent the "suffering poet."
Po Chü-i included him in a list of poets who did not meet with
worldly success in his famous letter to Yüan Chen,[73] and also mentioned him in the line, "Meng Chiao and Chang Chi suffered excessive poverty."[74] Wang Yü-ch'eng, who apparently had considerable admiration for Meng, also referred to him in a similar
context,[75] together with Chia Tao. Meng and Chia appear together
as suffering poets in Ou-yang Hsiu's *Liu-i shih-hua*:[76] "They both
lived in poverty because of poetry until their deaths. And yet all
their lives they amused themselves by writing lines about their suf-

fering." Ou-yang proceeds to quote several examples of these lines by both poets. In his preface to Mei's poetry, written after Mei's death,[77] Ou-yang added Mei Yao-ch'en to the ranks of suffering poets. In a note to one of his own poems,[78] probably dating from 1040, Mei already refers to Ou-yang's idea that many poets have suffered hardships, and also mentions Meng Chiao and Chia Tao, as well as Ch'ü Yüan, Su Wu, Tu Fu, Li Po, and Lu T'ung.

But there were specifically literary reasons for Mei to have taken an interest in Meng Chiao. Meng's concept of what poetry should be was close to Mei's. In his poem, On Reading the Works of Chang Pi (c.804),[79] Meng enunciates a theory of poetry which strikes a balance between Confucian ideals and aesthetic standards. Ever since the death of Li Po, he writes, the Six Principles which characterized the poetry of the Book of Odes have declined. Meng specifically laments the disappearance of the tradition of the Kuo Feng. But with the advent of Chang Pi, he feels, "this culture," that is, the Confucian literary tradition, will again flourish. Chang Pi writes of the rise and decline of states, a primarily Confucian concern, but also imbues his diction with the "wind" and "bone" said to be so important for literary style in the Wen-hsin tiao-lung.[80] Meng ends by wondering who will act as "Poetry Collector" for Chang. The significance of this term will be fully discussed later; here we need only note that it implies poetry of social comment.

In another poem,[81] this one sent to Wei Ying-wu, a poet who was also to exert considerable influence on Mei, Meng speaks of the poetry of Hsü Ling (507–583) and Yü Hsin (513–581) as "dirt and dust," while the fame of Ts'ao Chih (192–232) and Liu Chen (d.217) is like "gold and jade." In other words, the feminine, slightly decadent poetry of the "palace style" popular in the sixth centruy is rejected in favor of the "Chien-an (196–220) school," which was more powerful in its diction and wider in scope. The same poem goes on to say that poetic lines should be "refined and correct," terms also used by Wang Yü-ch'eng to praise the work of a fellow poet who he felt had helped to revitalize Sung poetry.[82] Mei might have seen a parallel between these ideas of Meng's and his own desire to revive the Confucian poetic tradition with its social commitment in response to the Hsi-k'un poetics which he rejected.

In pursuance of his views on poetry, Meng Chiao wrote a number of poems of social comment which may well have attracted Mei's attention. One of these, *Cold Ground: Song of the Peasants*,[83] relates the sufferings of the poor on cold nights when "there are no fires to warm the ground for sleeping." The wind pierces their skin like arrows or needles: "Frosty winds blow through the walls; / We cannot escape from our suffering!" But, ironically, they are able to smell the odor of roasting meats from the nearby homes of the rich, "drinking in their high halls to the sound of bells.'

Meng's poetic style is characterized by an interest in new, startling imagery. Cold, wintry scenes and crystalline or angular forms are frequently depicted. In one of a series of nine poems entitled *Cold Stream*,[84] three different kinds of jade are named, one to describe the sound of ice breaking up on a river, and two to describe the appearance of differently colored ice. The third poem of the same series [85] has the poet walking in the snow along the riverbank after drinking a cup of morning wine. He sees tht the waves have frozen into blade-like pieces of ice which cut and wound the waterbirds. The feathers of the birds are pared away, and the gurgling sound of their blood is heard as it flows into the muddy sand. It was probably such extraordinary imagery as this that prompted the southern Sung critic Ao T'ao-sun to compare Meng with "a broken sword lying at the bottom of a stream; a cold pine growing in a gulley." [86] Yen Shu seems to have been less happy with Meng's penchant for novelty. In a poem of 1046 which records Yen's literary opinions as expressed in a personal conversation,[87] Mei writes, "Rather follow the rustic quality of Magistrate T'ao [Ch'ien]; / Do not adopt the novelty of Meng Chiao." According to Mei's note on the second line, "His Excellency [i.e., Yen Shu] says that among Chiao's poems there occur lines in which all five characters are new (i.e., have never been used before in poetry)."

But it would be strange if Mei, a man whose search for new poetic material led him to write a poem on crows eating maggots in his privy,[88] did not take a more sympathetic view of Meng's work. That both Mei and Ou-yang were, in fact, interested in Meng as a poet is suggested by several poems they wrote in his style. For example, in 1047 Ou-yang wrote *In the Style of Meng Chiao: Autumn*

Thoughts—Two Poems Sent to Sheng-yü.[89] Here is the second of the poems:

Leaves fall on the empty plain from clustered trees;
The southern mountains tower loftily.
These craggy cliffs remind me of the Old Poet—
His jutting bones must stick out even further in the cold!
The Old Poet is like the autumn insects
Humming in autumn with a hundred sounds.
Cloaked in frost, he plucks the solitary flower;
Weeping for the past, he mourns at weed-grown graves.
Jade chiming against stone or metal;
His limpid tones bring awe when they are heard.
How may I have the pleasure of seeing him again
So he can wash away my pressing cares?
The birds that fly south-easterly
Should bring a letter before a day is past.

To this Mei responded with two poems entitled *Following the Rhymes of "Autumn Thoughts in the Style of Meng Chiao" Sent to Me by Ou-yang Yung-shu,*[90] of which the second is translated here:

How noble are your autumn meditations,
Tiered and clustered, lofty as mountains!
They find expression in words of autumn sadness
Like isolated peaks that tower ten thousand feet.
You think of me, grown old in poetry,
And indeed my hair is wispy with age.
Then follows a lament for our old friends,
Friends who have mostly gone to their graves.
Dark winds howl in nocturnal trees—
I hear in their sighing the voices of awesome ghosts.
Although I have put this body out of mind
The world's thronging cares still press upon me.
I lie sleepless as the frosty moon appears,
Fosty moon—I could almost pluck it down!

Both these poems indicate that Ou-yang and Mei were intimately familiar with Meng Chiao's great series of fifteen poems entitled *Autumn Thoughts.*[91] Ou-yang calls Mei "the Old Poet," a phrase which occurs in the sixth poem of Meng's series, and which Ou-yang applied to Mei frequently in their poetic correspondence.[92] Ou-yang refers to Mei's "jutting bones;" the image of bones occurs often in Meng's poems. The first of the series, for example, begins, "Lonely bones lie in the night and can't fall asleep." The second poem includes the superb line (in A. C. Graham's translation), "The cold wind harshly combs my bones." [93] The word *sou*, which is used by Ou-yang, also plays an important role in Meng Chiao: "Meagre and wrinkled, wilted as these" (Graham's translation of *sou-tsuan ju tz'u k'u* in the fifth poem).[94] Mei introduces ghosts in his poem, recalling such lines as "Phantoms crowd my dimmed hearing" (Graham),[95] in the fifth poem of Meng's series, and "Ghosts and spirits howl in the dark bamboo" in the tenth. Finally, the "frosty moon" of Mei's final couplet is reminiscent of Meng's "the face of the autumn moon freezes" (Graham) [96] in poem two. These examples, which could be multiplied, testify to the care with which Ou-yang and Mei read Meng Chiao.

Ten years later, in 1057, while the two friends were participating in the administration of the examinations in the Ministry of Justice, they exchanged poems to pass the time, as we have seen. One of the poems written by Ou-yang was *Viewing Bamboo in the Ministry of Justice, in the Manner of Meng Chiao.* [97] Mei's poem in response to this is entitled, *Viewing Bamboo in the Ministry of Justice, in the Manner of Meng Chiao. Echoing Yung-shu's Poem and Using its Rhymes.* [98] Perhaps because these poems are not inspired by particular originals by Meng, elements of his style are not so easily discerned in them as in the *Autumn Thoughts* examples. But the poems do show that Meng's poetry continued to interest Ou-yang and Mei for a considerable period of time.

It has been suggested by Ch'ien Chung-shu that Mei Yao-ch'en may not have been entirely happy about Ou-yang's comparison of himself with Meng Chiao.[99] He quotes a passage from the *Wen-chien hou-lu* by Shao Po (c.1122) in which a certain Tseng Chung-ch'eng says, "Sheng-yü said to Su Tzu-mei, 'Yung-shu would have it that he is Han T'ui-chih [Han yü] and I am Meng Chiao. Although this was only said in jest, it seems rather unfair to me.' " Ch'ien also quotes a poem to which we have already referred [100] in which Mei writes that Ou-yang, Shih Man-ch'ing, and Su Shun-ch'in are like Han Yü, Lu T'ung, and Chang Chi respectively, and that "I can be compared with Meng Chiao—alas! We are alike in our suffering!"

But the first of these passages in hearsay thrice removed from its putative source, and the second comes from a poem in which Meng Chiao is praised highly. More serious is Ch'ien's allegation that in fact Mei derived little inspiration from Meng Chiao's poetry. In a sensitive comparison of the two men's work, however, Ch'ien succeeds in showing that some of Mei's poetry at least is quite close indeed to Meng's. Even if it forms only "ten or twenty per cent" of his total output, this poetry demonstrates that Meng Chiao was one of the poets who influenced Mei.

References to other poets of the Han Yü circle are also frequently encountered in Mei's and Ou-yang's poetry. In a poem on an eclipse of the sun,[101] Mei refers to Lu T'ung (d. 835) and his famous poem on a lunar eclipse.[102] Lu, Mei says, was the only man of his time brave enough to write this scathing political allegory. Now that he is dead, only Mei is capable of composing a companion piece on a solar eclipse. The three-legged crow of the sun is impotent to prevent the eclipse, and is, in fact, responsible for it. The poet wants the mythological archer Hou-i to shoot the crow down so that the creatures of the four directions and the Five Elements will return to normalcy, and a sage emperor like Shun will be able to appear. "My achievement in writing this poem today can be compared with that of Lu T'ung!" As we have seen, in his poem *Echoing Yung-shu's Baby-Washing Song—following his rhymes*,[103] written on the occasion of his fifth son's birth, Mei again compares himself with Lu T'ung, because "he too had 'One More Boy' who was his son." Mei also associates Shih Man-ch'ing with Lu T'ung in a poem already referred to,[104] and expresses his approval of a friend's views on poetry by saying, "In your discussion of poetry you often speak of Meng [Chiao] and Lu [T'ung]." [105] Like Han Yü and Meng Chiao, Lu T'ung was known for his "new and strange" poetry (Mei's own words [106]) in which he frequently used awkward, prose-like diction.

Chang Chi (c.765–c.830) is still another poet of the Han Yü circle whose name often appears in Mei's poetry. In the poem which couples Shih Man-ch'ing and Lu T'ung, Su Shun-ch'in is said to resemble Chang Chi.[107] Chang is one of the four poets Mei names as representatives of the Han Yü school in another poem.[108] Mei

also refers to Chang Chi's eye illness in a poem on his own ailment: [109]

Already an impoverished Meng Chiao
I've become a blind Chang Chi as well.

Two aspects of Chang Chi's poetry are of particular interest for
the present study. Liu Pin (1022–1088), who knew Mei Yao-ch'en,
praised Chang's *Yüeh-fu* and his five-character regulated verse, ap-
plying to the latter Mei's favorite term, "even and bland." [110] He
may have had in mind such a poem as this:

COMING TO A FISHERMAN'S
HOUSE AT NIGHT [111]

A fisherman's house at the river mouth:
Tide-waters lap the bramble gate.
A traveler wants to stop for the night
But the fisherman hasn't come home.
The village path winds through deep bamboo;
The moon rises over scattered fishing boats.
Far in the distance, along the sandy bank
I see him—spring wind riffling his grass coat.

The simplicity of diction here, the intimacy of the imagery and
the subtle shift of tone as the poet spots the fisherman, all make it
easy to understand why Yang Shen regarded Chang Chi as the
founder of one of the two schools of Late T'ang poetry. They es-
tablish a relaxed, intimate mood which would have appealed to Mei
Yao-ch'en.

Chang Chi's importance as a poet of social comment was appreciated in Chang's own lifetime by Po Chü-i. In a poem entitled *On
Reading the Ancient-Style Yüeh-fu of Chang Chi*,[112] Po praises Chang
in the highest possible terms. He has been devoted to literature for
thirty years, and is especially good at writing *yüeh-fu*. None of his
writings are "empty," but all are in the tradition of the Six Principles, and the *Feng* and *Ya*, in other words, the *Book of Odes*. Po
proceeds to single out four particularly good examples of Chang's
yüeh-fu. The poem *Studying to Become an Immortal*,[113] a protest
against Taoist practices couched in narrative form, and possibly the
forerunner of Po's own *The Sea Is Wide*,[114] "can be used to criticize a

dissipated sovereign." The *Poem on Duke Tung*,[115] which praises a virtuous official, "can be used to instruct covetous and corrupt officials." The other two examples selected by Po appear to be lost. These *yüeh-fu*, Po says, have been cast aside like dirt because there exists no "Poetry Collector" to gather them and record them in the emperor's library.

Chang's protest poems are among the finest of the T'ang dynasty. *The Song of the Old Farmer* [116] will be translated as an example:

The old farmer lives with his poor family in the mountains,
Tilling and planting three or four *mou* of mountain land.
There are few sprouts and a lot of taxes: nothing's left to eat.
His tax-crops are stored in government granaries where they spoil and turn
   to dust.
Late in the year, hoe and plow lie unused in the empty room;
He calls his son to climb the mountain and gather nuts and fruits.
—On West River, a merchant with a hundred bushels of pearls
Keeps a pet dog in the boat, and feeds him meat everyday.

Although reminiscent of Tu Fu's protest poetry, the present example has a simplicity of diction and development, as well as a characteristic understatement, which adumbrate Mei Yao-ch'en's poetry in the same mode. Chang was a staunch supporter of Han Yü's program of opposition to Buddhism and Taoism, and revival of the Confucian tradition; [117] thus, both his intellectual position and his poetic practice would have attracted the attention of Mei and his friends.

Chia Tao, the poet who was most admired by P'an Lang and the Late T'ang school, appears together with Meng Chiao, Lu T'ung, and Chang Chi as one of the four poets of the Han Yü circle in a poem by Mei.[118] As early as 1034, Ou-yang was comparing Mei with Chia Tao: "Sheng-yü is good at reciting poetry, so we say in jest that he is like Lang-hsien [Chia Tao]." [119] Elsewhere, Ou-yang compares Mei's diction with that of Chia Tao and Wu-k'o, Chia's monk-friend.[120] Ou-yang himself wrote a poem entitled *Playing the Zither—in the Manner of Chia Tao* [121] in which the poet dreams of a dignified gentleman whose zither playing conjures up wind and clouds, and inspires the birds and animals to sing. When the poet awakens and finds that the musician has disappeared, he weeps copiously. The relationship of this poem to Chia Tao's style is obscure, but it does demonstrate an interest in Chia's poetry.

Mei Yao-ch'en's interests in mid-T'ang poetry were by no means limited to the poets of the Han Yü circle. Po Chü-i, whose influence appears to have been pervasive in the early Sung, was also admired by Mei. It has already been noted that the views expressed in one of Mei's poems about poetry are very close to those of Po's letter to Yüan Chen.[122] In a poem to a man who was setting out for a new official post near Chung-chou, where Po was once stationed,[123] he says, "The Inspector's talented brush is full of power; / He will certainly be like Po Chung-chou!" In another poem, written on a similar occasion,[124] he says, "Inspector Po of Chung-chou: / His *Bamboo Branch Poems* [125] are quite accomplished. / You must carry on this tradition of beauty. . . ." And in still another poem of this type: [126] "Who needs singers and wind instruments? Only poetry and wine! / Especially now that Po Lo-t'ien of Yü-hang has arrived." A poem Mei wrote on a friend's garden [127] begins, "Chanting and enjoying Lo-t'ien's *Poem Written by the Pond,*[128] / You have bought a pond ten *mou* in area, all planted with lotus." Later in the same poem, Mei speaks of the famous "gathering of the nine elders," a literary group over which Po presided.

While Mei never wrote a poem specifically stated to be in the Po Chü-i manner, his *Song of the Flower Girl,*[129] a lengthy narrative poem possibly written in 1044 which relates a young singing girl's love affair, is obviously modeled on Po's long narrative poems, *Everlasting Sorrow* and *Song of the P'i-p'a.*[130] The line,

Just as heaven and earth are eternal this sorrow will have no end,

is an "allusive variation" on

Heaven and earth may be long-lived, but they will end sometime;
This sorrow will go on forever and never end,

from *Everlasting Sorrow,* and the simple but expressive diction of Mei's poem in general is very close to Po.

Ou-yang Hsiu also admired Po Chü-i. In a passage from *Liu-i shih-hua* already quoted,[131] Po is associated with Tu Fu as one of the "T'ang worthies." Ou-yang once visited Po's grave and wrote a poignant *chüeh-chü* poem [132] on the experience, in which he describes pouring out a libation to Po's spirit. In another poem [133] he passes the site of Po's exile, and is struck by the realization that his own place of banishment is still far away.

In his letter to Yüan Chen,[134] Po Chü-i praises the poetry of Wei Ying-wu (c.736–c.790), calling it "calm and bland," a phrase suggestive of Mei's "even and bland." Elsewhere in his works, Po speaks highly of Wei, even linking his poetic style with T'ao Ch'ien.[135] In this respect as in others, Po anticipates the interests of the Sung poets. Although Ssu-k'ung T'u (837–908) associated Wei with Wang Wei as a poet whose style was "limpid and bland, finely structured," [136] it was only in the Sung dynasty that Wei really came to be appreciated. The *Ts'ang-lang shih-hua,* it will be recalled, named Sheng Tu as a poet who emulated the style of Wei Ying-wu.[137] Wang Yü-ch'eng also refers to Wei as a discerning critic of poetry.[138] According to Wu Ch'u-hou (d. c.1093), Yen Shu praised Wei's poetry.[139] But Mei Yao-ch'en appears to have been the first major poet who was seriously interested in Wei.

Liang K'un has suggested that the two poets who had the greatest influence on Mei were Han Yü and Wei Ying-wu.[140] In support of this view, he quotes a passage from the *Feng-yüeh-t'ang shih-hua* by Chu Pien (d. 1138 or 1154),[141] according to which, "In his youth, Sheng-yü exclusively emulated the style of Wei Su-chou [Wei Ying-wu]." Mei's works contain many references to Wei. In an early poem to a Buddhist monk who had visited Fan Chung-Yen,[142] Mei compares the monk with the great monk-poet of the T'ang dynasty, Chiao-jan (c.760), and Fan with Wei Ying-wu, who had admired Chiao-jan's poetry. When Ou-yang Hsiu was exiled to Ch'u-chou, Mei sent him a long poem [143] which begins.

Formerly I read the collected works of Mr. Wei [Ying-wu]
And found many poems about Ch'u-chou.
With great élan he describes local scenes and customs,
Seeking everywhere the hidden and unusual.
Now you have been appointed Prefect there,
As famous as this man of the past.

Later in the same poem, Mei approves of Ou-yang's calligraphy and poetry: "You do not make characters like a child's / Nor do you write 'wind and moon' poems." Mei thus felt that Ou-yang was carrying on the poetic tradition represented by Wei Ying-wu, "seeking everywhere the hidden and unusual." Ou-yang himself, as it happens, was not too fond of Wei's poetry, a point made quite early by Han Chü (c. 1086–1135).[144] The only evidence in Ou-yang's works for his opinion of Wei is provided by his little prose piece, *Written After Wei Ying-wu's "West Stream at Ch'u-chou"*,[145] in which he criticizes Wei for writing about a place that did not actually exist.

Among the poems in the styles of past poets collected in chapter twelve of Mei's works can be found a five-character *chüeh-chü* entitled *In Imitation of Wei Ying-wu's "Fading Lamp"*.[146] The original poem by Wei, actually called *Facing the Fading Lamp*,[147] describes how a recluse, unable to fall asleep, lies in the glimmering lamplight undoing and retying the sash of his robe. Mei's poem places more emphasis on the lamp and its light, introducing the recluse-poet only in the last line: "I pass the night alone, like the Mountain Spirit."

More helpful for judging the extent of Mei's familiarity with Wei Ying-wu is the long prose preface to his poem, *Climbing the Sun View Peak of Mount T'ai*, written in 1053:[148]

> When I anchored below Kua-pu Mountain, I dreamt that Wang Ching-i [Wang Ch'ou] asked me about the poem *Sun View Peak* by Wei Ying-wu. I recited the poem, but the words did not seem to fit, so I told Ching-i that we would have to consult Wei's collected works. Upon awakening, I immediately did so, but there was no poem of this title. And yet I could still remember that the first line of the poem I had recited in my dream was, "In the morning I climb Sun View Peak." I have therefore written a complete poem starting with this line.

Careful perusal of Wei's complete works reveals that there is indeed no poem of this title by him, nor does the line recited by Mei in his dream occur in any of Wei's poems. But the expression *ch'en teng* ("In the morning I climb") occurs at least twice:

In the morning I climb the frosty wilds.[149]

In the morning I climb to the western studio, and gaze about.[150]

The related expression *ch'en chi* also occurs.[151] This example, more than any of the others quoted above, suggests that Mei had read Wei Ying-wu with considerable care. He was even inspired to dream about reciting one of Wei's poems, and an expression which had been used at least twice by Wei, and was probably floating around in Mei's subconscious mind, came to the surface in this dream.[152]

Wei Ying-wu's poetry displays several features which would have been of interest to Mei. His best known works are quiet, understated poems on the poet's experience of the landscape or his relations with friends, of the kind that would have appealed to poets of the Late T'ang school. Here is an example: [153]

MEETING REGISTRAR LI OF LOYANG
ON THE RIVER HUAI
I've built a hut overlooking the old ferry;
Lying here, I watch the River Huai flow.
I grow old by the window;
Trees turn autumnal beyond the gate.
A wild goose passes the cold mountain;
In evening rain, a boat comes from afar.
As the sun goes down I meet the returning traveler:
I'll never forget those good times we had.

The simplicity of diction and intimacy of tone in such poetry might well have prompted Po Chü-i to characterize it as "calm and bland." They are also features held in common with Po's own poetry, and with the poetry of Chang Chi.

Like Chang Chi, Wei wrote poetry of social comment as well as poetry of the "Late T'ang" type. His *Song of Quarrying Jade* [154] is surprisingly different from the type of poetry usually associated with Wei:

The government is mustering commoners,
Telling them to quarry the jade of Lan River.
Homeless at night on the steep mountain ridge,
They sleep in thick forests in the falling rain.
—A lonely wife returns from bringing her husband food
And stands south of the hut, weeping.

This poem is obviously related to Li Ho's famous *Song of the Old Man Quarrying Jade*,[155] as Wang Ch'i (c. 1723) has already pointed out.[156] In both poems the jade gatherers suffer through a rain storm in the mountains. In Wei's poem, the wife of one of the gatherers is depicted bringing her husband food and then returning home to weep. Li Ho has the old jade quarrier think of his children at home in the cold. In addition, the related words *chen* ("grove") and *chen* ("acorns") are used by Wei and Li respectively, suggesting that one was influenced by the other. As Wei died around 790, and Li was born in 791, the credit for writing the original poem must go to Wei. Li's version is more elaborate, and introduces the fantastic and macabre elements ("dragon," "ghosts of the drowned") that are characteristic of his style. Wei's poem is simpler in diction, less passionate in tone, and entirely realistic in its imagery. In all these respects, his poem is much closer than Li's to the kind of social protest poetry that Mei Yao-ch'en was to write.

Two other aspects of Wei's poetry that would have attracted Mei's attention are the superb series of poems on the death of his wife, and a group of poems dealing with antiques. But as these are rather special *genres*, they will be discussed in the chapter on Mei's poetic practice.

Later Sung poets were to regard Wei Ying-wu as one of the great exponents of "even and bland" poetry. In fact, the Ming critic Wang Shih-chen (1526–1590), while able to appreciate Wei's poetry, felt that Wei's more enthusiastic Sung admirers praised him excessively.[157] Su Shih was one of these admirers, and his name apparently became associated with that of Wei Ying-wu, as Tseng Chi-li (c. 1147) claimed that no one had appreciated Wei's poetry before Su.[158] This view was corrected centuries later by Chao I (1727–1814), who pointed out that Po Chü-i had already recognized Wei's talent,[159] but even Chao failed to notice that Mei Yao-ch'en was largely responsible for introducing Wei's poetry to the Sung dynasty.

Mei, while especially interested in mid-T'ang poetry, was of course familiar with the great High T'ang masters as well. One of his poems seems to suggest, in fact, that he considered Tu Fu and Li Po to be superior to Han Yü.[160] The poem, which probably dates from 1056 or 1057, again names the *Book of Odes* (here referred to as the "two *nan*," i.e., the *Shao-nan* and *Chou-nan* sections of the *Kuo*

Feng) as the ancestor of the orthodox poetic tradition. This work of the sages was "cut up and fragmented" by later generations of poets, but "we (Mei and his colleagues) are striving to imitate it, although trying to paint a dragon we've ended up painting a lizard!" "In the T'ang dynasty," Mei continues, "literature flourished. Han [Yü] yielded to [Tu] Fu and [Li] Po. Fu and Po were all-encompassing, and strove to emulate completely Juan [Chi] and T'ao [Ch'ien]." [161] The significance of Juan Chi and T'ao Ch'ien for Mei will be discussed later. Here it is interesting to note his admiration for Tu Fu and Li Po, although toward the end of the same poem, Mei reasserts the particular importance of mid-T'ang poetry for him: "Again the style of the *Yüan-ho* period appears."

Li Po, Tu Fu, and Han Yü appear on an equal footing in one of the poems in which Mei proclaims the superiority of an "even and bland" style.[162] Here they represent outstanding poetry in general, and are named as a compliment to the man whose poetry Mei is praising. Elsewhere, Mei compares himself with Tu Fu, and Ou-yang Hsiu with Li Po: [163] "I grow old in poverty like Shao-ling [Tu Fu], / And you are like the Banished Immortal [Li Po]." Specific references to Tu Fu as a poet also occur: "As Shao-ling experienced frustration, his poetry tended to mature." [164]

Mei wrote one poem which he explicitly states to be based on a Tu Fu original: *In Imitation of "Jade Flower Palace" by Tu Fu*.[165] A detailed comparison between this poem and the Tu Fu original [166] reveals that Mei has been astonishingly faithful to his source. Nearly every line of Mei's poem contains a word or image which also appears in the Tu Fu poem, usually in the corresponding line. Mei's poem may have been a piece of apprentice work, but it shows that he read the poets in whom he took an interest with the greatest possible care.

Less closely related to Tu Fu but obviously inspired by one of his poems is Mei's *Lament for a Prince*.[167] As in Tu Fu's more elaborate original,[168] the poet meets a prince who has fallen on evil times. The poet is deeply moved by the prince's suffering, and gives him food and drink.

Mei's interest in Tu Fu was shared by Ou-yang Hsiu. Probably because Ou-yang stated in a well-known essay that he preferred Li

Po to Tu Fu,[169] later critics often claimed that he did not like Tu's poetry.[170] But the scholar Ch'en Yen-hsiao (c.1147) rejects this view.[171] Ch'en quotes three passages which testify to the high regard in which Ou-yang held Tu Fu. The first, an entry from *Liu-i shih-hua* [172] which has already been referred to, begins by praising Ch'en Ts'ung-i (c.1004) "for his pure Confucianism and scholarship in ancient matters" at "a time when modish literature was in fashion." There follows a brief reference to the Hsi-k'un school in which Ou-yang complains that because of the popularity of this school, the poetic works of the "T'ang worthies" nearly went out of circulation. The passage continues,

> Mr. Ch'en happened to get hold of an old edition of Tu's works, full of omissions and errors in the text. In the poem *Seeing Off the Superintendent Ts'ai* [173] there occurred the line, "Light of body, like a single bird _____." The last character was missing. Mr. Ch'en therefore had his guests complete the line by adding an appropriate character. One suggested "speeding," another, "falling," another, "arising," another, "swooping." None of them was sure. Afterwards, Mr. Ch'en came across a good text, and found that the line read, "Light of body, like a single bird *passing by*." Mr. Ch'en sighed in admiration, reflecting that all the gentlemen could not equal Tu in even a single word.

The second example given by Ch'en Yen-hsiao to demonstrate Ou-yang's admiration for Tu Fu also comes from *Liu-i shih-hua*,[174] and has already been quoted: "In the later years of the T'ang dynasty, poets no longer wrote in the heroic, expansive manner of Li and Tu, but devoted themselves to surpassing each other in precision of expression." Here Li and Tu again appear on an equal footing.

Ch'en's third and final example is a passage from the *Chi-ku lu*,[175] Ou-yang's archaeological catalogue, in which Ou-yang concludes that a certain stele is spurious on the testimony of Tu Fu.

Probably the most eloquent proof of Ou-yang's admiration for Tu is provided by a poem Ou-yang wrote on a portrait of him.[176] Tu is here associated with the tradition of the *Book of Odes*, and is called "a hero of poetry."

The name of Li Po has already appeared several times in quotations from Mei and Ou-yang. Ou-yang, it will be recalled, says in an essay on the two poets that he prefers Li to Tu. Also important is his poem, *A Playful Poem on T'ai-po for Sheng-yü*, also known as *On Reading Li Po's Works—in his style*.[177] The poem is a *tour de force* which depicts Li as the great romantic poet, writing only when drunk. Among his themes are the dangerous roads to Szechwan, a fantastic vision of roaring dragons and tigers, and a musical carousal in the palace. At the end of the poem, Li looks down from the sky at Meng Chiao and Chia Tao, "fireflies flying wet with dew, and chirping in the autumn grass." Ou-yang regarded Li Po primarily as a poet of the monumental and romantic. His poem *Mt. Lu is High*,[178] an exercise in Li's heroic mode, was admired by Mei.[179]

References to Li Po as a poet are fairly numerous in Mei's works. In a poem about a friend's white pheasant,[180] Mei mentions that Li Po also wrote a poem on this subject, probably referring to Li's poem, *Sent to Mr. Hu of the Yellow Mountains, Asking Him to Send Me His White Pheasants*.[181] In *Reading "[Cup in Hand] I Question the Moon,"*[182] Mei good-humoredly takes Li to task for some of the extravagant questions and assertions in his original poem.[183] His respect for Li, however, is evident: "And yet these words—'It will always glimmer in my golden cup'— / Will go unchallenged for ten thousand ages."

Mei actually appears to imitate Li Po's style in his long, seven-character poem, *Returning from Greendragon—presented to Hsieh Shih-chih* [Hsieh Ching-wen, the nephew of Mei's first wife],[184] written in 1044:

Three or four years since we last parted,
And your craggy bones are still jutting out!
The beard is fuller and darker than it was.
In learning you have long been without a peer.
I, alas, have grown old and quite useless;
Spreading white hairs will soon cover my head.
My writings seem at variance with the times;
My wife hungry, my children crying, I haven't a cent.
Happily I can pass the day with the *Documents* and the *Odes*;
Who cares about wealth and position, intimacy with high officials?
These days, too, I have been drinking little wine—
Before the second cup I burn inside!
The other night you and I drank joyfully together;

After only a cup or two I fell asleep.
The cackling of chickens and barking of dogs seemed to ring in my ears;
I raised my head—the room and ceiling whirled around!
I rose and fixed my headcloth, ill at ease,
Rigged my boat and sailed straight to the vast ocean shore.
I wanted to mount a whale and ride ten thousand miles,
But the lightning didn't lend me its thundering whip.
My spirits fell, depression came—there was nothing left but sleep.
My thoughts in dream were carried to a duckweed island. . . .
No more drinking parties with you, my friend:
Who can follow the Banished Immortal, get drunk and die?

This strange poem begins with eight lines of realistic description of Hsieh's physical appearance and Mei's present situation. The poet describes himself as old (he is actually forty-two!) and out of touch with the times. His family is suffering from poverty. But in the ninth and tenth lines he reflects that he can enjoy the life of a true Confucian scholar, reading the classics and holding worldly success in contempt. This couplet forms a transition to the remaining lines of the poem, which now seems to shift into the heroic, even fantastic mode associated with Li Po. The perspective changes, distances expand, and the imagery becomes grandiose: "vast ocean shore," "whale," "lightning," "thundering whip." But even in the midst of his dream, Mei introduces a touch of homely realism: the "room and ceiling whirling around" of line sixteen also appear in *Prefectural Judge Fan Urges Me To Give Up Drinking Wine*,[185] where they are clearly intended to describe a hangover. At the end of the dream, as in the *Li sao*, the poet's wanderlust is thwarted by depression. He realizes that he cannot emulate the Banished Immortal, Li Po, to the ultimate point of dying as he did.

We have seen that according to Mei, Tu Fu and Li Po "strove to emulate completely Juan [Chi] and T'ao [Ch'ien]."[186] This passage serves to introduce into the discussion two of Mei's favorite poets. It has even been asserted by Yokoyama Iseo that Juan Chi (210–263) and T'ao Chien (365–427) are the only poets repeatedly mentioned by Mei and therefore the only ones who really exerted any influence on him.[187] Although the examples quoted above would seem to indicate that Mei's interest in the mid-T'ang poets as well as Tu Fu and Li Po was at least equally great, there can be no doubt that Juan and T'ao were of considerable importance to him.

References to Juan Chi occur frequently in Mei's collection. A poem probably dating from 1049 [188] contains the line, "I chant the poems of Mr. Juan." Another, probably dating from 1053,[189] includes the couplet, "In poetry, able to be like Juan Chi, / In criticism, not yielding to Chung Hung." In a poem from 1054 or 1055 entitled *Night*,[190] the final couplet reads,

Juan Chi alone cannot sleep;
Restless, he rises to play the zither.

The reference here is to the first poem of Juan's famous series, *Singing My Feelings*,[191] which begins,

In the night I cannot sleep,
So I rise and sit down to play the singing zither.

Another allusive variation on these lines appears in a poem probably dating from 1045, entitled *Feelings on an Autumn Night:* [192]

I lie alone but can't fall asleep,
So I rise and sit down, agitated in my heart.

Finally, the poem *Sitting at Night*,[193] dating from 1049, will be translated in full as an example of the Juan Chi manner as interpreted by Mei:

Deep in the night I feel anxious and lonely;
The empty hall glimmers with lamp and candlelight.
A brief rustling of falling leaves is heard;
Hidden insects chirp on ceaselessly.
I have devoted myself to study, but not merely for myself;
Content with poverty, I pursue righteous fame.
Thus I have written this poem, *Singing My Feelings,*
Thinking of Infantryman Juan.

As Yokoyama Iseo has noted, this poem is probably based on the first of the series, *Singing My Feelings*.[194] It seems strange that the poet should pride himself on "pursuing fame," but he may have had in mind this passage from the *Prose Poem on the Owl*, quoted in the biography of Chia I in the *Han shu:* "The covetous man pursues wealth; the righteous man pursues fame."

Mei wrote a number of other poems in this mode. A group of four probably dating from 1054 is simply entitled *Singing My Feelings*.[195] Another poem, dating from 1052 or 1053 and preserved in the fragmentary Sung edition,[196] is called *In Imitation of Singing My Feelings*. Two further poems, *In Imitation of Infantryman Juan's "A Day and Then Another Day"*,[197] probably date from 1053 and are based on one of the poems in the series *Singing My Feelings*.[198]

The earliest of Mei's poems in the Juan Chi manner, and the best, was written in 1044:[199]

HSIEH SHIH-HOU [HSIEH CHING-CH'U, THE NEPHEW OF
MEI'S FIRST WIFE] RETURNS TO NAN-YANG—
IN THE MANNER OF INFANTRYMAN JUAN

A day and then a morning,
The evening then the dawn:
This is the time I spent with you,
A brief visit when we didn't speak of parting.
My feelings are unending
But now the year draws to its close.
The neighing horses are impatient for the road;
The solitary bird pursues his mate ahead.
You harness up the carriage, longing for your wife,
Ice and charcoal fit image for your love.
South you face the white river's shore;
Wind and snow beat the high banks.
Thinking of your loving mother's fears,
You gallop swiftly home as the seasons change.
Sword unbuckled, you climb to the northern chamber
Where your young wife smiles brilliantly.
She sews and patches your tattered coat,
Cleaning off the journey's dust.
But I, a stranger in the capital,
Grieve to wear an unwashed robe.

The use of "ice and charcoal" in line ten derives from a passage in the *Huai-nan Tzu*:[200] "No two things in the world love each other more than ice and charcoal." The welcome annotation to this statement explains that "when ice comes in contact with charcoal, it melts into water, thus returning to its original nature. When charcoal comes in contact with ice, it preserves its [form as] charcoal. For this reason, it is said that they love each other."

The elements of Juan Chi's style in *Hsieh Shih-hou Returns to Nan-yang* are fairly easy to identify. The two opening lines are variations on Juan's "A day and then another day," and "A day and then an evening." Lines seven and eight introduce the quasi-allegoric mode which is characteristic of early Six Dynasties poetry. The horse and bird are used to represent Hsieh Shih-hou, returning to see his wife, but at the same time they are sensed as real animals, participating in the action of the poem. Some of the landscape of Hsieh's return route is then sketched, and the subsequent meeting with his wife is narrated. But at this point a subtle change seems to occur. Hsieh's wife mends and cleans his clothes for him, a homely touch foreign to Juan Chi. And then in the final couplet, significantly removed from the rest of the poem by the particle *erh*, Mei's personal tragedy comes to the surface, called forth by the thought of Hsieh's marital happiness: Mei's wife had died earlier in the year, and there is no one to wash his robe for him now. The poignancy of this ending is especially effective for its contrast with the somewhat aloof tone, characteristic of Juan Chi, maintained in the preceding lines. In this poem, then, Mei transcends his model, assimilating certain elements of style and tone, but adapting them to his own needs as a poet.

T'ao Ch'ien is probably the poet to whom Mei refers most frequently. And a large number of these references deal specifically with poetry. In a poem probably dating from 1043,[201] for example, Mei praises a monk-poet for writing in T'ao's style, while most monk-poets only grow old "chirping like crickets before windows or under trees," and never write in the old *Chien-an* style, here apparently used somewhat anachronistically as a general cognomen for early Six Dynasties poetry. In a late poem from 1058 or 1059,[202] Mei says, "Whenever one reads the poetry of T'ao Ch'ien / It makes one forget the troubles of the world," a statement which recalls his praise of Lin Pu's poems: "Reading them made one forget the hundred affairs." [203]

Other references to T'ao are more specific as to the aspects of his style which Mei admired. A couplet already quoted from a poem based on Yen Shu's statements on poetry [204] reads, "Rather follow the rustic quality of Magistrate T'ao; / Do not adopt the novelty of

Meng Chiao." That Mei agreed with at least the first half of this couplet is suggested by a poem written around 1050 [205] in which he says of his own poetry, "It is just like T'ao Yüan-ming: / Harsh diction close to that of farmers." We have seen that Wang Yü-ch'eng wrote a series of poems in which he purposely employed "low" diction, "so that the mountain farmers can easily understand them." [206] According to the preface to *The Farmers' Words*, translated and discussed in chapter 5, Mei based this poem on the actual statements of farmers. T'ao Ch'ien thus appealed to Mei partly because of the quality of his diction.

It is of particular significance that Mei twice associates T'ao Ch'ien with his own poetic ideal of *p'ing-tan* ("even and bland"). T'ao figures in one of Mei's most important statements on poetry, included in a poem of 1045 [207] in which he seems to be criticizing his friend Sung Chung-tao for not taking sufficient care of himself while ill:

Poetry is basically stating one's feelings;
There's no need to shout them out loud!
When you realize that the poem should be even and bland,
You'll devote yourself to Yüan-ming morning and evening.
He should be in your dreams when you sleep
And in your broth when you eat.
If Yüan-ming has a spirit
He's probably feeling upset about you. . . .

In another poem of 1045,[208] sent to Sung Chung-tao and his more famous brother Sung Min-ch'iu, Mei says of their writings, "Among them are poems like those of Yüan-ming, / Even and bland, in the same class as his."

Mei himself wrote poems in the manner of T'ao Ch'ien. *In Imitation of T'ao Ch'ien's "Stopping Wine"* [209] is based on a *tour de force* by T'ao [210] in which the character *chih* appears in every line and alternately takes on the meanings "to give up or put an end to," "to stop (in a place)," and "only." Mei, by including two *chih*'s in one line, comes out one ahead of T'ao! Also written with tongue in cheek are the *Three Poems In the Style of T'ao* [211] of 1045. These poems, entitled *The Hand Questions the Foot*, *The Foot Answers the Hand*, and *The Eye Explains*, are obviously based on T'ao's trilogy,

Body, Shadow, and Spirit: [212] *Sent By the Body to the Shadow, The Shadow Answers the Body,* and *The Spirit Explains,* as Yokoyama has pointed out.[213] While T'ao's original series touches on some of the most profound problems of the human condition, Mei has narrowed his scope somewhat. After the hand and foot insult each other, the eyes plead with them to cooperate and perform their allotted functions, just as the two eyes work together. Mei also reveals his familiarity with T'ao's trilogy in this couplet: [214] "Whenever I see the *Body, Shadow, and Spirit* poems, / I wonder if this is not the truth explained by Spirit."

T'ao's famous poem and prose piece on the *Peach Blossom Spring* [215] inspired Mei to write two poems based on this story. The first, *Song of Wu-ling,*[216] is one of his earlier works, possibly dating from around 1034. The second, simply called *Peach Blossom Spring,*[217] was written in 1056 at the request of a friend of Mei's. At first, Mei thought that his earlier poem on the subject would do, but on rereading it he found that he was "quite dissatisfied with it," and so produced an entirely new work. As the preface to this new poem notes, "It was T'ao Ch'ien who first wrote a prose account and a poem about Wu-ling, and after him there came an unbroken line of authors who composed verses on the subject."

Although fragmentary and far from conclusive, the lines and poems quoted in this chapter suggest that Mei Yao-ch'en and Ou-yang Hsiu had catholic tastes in poetry. For them, the correct poetic tradition originated in the *Book of Odes* and *Li sao.* It was developed in the Six Dynasties by Juan Chi and T'ao Ch'ien, and was practiced in the T'ang dynasty by Tu Fu and Li Po, and by the outstanding poets of the mid-T'ang period, most notably Han Yü and his circle. Mei and Ou-yang did not, of course, agree in every particular. Mei seems to have been much more interested in Juan Chi and T'ao Ch'ien than Ou-yang, and Ou-yang did not share Mei's enthusiasm for Wei Ying-wu. But they were agreed in feeling that the tradition had waned during the late T'ang, Five Dynasties, and early Sung.

Their very catholicity of taste, however, made it possible for them to recognize that early Sung poetry had its merits, and they did not reject all of it by any means. It was their purpose to revitalize poetic practice by selecting elements from a number of different styles which coexisted within the orthodox mainstream, and some of which had been preserved by certain of the early Sung poets, especially Wang Yü-ch'eng. This eclecticism led them to eschew the extremist polemics of Shih Chieh, whose opinions they may have shared to a milder degree.

If the actual poetry which Mei and Ou-yang wrote cannot be categorized simply and encompasses a variety of expressive modes, it is because the sources from which it derived were so various, ranging from the versified prose of Han Yü to the lucid diction of Chang Chi and Wei Ying-wu, from the rustic simplicity of T'ao Ch'ien to the fantastic visions of Li Po, and from the intimate landscape scenes of Chia Tao to the grim social commentary of Tu Fu and Po Chü-i.

Chapter Four

THEORY

Few CHINESE POETS set down their views on the nature of poetry in systematic, logically structured monographs. Mei Yao-ch'en is no exception. As in the previous chapter, we must therefore depend on a few scattered lines in Mei's poems and on a handful of quotations from Mei in Ou-yang Hsiu's *Liu-i shih-hua* to form some idea of his poetic theory. A small book on poetry entitled *Hsü chin-chen shih-ko* [1] and purporting to be a work of Mei's does exist, but Ka-kehi is certainly correct in his suggestion that it is a forgery.[2] The book opens with a preface which relates how a Buddhist monk praised the poetry of Po Chü-i to Mei, and showed him a copy of Po's *Chin-chen shih-ko*. Mei was impressed by this work and decided to write the present one to continue and expand on Po's. The test presents various tersely stated poetic principles, illustrating them with couplets and some *chüeh-chü* poems by mostly unidentified authors. Among the poets who are named are Chia Tao, Li Po, and Chou P'u (d. 878), a Late T'ang poet. The lines quoted are given rather forced symbolic or allegoric interpretations. For example, the couplet, "The sun has risen ten feet above the mountain; / The wind has blown many plants into blossom," is interpreted to mean that "a wise lord has put the state in order; his instructions and statutes have been issued, and the common men are all content in their places."

The text also gives a number of illustrations for the Eight Defects enumerated by Shen Yüeh, as well as other categories such as the Five Principles, the Three Styles, the Seven Don't's, and the Eight Modes. Few of the statements made in the work could possibly be construed as characteristic of Mei's views. One of the Five Principles is said to be "protest," and is illustrated by this couplet from *The Widow in the Mountains* by Tu Hsün-ho: [3] "Even though the mulberries have been abandoned, they still impose taxes; / The fields and gardens have gone to weed, but they keep collecting tax-sprouts." According to the author of the text, this couplet "protests the government's cruel exaction of heavy taxes." It is possible to see in this example a reflection of the important role played by protest poetry in Mei's work. Elsewhere in the text, the "upper, middle, and lower" types of poetry are described. The middle type is said to be "bland and yet flavorful," and is illustrated by the lines, "Leisurely I lean on a Great Lake rock, / Drunkenly listening to the Tung-t'ing autumn," a perfectly parallel, Late T'ang couplet of the kind later critics were to associate with the "even and bland" style, as shall be shown later in this chapter. Aside from these two examples, nothing in the *Hsü chin-chen shih-ko* is particularly representative of Mei's ideas.

The most extensive existing statement on poetry by Mei Yao-ch'en is recorded in Ou-yang Hsiu's *Liu-i shih-hua*. [4] As this passage is of great importance, it will be quoted here in full. The first part of the translation (until the Chia Tao couplet is introduced) is partly based on that of Burton Watson: [5]

> Sheng-yü once said to me, "Though the poet may emphasize meaning,[6] it is also difficult to choose the proper diction. If he manages to use words with a fresh skill and to achieve some effect that no one has ever achieved, then he may consider that he has done well. He must be able to depict a scene that is difficult to describe, in such a way that it seems to be right before the eyes of the reader, and to express inexhaustible meaning which exists beyond the words themselves—only then can he be regarded as great.
>
> "Chia Tao has written, 'I gather mountain fruits with a bamboo basket, / Carry water from rocky streams in a clay jar.' [7] Yao Ho has written, 'My horse follows the mountain deer, running free; / My chickens fly to perch with the wild birds.' [8] Both these couplets describe lonely, out-of-

the-way mountain towns where there is little official business. But neither is as skillful as, 'The district is ancient; locust roots protrude. / The
official is virtuous; the horse's bones jut out.' "

I [i.e., Ou-yang Hsiu] said, "These are indeed examples of skillful diction. But what poems illustrate 'depicting a scene that is difficult to
describe,' and 'expressing inexhaustible meaning'?"

Sheng-yü replied, "The author must get it in his mind; the reader
must comprehend his meaning. Examples of this kind are hard to enu-
merate. I can, however, give a general idea of what I mean. Consider
these lines by Yen Wei (c.756): 'By the willow bank, spring waters are
wide; / On the flower beds, evening sunlight lingers.' [9] Are not the atmosphere and the seasonal landscape—their warm harmony and lambent charm—depicted here in such a way that they seem to be right
before the eyes of the reader? Again, in this couplet of Wen T'ing-yün:
'A cock crows—moon above the thatch-roofed shop; / Footprints in the
frost on the wood-plank bridge,' [10] and in this one of Chia Tao: 'Strange
birds screech in the vast plains; / The traveler is frightened in the setting
sun,' [11] are not the hardships of the road and the sad thoughts of a traveler expressed in such a way that they are felt beyond the words themselves?"

This important passage opens with a statement which might have
been intended as a retort to an attitude expressed by Liu Pin, who
knew Mei: "In poetry it is the meaning which is paramount. Diction is of secondary importance. A poem whose meaning is profound and whose purport is exalted is naturally a masterpiece, even
though its diction may be facile." [12] Mei protests that attention
must also be paid to diction. He then presents his criteria for outstanding poetry: it must be new, in the sense that it says things
which have never been said before; it must be accurate and evocative in its descriptive passages; and it must be able to conjure up a
desired mood that transcends the actual words of the poem. Mei il-
lustrates his views with three couplets describing the leisurely life
of an official in an obscure district. The third, which I have not
been able to identify,[13] is declared to be superior to the Chia Tao
and Yao Ho examples, possibly because the locust roots and the
horse with jutting bones are felt to represent or symbolize the ancient district and the leisured official respectively, while at the same
time they are sensuously experienced as actual images. But this
does not necessarily mean that Mei is rejecting the Late T'ang cou-

plet. He quotes three more—another by Chia Tao, one by Yen Wei, and one by Wen T'ing-yün—with approval as further illustrations at the request of Ou-yang Hsiu.

The poets of the Late T'ang school, concerned as they were with the creation of charming, evocative landscapes, would have accepted Mei's concept of "depicting a scene that is difficult to describe in such a way that it seems to be right before the eyes of the reader." In fact, the words "difficult to describe" appear in a poem on river scenery by Lin Pu, one of the chief poets who wrote in the Late T'ang style: [14]

Hidden poetic scenes strike my eyes;
I know they will be difficult to describe.

This concept did not originate with the Late T'ang school, but was first expressed by Lu Chi (261–303) in his *Prosepoem on Literature* (in the translation of Achilles Fang): [15] "Topsy-turvy and fleeting, shapes are hard to delineate."

The concept of "inexhaustible meaning which exists beyond the words themselves" is also not entirely original. It is implicit, for example, in this famous passage from *Chuang Tzu* (in the translation of Burton Watson):

> The fish trap exists because of the fish; once you've gotten the fish, you can forget the trap. . . . Words exist because of meaning; once you've gotten the meaning, you can forget the words. Where can I find a man who has forgotten words so I can have a word with him?

A passage suggestive in its wording of Mei's statement occurs in the preface to the *Shih-p'in* of Chung Hung (c.505). [16] Here, Chung defines the difficult term *hsing* (as in the *Great Preface* to the *Book of Odes*) as follows: "The text has ended and yet the meaning continues." It should be noted, however, that Chung is concerned here with a particular term and not with poetry in general.

Chu Tung-jun has suggested that Mei's dictum is related to an interesting passage in the *Letter on Poetry to Mr. Li* by Ssu-k'ung T'u (837–908): [17]

> There have been many metaphors past and present to explain why poetry is the most difficult of the difficult literary arts. It is my humble

opinion that one can speak of poetry in terms of differentiating flavors. Of the foods worth eating south of the Chiang-ling region [i.e., in the land of the "southern barbarians"], it's not that the vinegar is not sour, but it stops at being sour and does not go beyond; and it's not that the salt is not salty, but it stops at being salty and does not go beyond. The reason Chinese people only eat enough of these things to satisfy their hunger is that they realize that an exquisite flavor which lies beyond saltiness and sourness is lacking. How appropriate, however, that the people of Chiang-ling should not understand this distinction, as they themselves practice such cooking!

While not without adumbration in earlier critical writings, Mei's two dicta entered the repertoire of critical formulae almost immediately in the form given them by Mei, although interpretations of their meaning sometimes differed. Ssu-ma Kuang, for example, states that "when the ancients wrote poetry, they prized 'meaning which exists beyond the words themselves.' " [18] As an example of such poetry, he quotes Tu Fu's poem, *Spring View*. [19] Commenting on the first two couplets of the poem, he says, "From 'mountains and rivers remain' we realize that nothing else remains; from 'grasses and trees are thick,' we realize that there are no people. In ordinary times, flowers and birds are enjoyable things, but from the fact that when the poet sees the former he weeps, and when he hears the latter he grieves, the nature of the times can be known." That is, for Ssu-ma Kuang "meaning which exists beyond the words" implies a poetics of suggestiveness and oblique expression.

Ko Li-fang (d. 1164) gives couplets by Mei himself to illustrate the two dicta. [20] After quoting a slightly abbreviated version of Mei's statement, duly noting it to be by "Mei Sheng-yü," Ko continues,

This is a truly famous statement. Consider his [i.e., Mei's] *Seeing Off Mr. Su of the Ministry of Finance to Become Vice-Prefect of Hung-chou*, which says, "Sand birds dip as I watch them fly toward me; / Cloudy mountains: I love how they seem to move in the background!" And his *Seeing Off Chang Tzu-yeh to Take Up an Official Post at Cheng-chou*, which says, "Autumn rains stir up waters by the embankment; / High winds blow off the leaves of the temple *wu-t'ung* trees." His *Seeing Off the Assistant in the Department of the Imperial Wardrobe, Ma, to Become Vice-Prefect of Mi-chou* says, "Your high sail sets off on the Huai; / Ancient trees are autumnal by the seaside." And his *Echoing a Poem Sent to Me by the Collator of Texts, Ch'en, Following His Rhymes* says, "How

many years passed on the River's waters; / No longer a youthful face in
the mirror!"
  These are examples of "expressing inexhaustible meaning." [21]

The first two examples given by Ko are quite clearly couplets
which depict natural scenes in the Late T'ang manner, as indeed
were the lines quoted by Mei himself in his original statement.
Why the last two examples are felt by Ko to "express inexhaustible
meaning" is not immediately apparent.

In the previous chapter, examples were quoted from Mei's poetry
to give some idea of his views on poetic history. Occasional passages, though they are few and far between, can also be used to determine his poetic ideals. The term which occurs with the greatest
frequency in these passages is p'ing-tan, rendered here as "even
and bland" for lack of a better translation. It will be recalled that
Mei wrote of Lin Pu that "when he was in harmony with things,
enjoying his feelings, he would write poems which were even and
bland, profound and beautiful. Reading them made one forget the
hundred affairs. The words achieved the ultimate in calm and correctness, and did not stress satire and protest. Thus I realized that
his taste was comprehensive and far-reaching, and that he was simply expressing his happiness through poetry." [22] Other passages
make it quite clear that "even and bland" was Mei's highest poetic
ideal. In one of his poems to Yen Shu written in 1046,[23] he says, "I
write poems about that which is in harmony with my feelings and
nature, trying as best I can to achieve the 'even and bland.' My
rough diction is not rounded or smoothed, but sticks in the mouth
more harshly than water-chestnut or prickly water-lily." Mei goes
on to express discouragement at his inability to perform the great
task of carrying on the tradition of the Book of Odes. The first part of
this passage is reminiscent of Mei's characterization of Lin Pu, who
wrote "even and bland" poetry "when he was in harmony with
things." It is of considerable interest that the even and bland style
is associated here with "rough diction" and with the orthodox Confucian poetic tradition of the Book of Odes. This latter association
recurs in a poem probably dating from 1055,[24] in which Mei expresses his own admiration, and that of his friend Tu T'ing-chih,

for the poetry of Shao Pi, *tzu* Pu-i.[25] In the course of this poem, Mei asserts that "In writing poetry, no matter whether past or present, it is only achieving the 'even and bland' that is difficult." It will be shown later in this chapter that the phrase "achieving the 'even and bland' " had already been used by at least three T'ang writers. But none of them gave it the prominence which it has in this passage. In the same poem, Mei rejoices that the tradition of the *Book of Odes* has not ended. Shao Pi's poems are like pearls falling in a plate, or like moonlight, suffusing his pillow and mat with cold. Tu T'ing-chih shares Mei's enthusiasm, and feels that the poems are worthy of Li Po, Tu Fu, or Han Yü. He and Mei declare their intention of clutching spear and halberd, and fighting to the death at the "altar of generals."

According to Ou-yang Hsiu,

> At first he [Mei] liked to write poetry which was fresh and beautiful, relaxed and free, *even and bland*. After a long time, it became deeply imbued with a profound, detached quality. Sometimes he carefully worked his poems over to obtain strange and skillful effects. But the spirit was complete and the strength ample, so his poetry became more and more forceful as he grew older.[26]

This passage seems to suggest that the even and bland style was more characteristic of Mei's earlier poetry than of his later. If, however, the actual occurrence of the term "even and bland" in Mei's works provides an accurate indication of his interest in the style, it would appear that precisely the opposite was the case. As Kakehi has noted,[27] the term "even and bland" appears very frequently in the poetry of 1045/46, and then consistently thereafter, as in the Lin Pu preface of 1053, and the poem on Shao Pi's poetry of 1056. On the other hand, I am aware of only one relatively early occurrence of the term. In a poem which probably dates from 1037,[28] Mei praises a poem by a friend of his on the Ch'i Mountain Temple. The previous poets who wrote on this subject can be numbered, Mei says. But now the scenes of Ch'i Mountain will be recorded in "beautiful lines" with "diction and rhymes" that are "difficult and outstanding," surpassing those written in the past by Tu Mu (803–852).[29] And, Mei continues, the poem in question is characterized by an "even and bland" manner, "like ancient music."

Aside from this one early example, the use of the term *p'ing-tan* appears to be limited to Mei's middle and late years. These were also the periods when Mei was most interested in T'ao Ch'ien, and as we have seen, he associated T'ao with the *p'ing-tan* manner, as in a poem of 1045 which has already been quoted: [30]

Poetry is basically stating one's feelings;
There's no need to shout them out loud!
When you realize that the poem should be even and bland,
You'll devote yourself to Yüan-ming morning and evening.

In the following year, describing the poetry of Chiang Hsiu-fu (1005–1060), Mei wrote, "You have sent from far away your 'even and bland' words." [31] Mei's pupil Han Wei (1017–1098) was of the opinion that "many of Chiang's poems are in the manner of T'ao Ch'ien." [32]

The question which obviously presents itself is the extent of Mei's originality in placing such emphasis on the *p'ing-tan* concept. Writers on the subject appear to be agreed that the earliest use of *p'ing-tan* as a term of literary criticism occurs in the *Shih p'in* of Chung Hung (c.505).[33] In the entry on Kuo P'u (276–324) in this work, Kuo is said to be one of the poets who first "transformed the 'even and bland' style of the *Yung-chia* period (307–313)." [34] In the preface to the *Shih p'in*, we are told that "in the *Yung-chia* period, poets esteemed Huang [-ti] and Lao [Tzu], and tended toward vapid discussions. At that time, the content of their poetry exceeded its diction; their work was 'bland and had little flavor.' " [35] There can be little doubt that the term "even and bland" in the Kuo P'u entry is used in a pejorative sense, meaning something like "insipid." As *p'ing-tan* later came to be considered a desideratum of poetry, it is similar in its history to such terms of European art criticism as "Impressionism" and "Fauvism," both of which were originally pejorative or mocking in tone, but have since been used as the legitimate names for two schools of French painting.

Mei must have been familiar with the use of *p'ing tan* in the *Shih p'in;* he refers at least three times to Chung Hung, as Kakehi has noted.[36] A poem probably dating from 1053, for example, contains this couplet, already quoted earlier: [37] "In poetry, able to be like

Juan Chi; / In criticism, not yielding to Chung Hung." Another poem of the same period [38] includes this line: "Naturally possessing the critical acumen of Chung Hung." An even later poem, written in 1057 or 1058,[39] also invokes the name of Chung Hung: "Loving to discuss the poetry of past and present, / Laughing at Chung Hung in our critical judgments."

Although *p'ing-tan* does not seem to have been used again as a term of literary criticism until relatively late in the T'ang dynasty, early non-literary uses are well attested. Related terms occur as early as the Taoist classics. The phrase "bland and with little flavor" aptly applied by Chung Hung to the Taoist poetry of the *Yung-chia* period, is modeled on the phrase "bland and flavorless" from the *Lao Tzu*,[40] where it describes the ineffable Tao. Several passages in Chuang Tzu are relevant. The Nameless Man advises T'ien Ken (in Burton Watson's translation) [41] to "let your mind wander in simplicity (*tan*), blend your spirit with the vastness, follow along with things the way they are (*shun-wu tzu-jan*)." That this passage may have influenced Mei's conception of "blandness" is suggested by a passage from his Lin Pu preface which has already been quoted twice: [42] "When he was in harmony with things (*shun-wu*), enjoying his feelings, he would write poems which were even and bland . . ." Here as in the Chuang Tzu example, the concepts of "blandness" and "harmony with things" are associated, and the same words are used to express them in both passages.

The *Chuang Tzu* also uses the compound *t'ien-tan*, "calm and bland," as in this passage from the *Way of Heaven* chapter: [43]

> Emptiness, stillness, limpidity (*t'ien-tan*), silence, inaction are the root of the ten thousand things.

It will be noted that in these Taoist examples, the concept of "blandness" is used in a positive sense. It is, in fact, one of the attributes of the absolute. Giving a positive meaning to a quality which is overlooked or even despised by most men is typical of Taoist irony, a mood which would not have been uncongenial to Mei Yao-ch'en and his friends.

Positive, though non-literary, uses of *p'ing-tan* occur several times in Three Kingdoms and Six Dynasties sources. A work entitled *Monograph on Personalities* by the Wei scholar Liu Shao contains a relevant passage [44] which has been noticed by Kakehi.[45] The passage reads,

> In a man's character, it is balance and harmony that are most prized. A character which is balanced and harmonious must be even, bland, and flavorless. Thus, such a man is able to develop in equal measure the five virtues [i.e., courage, wisdom, humanity, faithfulness, and loyalty] and to adapt himself flexibly to the situation. For this reason, in observing a man and judging his character, one must first look for the "even and bland," and then seek intelligence.

Two notes to this passage by a certain Liu Ping explain that

> When something is "bland," the five flavors are able to be in harmony. If something is [too] bitter, then it cannot be sweet. If it is [too] sour, then it cannot be salty. . . . When a man is "even and bland," without prejudices, then he will as a matter of course be in control of all the virtues. He will be able to use them appropriately, adapting comprehensively, unimpeded, to all situations.

In these passages it is fairly clear that "even and bland" means "in perfect balance or harmony," a state in which no one quality is in evidence to the exclusion of any other, but all exist together in equilibrium. It may be wondered, as by Kakehi, whether Mei Yao-ch'en would have been familiar with Liu Shao's book,[46] but a reference to the work in the *Wang-shih t'an-lu* by Wang Ch'in-ch'en,[47] the son of Wang Shu (997–1057), at least proves that it was known to scholars of the generation immediately after Mei. (According to Wang Ch'in-ch'en's SS biography, his writings were admired by Ou-yang Hsiu. It will be recalled that Wang's father, Wang Shu, was one of the men who visited Mei together with Ou-yang in 1056.) The passage in question reads, "In human nature, it is the 'even and bland' that is prized. . . . Formerly, in his discussion of personalities, Liu Shao also considered the 'even and bland' to be of primary importance."

Another occurrence of *p'ing-tan*, also noticed by Kakehi,[48] is found in the *Essay on Music* by Juan Chi: [49]

> The Male Principle and Female Principle are easy and simple; therefore refined music is not cumbersome. The Way and its Power are even and bland; therefore it [i.e., refined music] is soundless and flavorless.

Because it is not cumbersome, Yin and Yang circulate naturally. Because it is flavorless, the hundred creatures are naturally joyful.

Here the precise meaning of *p'ing-tan* is somewhat more difficult to determine. The parallelism with "easy and simple," and the association with the qualities "soundless and flavorless" would seem to suggest that the term is used to emphasize the purity, subtlety, and simplicity of the highest music. Again, the problem of Mei Yao-ch'en's familiarity with this text has been raised by Kakehi.[50] It does not appear impossible, however, that Mei would have read an essay by a poet who interested him as greatly as did Juan Chi.

A final example of this kind occurs in the biography of Hsi Chien in the *Chin shu*. The relevant passage reads, "Yüeh Yen-fu [Yüeh Kuang (d. 304)] is 'even and bland' in his moral tone, and calm and pure in his knowledge derived from experience." Here, as in Liu Shao, *p'ing-tan* is used to describe a man's character.

In his article on the term *p'ing-tan* in Sung literary criticism, Yokoyama states that T'ang examples of *p'ing-tan* as a literary term are not to be found. He does, however, call attention in a footnote to the "unemphatic" (*ch'ung-tan*) mode which appears in *The Twenty-Four Modes of Poetry* of Ssu-k'ung T'u (837–908).[51] Although Ssu-k'ung's poetic descriptions of his twenty-four modes are extremely vague, some idea of what this particular mode meant to him is conveyed by these lines (in the translation of Yang Hsien-yi and Gladys Yang):[52]

It dwells in quiet, in simplicity;
For inspiration is subtle, fugitive;
. . . Gentle as the breath of wind
That brushes your gown.
. . . When you grope for it,
It slips through your hands and is gone!

In his analysis of the twenty-four modes, Chu Tung-jun lists the "unemphatic" mode as one of those which "relate to the poet's life."[53]

In addition, the character *tan* occurs three times in *The Twenty-Four Modes of Poetry* (the translations are those of the Yangs):[54]

The man, serene (*tan*) as the chrysanthemum. (from the "polished" mode)

But light (*tan*) shades grow in depth. (from the "exquisite" mode)

Too ethereal (*tan*) to recall. (from the "distinctive" mode)

Finally, it will be recalled that Ssu-k'ung T'u described Wei Ying-wu's poetry as "limpid and bland, finely structured." [55]

Yokoyama happens to be wrong in his statement that *p'ing-tan* was not used as a term of literary criticism in the T'ang dynasty. The term occurs, for example, in a particularly important passage from a poem sent by Han Yü to Chia Tao, and quoted by Kakehi. [56] The language of the passage in question is unfortunately quite obscure, but the gist seems to be that Chia Tao expresses himself freely with "wild words," "often achieving the 'even and bland.' " As Kakehi points out, *p'ing-tan* is here given an unmistakably positive sense. Precisely what is meant for Han Yü is another matter; it is not easy to understand how an "even and bland" style is consistent with "wild words." A similar association occurs in a poem in which Han Yü praises the literary talents of various friends of his. [57] "Chang Chi," he tells us, "emulates the 'ancient and bland.' " In the same poem, Han expresses his admiration for "difficult diction." That the term "ancient and bland" is close to "even and bland" is suggested by the fact that Ou-yang Hsiu uses it to describe Mei Yao-ch'en's poetic style: [58] "Sheng-yü has worked hard at poetry all his life, writing with feeling that is calm and detached, ancient and bland."

Kakehi maintains that Mei was conscious of following Han Yü in his use of *p'ing-tan* as a positive term of literary criticism. [59] Not only is Mei's and Ou-yang's veneration for Han Yü well attested to by the passages quoted in the previous chapter, but Chia Tao and Chang Chi, the two poets to whom Han applied the terms *p'ing-tan* and *ku-t'an*, were also among the poets in whom they took considerable interest.

Although Po-Chü-i does not use the term *p'ing-tan* to my knowledge, related expressions are used by him in interesting contexts. In the letter to Yüan Chen, [60] Wei Ying-wu's poetry is described as "exalted and refined, calm and bland." In the same letter there occurs the phrase "thought bland and diction unusual." Elsewhere, [61] Po applies the phrase "bland and flavorless" to his own poetry, as well as to the ancient music of the zither (ch'in),[62] in both cases with a sense of irony entirely in the Taoist tradition from which this use of "bland" originally derived. Su Shun-ch'in also describes the music of the zither as "sparse and bland." [63] In a poem about an old instrument in his possession, he relates how a great zither master performed on it for him: "Occasionally he expresses deep meaning with sparse and bland sound; / Deep meaning, thin flavor—I alone understand."

The phrase "achieving the 'even and bland' " (which forms part of Han Yü's line, "Often achieving the 'even and bland' ") occurs, as noted previously, in Mei Yao-ch'en's couplet, "In writing poetry, no matter whether past or present, / It is only achieving the 'even and bland' that is difficult." The same phrase, as it happens, had also been used toward the end of the T'ang dynasty by the famous poet-friends Lu Kuei-meng (d. c.881) and P'i Jih-hsiu (d. c.881). Lu's use of the phrase is literary, and therefore provides another instance of the use of p'ing-tan as a positive term of literary criticism in the T'ang dynasty. In his autobiographical sketch, An Account of Mr. Fu-li,[64] Lu writes, "When young, he [i.e., Lu himself] worked at songs and poetry, wishing to compete with the Creator himself. Whenever he encountered suitable material, he would transform it into any number of stylistic forms." This is followed by impressionistic descriptions of some of these "stylistic forms," one of which involves "imprisoning and fettering the strange and unusual." "But," Lu continues, "it was only when he had achieved the 'even and bland' that he stopped." In making p'ing-tan the ultimate goal of poetic endeavor, Lu Kuei-meng comes closer to Mei Yao-ch'en's apotheosis of the "even and bland" style than any other writer prior to Mei.

The idea, implicit in An Account of Mr. Fu-li, that the poet only achieves the p'ing-tan style after a long period of development, adumbrates a Sung concept. Although, as we have seen, Ou-yang Hsiu considered that the style was characteristic of Mei's early period ("At first he liked to write poetry which was . . . even and bland."), Wu K'o (c.1126), writing at a time when Su Shih's approval of the style had ensured its permanent influence, clearly expressed the view that it represented the culmination of a poet's development. Tu Fu's poetry, for example, was, according to Wu, "flowery and beautiful" in his youth, but became "even and bland" as he grew older.[65] Elsewhere, Wu states this principle in general terms: [66]

> All literature is first flowery and beautiful, and later even and bland. It is like the sequence of the four seasons. In spring, things are flowery and beautiful; in summer, flourishing and ripe. In autumn and winter they withdraw and hibernate. It is like something which is withered outside but rich inside. The flowery and beautiful, flourishing and ripe, are enclosed within.

The idea that *p'ing-tan* develops late in a poet's life has been discussed by Yokoyama.[67] Another modern writer, Chu Tung-jun, has actually divided Mei Yao-ch'en's poetic life into two general periods: an early one, during which he was moved by the sufferings of the people and the incursions of the Hsi Hsia troops to write poetry in which he frankly expressed his anger; and a late one, during which he matured and evolved the *p'ing-tan* style.[68] Lu Yu also passed through two such stages of development, according to Chu.

Lu Kuei-meng's friend, P'i Jih-hsiu, also used the phrase *tsao p'ing-tan*, but in an entirely different context. In the course of a poem describing a visit to the famous Lin-wu Cave,[69] P'i relates in considerable detail how he passed through the fantastic chambers and corridors of the cave. Then, immediately after a couplet in which he has squeezed his way through a narrow opening like the mouth of a jar, these lines occur: *"O-erh tsao p'ing-tan; / Huo-jan feng kuang-ching."* Given the context of the poem, these lines must mean something like, "Suddenly we came upon a level, smooth area; / Brilliant light burst into view ahead." But another line by P'i indicates that for him too *tan* (here used in the closely related sense of "limpid") was a desirable quality in poetry. In the middle of a lengthy poem on the history of poetry,[70] there occurs the line, "Meng [Hao-jan] is limpid, like rippling wavelets."

As a final T'ang example, mention should be made of an interesting entry in the *Shih-shih*, attributed to the monk Chiao-jan (c.760).[71] One of the styles or modes of poetry listed by him is entitled "the bland and common" (*tan-su*), and is described as follows:

This way is like Hsia-chi [72] at the wine counter: she seems loose in her morals but is actually chaste. In this mode, the styles of Wu and Ch'u are adopted. Although common, it is quite correct. An ancient song says,

There's a hundred-foot well
> at the top of Hua-yin Mountain;
Below is a flowing spring,
> bone-piercingly cold.
How lovable, the girl who comes to look
> at her reflection:
She only sees her slanting neck,
> and nothing else!

This curious passage suggests that for Chiao-jan, the "bland and common" mode of poetry encompasses popular and folk songs, often dealing with young girls and their amours, of the kind usually referred to as "Songs of Wu." The "blandness" of such poetry would lie in its light, easily comprehensible diction, unencumbered by weighty allusions or difficult imagery. Although only slightly related to the sequence of usages leading to Mei Yao-ch'en's emphasis on the "even and bland" style, in point of time the present example may well have been the earliest positive, literary critical use of a compound including the character *tan*.

Among the early Sung poets, Wang Yü-ch'eng is notable for his use of *tan* (or compounds including it) with reference to poetry. In an extremely long poem sent to Ch'ung Fang (d. 1015),[73] Wang describes a "divine work" as "ancient and bland, like sipping broth from a cauldron." "Ancient and bland" is a term first used by Han Yü with reference to Chang Chi's poetry, and later used by Ou-yang Hsiu for Mei Yao-ch'en. In another poem,[74] Wang describes the poetry of Meng Pin-yü (c.904–c.983) as being written in a "refined and bland style."

The examples quoted above make it quite clear that Mei Yao-ch'en was far from being the first poet to use *p'ing-tan* or related expressions as terms of literary criticism. But even if they give some idea of the sources which might have influenced Mei, the problem remains of what precisely "even and bland" meant for him. One of the important passages for the understanding of Mei's views on poetry, already quoted twice, is worth repeating here:[75]

Poetry is basically stating one's feelings;
There's no need to shout them out loud!
When you realize that the poem should be even and bland,
You'll devote yourself to Yüan-ming morning and evening.

Here, *p'ing-tan* appears to refer to poetry which is based on the poet's real, personal emotion, but which expresses that emotion in understated terms. By contrast, the poetry of the Hsi-k'un school was based on artificial emotion, and was extravagant in its expressive tenchniques.

The poet's feelings are also stressed in one of Mei's poems to Yen Shu,[76] quoted previously but repeated here: "I write poems about that which is in harmony with my feelings and nature, trying as best I can to achieve the 'even and bland.' My rough diction is not rounded or smoothed, but sticks in the mouth more harshly than water-chestnut or prickly water-lily." This example goes a step further in suggesting that *p'ing-tan* refers specifically to diction. A similar, apparently paradoxical association of "wild words" and "even and bland" style occurred in Han Yü's poem to Chia Tao.[77] In what is possibly Mei's earliest use of the term *p'ing-tan*, it is again juxtaposed with "difficult and outstanding diction and rhymes." [78]

Mei himself emphasized the importance of diction in poetry in his famous statement: "Though the poet may emphasize meaning, it is also difficult to choose the proper diction." In a poem of 1045,[79] already referred to in another context, Mei exclaims, "How can it be thought that my interest in poetry is merely superficial? When I am inspired by some affair, I write my short poems, and though the diction may be low and coarse, they are the result of effort and devotion." The same poem goes on to extol the tradition of the *Book of Odes*, which Mei is striving to emulate, and to castigate "those few poets of the late T'ang who wore away their years trifling with natural images." Here, Mei seems to be advocating a rough, even vulgar diction as a reaction against the excessive refinements of Late T'ang and Hsi-k'un poetry. On the other hand, the fact that Mei applied the term *p'ing-tan* to the poetry of Lin Pu, perhaps the greatest of the early Sung practitioners of the Late T'ang style, should preclude any hasty or overly simple conclusions as to what "even and bland" meant for him.

Once established by Mei Yao-ch'en as a *sine qua non* of poetics, *p'ing-tan* quickly became one of the most important terms in Sung literary criticism. Su Shih insured the prestige of the concept of "blandness" in poetry by his approval of it. "What is prized in the 'withered and bland;' " he wrote,[80] "is that the external is withered but the internal is rich. It seems bland but is actually beautiful. Such poets as Yüan-ming [T'ao Ch'ien] and Tzu-hou [Liu Tsung-yüan] are examples of this. If the internal and the external are both withered and bland, is this worth taking into consideration?" The term *p'ing-tan* was finally canonized by having a section devoted to it in the great encyclopedia of poetics, *Shih-jen yü-hsieh* by Wei Ch'ing-chih (c. 1240).[81]

The question of diction has been touched upon in the preceding paragraphs. Other passages referring to diction can be found in Mei's works. Mention has already been made of a poem written around 1050 [82] in which Mei says of his own poetry, "It is just like T'ao Yüan-ming: / Rough diction close to that of farmers." In a poem of 1055 or 1056,[83] one of a series in which he discusses the poetry of various acquaintances who had sent their works to him for his comments, Mei says, "Although my words are very simple, / My meaning is trenchant—who understands?" Another poem of 1055 or 1056 answers this question: [84] "Ou-yang understands me best. . . . He has compared by poetry with olives!" Later in this poem, Mei describes his own lines as "bitter and hard." Both this phrase (*k'u-ying*) and the simile of the olives occur in a poem by Ou-yang Hsiu written over ten years earlier, in 1044.[85] The relevant portion of this poem, in which Ou-yang characterizes the styles of both Su Shun-ch'in and Mei Yao-ch'en, reads (in the translation of Burton Watson),[86]

Master Mei valued what is clean and succinct,
Washing his stone teeth in the cold stream.
He has written poetry for thirty years
And looks on us as his juniors in school.
His diction grows fresher and cleaner than ever;
His thought becomes more profound with age.
He is like a beautiful woman
Whose charm does not fade with the years.
His recent poems are dry and hard;

Try chewing on some—a bitter mouthful!
The first reading is like eating olives,
But the longer you suck on them, the better the taste.

The idea of comparing the effect of words with the taste of olives did not originate with Ou-yang Hsiu. Wang Yü-ch'eng, in a poem entitled *Olives*,[87] describes how olives taste bitter at first, but become sweet after they have been chewed for a while. "What am I using this as an analogy for?" asks Wang rhetorically, "For the words of a loyal official." He then explains that the loyal official's words may at first be displeasing to the sovereign, and possibly even result in the official's banishment (Wang was exiled three times). But later, at a time of crisis, the sovereign will recall these words and regret that he did not pay heed to them. Wang concludes, "I send word to the Poetry Collector: do not look lightly on this poem, *Olives!*" Ou-yang Hsiu was familiar with Wang's poem. In a poem of his own, also entitled *Olives*,[88] Ou-yang writes,

Loyal words are at first despised,
But when a crisis occurs, how useless is regret!
There is no longer a Poetry Collector in the world,
So I'll recite this completed poem for you.

But Wang Yü-ch'eng's *Olives* is concerned with the *meaning* of words, whereas, in his poem on Su Shun-ch'in and Mei, Ou-yang seems to stress diction: "His [Mei's] diction grows fresher and cleaner than ever. . . . His recent poems are dry and hard; / Try chewing on some—a bitter mouthful! / The first reading is like eating olives, / But the longer you suck on them, the better the taste."

Partly, perhaps, because Hsi-k'un poetry was often quite obscure, one of Mei's concerns was that poetic diction should not be excessively difficult to understand. Commenting on the poems of a certain "Magistrate Chang," [89] Mei complains, "Although I have not allowed myself to become inattentive while reading them, I cannot understand one out of ten!" On the other hand, Mei was not unaware of the pitfalls awaiting the poet who attempts to make his diction *too* low. Ou-yang Hsiu records a statement by Mei on this matter: [90]

Sheng-yü once said, "When lines of poetry make sense, but have diction which approaches shallowness and vulgarity, and is laughable, this is a defect. For example, here is a couplet from a poem *Sent to a Fisherman:*

His eyes see nothing of market business;
His ears hear only the sound of wind and water.

Someone has said of this that it refers to disorders of the liver and kidney! And here is another from a poem *On Poetry:*

I search for it [i.e., a good line] all day long, but in vain;
Then sometimes it will come of itself.

This actually has to do with the difficulty of hitting upon a good line, but someone has said that it refers to a person who has lost his cat!" Everyone had a good laugh at this.

As it happens, Mei himself did not escape criticism for his "vulgar diction." the critic Chang Chieh (c. 1135), in a passage beginning, "Every man's talent has its limitations," [91] quotes excerpts from a group of poems on climbing pagodas and the like, arranged in a sequence from worst to best. The second worst of the series is Mei's

ON HEARING THAT TZU-MEI [Su Shun-ch'in], TZ'U-TAO
[Sung Min-ch'iu], AND SHIH-HOU [Hsieh Ching-ch'u] CLIMBED
THE PAGODA OF SKY CLEAR MONASTERY [92]

You three friends, young and strong,
Ascended the pagoda's topmost tier.
But why did you waste your thoughts on me?
I barely move along on level ground!
Even if I could have climbed with you
My legs would surely have buckled in pain.
And then I imagine the dizzy descent,
Panting, sweating, head and eyes aswim . . .
Wiser for me to stay quietly at home;
No use peering at the clouds and mist.

This poem, dating from 1044, is in fact an excellent example of the kind of simple but expressive diction Mei adopted for much of his personal poetry. The influence of Po Chü-i is apparent. But Chang Chieh, after quoting the last four lines of the poem, exclaims in disgust, "What vulgar diction!"—perhaps the first recorded adverse criticism of Mei's poetry. Chang is especially offended by the expression, "head and eyes aswim."

Chu Tung-jun is of the opinion that the influence of prose on the diction of Sung poetry began with Mei Yao-ch'en.[93] Mention has been made of the prose-like diction of Han Yü's poetry and the influence it exerted on Mei and Ou-yang. If asked why his diction was often so rough and seemingly awkward, Mei might have answered, with Dryden,

And this unpolished, rugged verse I chose,
As fittest for discourse, and nearest prose.[94]

As a poet of essentially Confucian persuasion involved in a literary movement which had as one of its aims the revival of the orthodox literary tradition, Mei felt a need for a poetic style which would allow him to present his ideas in verse, in other words, a discursive style. The diction of the poems in which Mei presents his views on poetry, several of which have been quoted in this and the previous chapter, is so strongly influenced by prose that these poems are usually best rendered in English prose paraphrase. Prose-like diction will constantly recur in the poems translated and discussed in the following chapter, especially in those which deal with contemporary events and works of art. This fact suggests that when Mei is concerned with actual events or objects which he is observing close at hand, he chooses to make extensive use of prose-like phrases which are better suited to precise, detailed description than the vaguer expressions characteristic of lyric diction. Thus one of Mei's goals was greater flexibility in the use of poetry for discourse and description, and he approached this problem by expanding the range of his diction.

It is not surprising that a poet who gave so much thought to the actual craft of poetry should also have been known as a literary critic. Ko Li-fang, writing in the mid-twelfth century, had this to say: [95]

Mei Sheng-yü quickly earned himself a reputation as a poet. Those scholars, therefore, who could compose poetry would often write out scrolls of their work and send them to him to get his opinion on their good and bad points. Mei would always send poems in reply, never letting the would-be poets off lightly. For example, in *Reading the Poetry Scroll of the Collator of Texts, Huang Shen* (1021–1085), he says,

The phoenixes are raising fledglings, but they still can't fly high;
The chickens and ducks are forming flocks, but their wings are still
    short.

In *Reading the Poetry Scroll of the Director of the Imperial Workshops, Hsiao Yüan,* he says,

The wild pheasant has five colors, but he is not a phoenix;
In knowing the hours and crowing well, how can he compare with the
    rooster?

In *Reading the Poetry Scroll of the Auxiliary Secretary Sun Chih-yen,* he says,

When drawing well-water, go down deep;
When polishing a mirror, rub off every speck of dust.

In *Reading the Poetry Scroll of Magistrate Chang,* he says,

Although I have not allowed myself to become inattentive while reading
    them,
I cannot understand one out of ten!

And in *Reading the Poetry Scroll of the Scholar Shao Pu-i . . . ,* he says,

After seeing them, he [i.e., Tu T'ing-chih] sighs involuntarily,
And says they remind him of Li [Po], Tu [Fu] and Han [Yü].

In all these passages, Mei instructs the aspiring poets on the basis of their shortcomings.

The examples quoted here by Ko Li-fang all come from chapters forty-five and forty-six of the *Wan-ling chi,*[96] and thus date from 1055 or 1056. The first couplet has been explained in this way by Hsia Ching-kuan:[97] "This means that the poet's work is not mature, although Mei praises his innate talent." Hsia also comments on the second example:[98] "This means that although the pheasant has lovely feathers, he is not a phoenix, nor is he as good as the rooster at knowing the hours and crowing. This is what is meant by [my comment on the first line of the previous couplet in this poem,] 'Prizing what is close to the vulgar.' "

The metaphors of drawing well-water and polishing a mirror are undoubtedly meant to express the unremitting effort which is necessary to become an accomplished poet. Ko Li-fang takes the lines as a reprimand to Sun Chih-yen, presumably for not working hard enough. The following couplet has already been discussed; it criticizes the poet for his excessive obscurity. It is hard to see in what sense Mei is "instructing" Shao Pu-i "on the basis of his shortcomings" in the final couplet. On the contrary, this passage would appear to praise Shao in the highest possible terms. At any rate, the Ko Li-fang entry shows that Mei was a respected critic of poetry.[99]

Something of Mei's style as a teacher can be sensed from the poem *Drinking On Sheng-yü's Western Porch* by Han Wei (1017–1098).[100] Aside from being one of the best portraits of Mei available to us, this poem (translated here in prose) is of interest because it reveals that Mei thought of T'ang poetry in terms of distinguishable schools. After relating how "two or three of us" have gathered for a drinking party at Mei's, Han continues,

> Our host is a doyen of Confucians; his words are worthy of the two *Ya*'s [of the *Book of Odes*]. He enunciates noble principles on how to conduct oneself while drinking, and summarizes the confusing details of literature. First he says that in judging a man's character, one must base oneself on that which is internal. Then he criticizes our scholarship, saying we should never be satisfied with ourselves. All the poets of the T'ang dynasty he analyzes into their respective schools. Once they have been subjected to the master's criticism, the wheat is separated from the chaff, and the chaff rejected.
>
> I say, "Our Sheng-yü deserves to be famous in succeeding generations." He answers by saying my writings are like those of Han Yü, and also show the influence of the Six Classics. But what have I done to establish myself? When I hear such praise, I feel as if I'm holding a scorpion! Sheng-yü is excellent at encouraging and counselling; these words of his are meant to exhort us. His intention is to urge us all to advance and improve in our work. Although I am dull and untalented, when I hear him I feel vigorous and intelligent.
>
> I call for a cup and pour myself a full measure, not caring if the other guests think me strange. Then back home to write this little poem, just to tell why I admire him so much.

Although it is possible to arrive at some notion of Mei's views on poetry by piecing together a line here and a couplet there, as I have attempted to do in chapters 3 and 4, one still misses an overall statement on the nature of poetry comprehensive enough to embrace these fragmentary ideas. Interestingly enough, it is a modern American poet who seems best to express an attitude toward poetry which, *mutatis mutandis*, might serve to characterize the new sensibility of Mei and his fellow poets. Wallace Stevens's *The Poems of Our Climate*,[101] published in 1938, is worth quoting in full:

I

Clear water in a brilliant bowl,
Pink and white carnations. The light
In the room more like a snowy air,
Reflecting snow. A newly-fallen snow
At the end of winter when afternoons return.
Pink and white carnations—one desires
So much more than that. The day itself
Is simplified: a bowl of white,
Cold, a cold porcelain, low and round,
With nothing more than the carnations there.

II

Say even that this complete simplicity
Stripped one of all one's torments, concealed
The evilly compounded, vital I
And made it fresh in a world of white,
A world of clear water brilliant-edged,
Still one would want more, one would need more,
More than a world of white and snowy scents.

III

There would still remain the never-resting mind,
So that one would want to escape, come back
To what had been so long composed.
The imperfect is our paradise.
Note that, in this bitterness, delight,
Since the imperfect is so hot in us,
Lies in flawed words and stubborn sounds.

It would be hard to find a better image for the Hsi-k'un poetry which was so popular in the early eleventh century than "a bowl of white, / Cold, a cold porcelain, low and round," filled with "pink and white carnations." Lovely, to be sure, but unreal, unrelated to human passion. In such a literary climate, Mei Yao-ch'en and Ou-yang Hsiu felt a need for "so much more," a return to the actual human being, "the evilly compounded, vital I" with his never-rest-

ing mind." They wished, like Stevens, to express the very imperfection which characterizes our personal and social existence in poetry
whose diction was a mimesis of that imperfection, diction "harsher
than water-chestnut or prickly water-lily," "flawed words and stubborn sounds." Such a conception of poetry informs the poems
which are discussed in the following chapter, and was passed on by
Mei to Han Wei and his other students.

Chapter Five

PRACTICE

I N THE PREVIOUS CHAPTER, it was shown that the *p'ing-tan* concept was of primary importance for Mei Yao-ch'en. But it was also suggested that the precise meaning of this term is less than clear. Some passages in which it appears seem to associate it with unpolished, "natural" diction; others, sometimes using it to describe poetry of the Late T'ang type, imply that *p'ing-tan* means a quiet, intimate tone. It is possible, though, to see in both these aspects a common factor: the desire to avoid hyperbole and self-consciously "poetic" writing of the kind that was prized by Hsi-k'un poets. Mei Yao-ch'en may thus have used the term *p'ing-tan* as a sobriquet for realistic poetry, poetry which took its main inspiration from the experience of the real world, rather than from a corpus of conventional images and allusions. Mei's emphasis on the ability to "depict a scene that is difficult to describe in such a way that it seems to be right before the eyes of the reader" also indicates that for him, the description of the physical world was one of the poet's chief concerns.

A reading of Mei's poetry reveals that, like all Chinese poets, he wrote a great many occasional poems at farewell dinners or other social gatherings, as well as hundreds of poems on standard themes which are indistinguishable from poems on these subjects by other poets. But in his best work, Mei emerges as an essentially realistic poet with a voice of his own. The present chapter is a brief anthology of Mei's most important poems, with commentary and notes, arranged under five headings: 1) Poems Describing Everyday Life; 2) Poems of Personal Emotion; 3) Poems of Social Comment; 4) Moralizing Poems on Living Creatures; 5) Poems on Antiquities and Works of Art. These categories are not meant to comprise an outline encompassing all of Mei's poems. Nor are they always mutually exclusive—a number of poems in category 2, for example, might have been placed in category 1. They are simply intended to call attention to the poetic modes and themes which are of particular importance in Mei's best work.

1 POEMS DESCRIBING EVERYDAY LIFE

It was suggested in a previous chapter that the Sung poet typically moved closer to his materials, that the "aesthetic distance" between the poet and his subject tended to decrease. One of the chief signs of this tendency in Mei Yao-ch'en's poetry is the frequent occurrence of poems which describe events or scenes of ordinary life without attempting in any way to glorify them or make them "poetic" in the conventional sense. In this section, a group of twelve such poems, ranging in date from 1035 to 1058, will be translated and discussed in chronological order. These poems deal with a wide variety of subjects, but in all of them the poet is facing the realities of actual life, and simply describing them as best he can, occasionally adducing an appropriate literary allusion or drawing a moral. The tendency of most T'ang poets to heighten or intensify their materials, even when these are drawn from everyday experience, is notably absent.

According to the *Nien-p'u*,[1] in 1035 Mei "became Magistrate of Chien-te subprefecture. Prior to this, the subprefectural office was protected by a hedge; an earthen wall had never been built. The sub-officials were thus able to collect taxes for their own selfish ends. Mei Yao-ch'en was the first magistrate to build a new wall, and he wrote a poem on the subject." The poem, which can be dated to 1035 from this entry, is entitled

THE NEW WALL AT CHIEN-TE [2]

There was no wall around my rustic office—
Bamboos formed a natural hedge.
They grew thick at the beginning of the year
But drooped and bowed in the last months.
Rotted away by nesting bees,
Tied and tangled by wild vines,
Weak and brittle after long summer rains,
Bent and crushed in the autumn wind.
Ducks and chickens would waddle through;
Sheep and oxen would stamp in for a look.
When I proposed building an earthen wall,
My underlings were all upset.
The chief clerk reported first:
"The earth here is crumbly; it can't be done!
When the heavy rains burst out in flood
The wall will float off like a galloping horse."
Now I realize his true intent;
His words were aimed at deceiving me.
They collected taxes for a bamboo fence
And used the funds for their own selfish ends.[3]
They taxed in winter to fix the western corner,
And again in spring to patch the northern side.
Everyday some part collapsed;
The people were never free from their troublesome demands.
Finally, I decided to delay no longer,
And had them clear space for a new foundation.
Thorns and weeds were cut away,
Spades and baskets cheerfully plied their tasks.
The rich earth did not crumble, but packed high and strong;
The wall seemed to be pounded with metal mailets.[4]
Time passed, and in less than a month
The completed wall rose like a lofty cloudbank.
A moat was dug to protect us from floods;
The wall was plastered and topped with thatch.
Now it guards against leopards and badgers,
Keeps us safe from wildcats and foxes.
The inside is cut off from the outside:
We're no longer bothered by the vulgar sounds of the street.
Now I'll relax in peace;
Men of the future, don't knock down my wall!

The New Wall at Chien-te offers a sensitively observed "slice of life" in and around a local government office. Nothing is idealized. The "weak, brittle" bamboo hedge, and the various animals, insects and natural forces that beleaguer it, are described in loving detail (lines one through ten). The vignette of petty bureaucratic corruption which follows is also realistically depicted (lines eleven through twenty-four). The rest of the poem relates how the new wall was actually built: "thorns and weeds" are removed, earth is packed, a moat is dug, and the wall is plastered and thatched. Now the office is protected from wild animals and disturbing sounds (lines twenty-four through forty). Throughout this poem, the poet's chief intention is to record reality in verse, although there is a note of social comment as well.

Mei's interest in recording the details of everyday experience in poetry led him to write a number of long narrative poems in which the events follow one another like the unfolding landscape of a scroll painting. The finest of these, and one of Mei's best poems, was written in the autumn of 1040: [5]

WHEN I WAS ESCORTING SHIH-HOU ON HIS RETURN TO
NAN-YANG WE ENCOUNTERED A GREAT WINDSTORM AND
STAYED OVERNIGHT AT KAO-YANG MOUNTAIN MONASTERY—
THE NEXT DAY WE TRAVELED TOGETHER TO CHIANG INN VILLAGE

Once before I had escorted you in the spring wind,
The spring wind in its full intoxication,
    the apricot at the peak of its charm.
Now I was to see you home in the autumn wind,
The autumn wind sadly whistling,
    riverbeds filled with sand.
Our horses' manes were swept aslant,
    their hair shrivelled and curled;
The servants' teeth kept chattering
    as their feet stumbled along.
Our worn-out furs were blown to tatters,
    the cold cut to our bones;
Withered treetrunks rubbed and struck,
    nearly bursting into flame.
Suddenly we came upon an old temple,
    jutting from the belly of a cliff.

There we dismounted from our horses
    and rested together.
The halls and chambers rose and fell,
    following the mountain's curve;
Pines and cedars soared skyward,
    piercing the cloudbanks.
Fallen leaves twirled down long galleries
    as if swept by a broom;
In the abbot's quarters, a curtain flapped
    as though shaken by a hand.
A clay image showed Hariti,
    breastfeeding nine children,
Fondling and embracing, playing with them,
    loveable each one:
The sight brought remembrance to a distance traveler's
    heart,
And I burned with longing to see my own young ones
    at home.
We sat huddled close to the brazier
    as sunlight yielded to darkness;
Borrowed beds and slept together
    in the glimmer of shrine lamps.
Although we were covered with blankets,
    they were as cold as iron;
Better to be home in poverty
    with no bedclothes at all!
Pillowed on our arms, unable to sleep,
    we hoped for the dawn;
Our legs were frozen to numbness, our sinews were
    cramped.
Then *bok-bok* sounded the wooden fish,
    announcing the end of the night;
We rose to see the Pleiades and Hyades moving westward.
The wind's angry howl stopped quickly,
    the east became bright;
The servants got our things together
    and we prepared to leave.
An old monk wiped the dust from the wall,
    brought me inkstone and brush,
And asked if I would take the trouble
    to inscribe the time of year.
Then together we rode out the gate
    and came to a mountain inn

Where the thatched roof had been blown off,
    leaving the roofbeams exposed.
Again we chatted and laughed for a while,
    sitting on foreign chairs,
And held a little party, even though you can't drink.
Less than five hundred *li* remained for you to travel,
And surely you had a purse-full of cash in your
    traveling case;
Yet you kept shaking out your robe and rising,
    fearful of the sun's decline,
Afraid, no doubt, that an anxious mother
    was awaiting your return.
But I had to go the way of the rivers and the seas,
Never knowing why my thoughts would return so often
    to these scenes.

Kakehi relates this poem to Tu Fu's *Song of the Autumn Wind Blowing Off My Thatched Roof*,[6] and to Han Yü's *Mountain Stones*.[7] The only connection between the Mei Yao-ch'en and Tu Fu poems would appear to lie in certain expressions which occur in both: "Cold as iron" (of bedclothes), and "angry howl" (of wind). Tu's second line, "Blows the three-layered thatch off my roof," may also be compared with Mei's thirty-second line, "Where the thatched roof had been blown off, leaving the roofbeams exposed." But the relationship between these two poems appears to end here. It is also difficult to see why Han Yü's *Mountain Stones* should be mentioned in connection with the present poem. In *Mountain Stones*, the poet visits a temple in the rain at dusk. He views the Buddhist paintings there, as well as the natural sights of the area. But the Han Yü poem, fine as it is, does not have the sweep and grandeur of Mei's poem, in which the episode of the visit to the temple is only one of several episodes which constitute the narrative line. Nor is Mei's poem entirely similar to such long narrative pieces by Tu Fu as *The Journey North*, in which the poet's personal experience, while magnificently evoked, forms only one part of a vast tapestry which also includes matters of national importance. Mei limits himself to an account of his own experiences during a journey; there is no social comment. The superb descriptions of the mountains and trees, the temple precincts, and the effect of the windstorm on servants and horses, are presented for their own sake. Especially moving is the passage where, looking at a statue of Hariti, the Buddhist protectress of children, Mei is reminded of his own children, and feels a sudden pang of homesickness. The poet's most intimate personal emotions are woven into the texture of a narrative which unfolds in a setting of awesome nobility, just as the great painters of the northern Sung somehow infused with humanity the tiny figures who travel through their monumental landscapes.

Contrasting with the dramatic sweep of *When I Was Escorting Shih-hou . . .* is the seemingly trivial incident which inspired the following poem: [8]

WHEN HSIEH SHIH-HOU AND I STAYED OVERNIGHT IN THE LIBRARY OF
MR. HSÜ, WE HEARD THE SOUND OF RATS AND WERE GREATLY ALARMED

The lamp is dim; everyone's asleep.
Now famished rats come scurrying from their holes.
The crash of toppled bowls and plates
Wakes us with a jolt from our dreams.
I fear they may knock down the inkstone on the desk
Or gnaw the volumes on the bookshelves.
My foolish son tries meowing like a cat—
Certainly not a very bright idea!

Hsü Yen, as we have seen, was the father-in-law of Hsieh Ching-ch'u (Shih-hou). According to his biography in the *Sung shih,* Hsü admired the writings of Liu K'ai, and was thus in sympathy with the literary tastes of Mei and his circle. In 1044, while Mei was in the capital, he and Hsieh stayed overnight in Hsü's library and had the experience that is described in this poem. No moral is drawn; nothing is idealized. The actions of the rats and the poet's fears are described, and the poem ends on a humorous note.

Mei's dry sense of humor is also evident in a poem probably written in 1046: [9]

PREFECTURAL JUDGE FAN URGES ME TO GIVE UP
DRINKING WINE

I loved to drink wine in my youth;
Hardly anyone could out-drink me then.

Now my hair is turning white and my teeth are loose;
I still like drinking, but can't drink too much.
Every time I drink I vomit it up;
My insides are never at peace.
And then the morning hangover—
        can't even lift my head,
The room spinning around like a whirlpool. . . .
Try to find pleasure and you end up sick in bed.
Who says it's good for your health?
From now on I will try to give it up,
But I fear that others will make fun of me.
Mr. Fan is good at exhortation;
He speaks sternly, mincing no words.
And so I learn that giving up is right;
No telling what will happen if I don't.

Poems which praise the power of wine to lift the poet from the mundane world are legion in Chinese literature, but descriptions of hangovers are not easy to find. Another poem of Mei's [10] relates how he became ill after drinking three or four rounds of wine with a friend in his boat; Mei vomited, and had to retire to bed. Apparently Judge Fan's warnings did not go unheeded, and for a while Mei stopped drinking. But another friend, a certain Wang, felt that he was making a mistake. A poem written later in the year [11] answers one sent by Wang in which Wang had urged Mei to resume drinking. In paraphrase, the first part of Mei's poem says,

> Formerly I drank too much wine, and my health was impaired. I vomited up several litres of blood, and almost developed lung disease. I reflected that above, there were my old father and mother, and below, my young wife and children. Even if I did not die, if I were to be perpetually ill, was this the proper way to care for my body? Mr. Fan came to exhort me to give up drinking wine, and what he said seemed to make sense. But now you have sent me a poem in which you criticize me with forceful words. You point out that I am growing old; how can I nourish my vital force if not with wine?

Convinced by Wang's arguments, Mei concludes, "From now on I'll drink a little, if only to keep my illness from getting any worse!" In all these poems, Mei shows unusual courage in dealing with the more unpleasant aspects of drinking. Few Chinese poets before him, if any, had written about vomiting blood after drinking wine.

Also dating from 1046 is the poem,

MY SON CAPTURES A BABY SPARROW [12]

Little sparrow—fledgling in the eaves,
Still not grown to the age of strength:
Learning to use his wings, he flutters in the sunlight,
When suddenly—caught hanging in the spider's web!
His mother cannot save him;
Helplessly she darts about with pitiful chirps.
But soon he's taken by human hands;
It's no insect's web that traps him now!

As in the poem on the rats in Mr. Hsü's library, Mei here concerns himself with a relatively minor experience, and turns it into a charming vignette of everyday life. One of the autumn poems in the *Field and Garden Poems* by Fan Ch'eng-ta (1126–1193) [13] relates how the poet had his boy servant destroy a spider's web in the eaves of his house to save the dragonflies and bees which had been caught in it. The motive of Mei's son in the present poem is not quite so beneficent! But the tone of domestic intimacy does look ahead to a kind of Sung poetry that was to reach its culmination in Fan's *Field and Garden* series.

Still another poem of 1046 is

THE PIEBALD HORSE [14]

I moor my boat to eat in a lonely village;
Across the river I see a piebald horse.
He stands there, hungry in the barren pasture;
Scarred birds swoop down to peck at him.
Deeply moved, without a bow to shoot,
I uselessly fling clods of earth at them.
But I'm too weak; I can't reach the bank.
My sweating face burns red with shame.

The fourth line of this poem, literally, "Scarred birds swoop down to peck," has been interpreted by Kakehi to mean that the birds peck at the horse's feed. Watson, following this interpretation, translates, "Scruffy birds flocking down to peck his feed." But lines by Tu Fu and Wang Yü-ch'eng which were discussed in chap-

ter 2 suggest rather strongly that Mei intended the birds to be pecking at the horse himself.[15] The memory of these lines probably influenced Mei when he wrote his poem, although he turned the
word *ch'uang*, "scar," which appears in both the Tu Fu and Wang
Yü-ch'eng poems as a noun meaning the scars of the horse and
donkey, into an adjective modifying "birds." Such an interpretation is not necessarily inconsistent with the view that this poem
records an actual event; the Chinese poet constantly mines the literary tradition for words and images with which to express his personal experience. The tone of anger and frustration which informs
this poem could not differ more from the intimate humor of *My Son
Captures a Baby Sparrow*, but the two poems are alike in deriving
from actual experience, and in remaining faithful to that experience
and avoiding romantic hyperbole of any kind.

In the following year, 1047, like many other aging Chinese
scholars, Mei began to have trouble with his eyesight. Characteristically, he refers to this problem in a number of poems, of which
two, the first dating from 1047 and the second from 1048, will be
translated here:

MY EYES GO DIM [16]

My eyes have suddenly gone dim;
In broad daylight I seem to walk through fog.
Amazing, but things double as I peer at them;
I make mistakes in brushwork when I write.
People coming toward me are barely recognizable;
Birds go flying by in a haze.
Who can distinguish things in this confusion?
I've already forgotten what's attractive and what isn't!

ON MY EYE ILLNESS [17]

Already an impoverished Meng Chiao,
I've become a blind Chang Chi as well.
Lines of poetry must be chanted out loud;
The things of this world are no longer visible.
Although I know what's attractive and what isn't,
It's hard to show the whites or pupils of my eyes.
Now my son must read my books to me—
The sound is unceasing, day and night.

In the course of the second poem, Mei refers explicitly to two of his favorite poets (Meng Chiao, Chang Chi), and implicitly to a third (line six: Juan Chi was able to show the pupils of his eyes to friends, and the whites to those he held in contempt). References to Chang Chi's bad eyesight occur in other early Sung poems. Wang Yü-ch'eng says of himself, "Like Chang Chi, my eyes are nearly blind," [18] and Wei Yeh, in a poem to Hui-ch'ung, one of the "Nine Monks," writes, "Chang Chi's eyes were dim, but his mind was not obscured; / Hui-ch'ung's ears are deaf, but he is naturally perceptive." [19] Despite these allusions, this poem, like the previous one, is a convincing account of Mei's personal experience, delivered again in a humorous tone tinged with sadness.

Related to the poems on his eye illness is a poem probably written in 1049 in which Mei describes his feelings on seeing his first white hair: [20]

ON THE SEVENTH DAY OF THE EIGHTH MONTH I SAW THE
FIRST WHITE HAIR IN MY MOUSTACHE

Others have been frightened to see a white hair
    in their moustache,
But I am happy to see one!
Anyone else would pluck it out,
But I intend to do nothing of the sort.
Pluck it out and it just grows again;
Why be ashamed to leave it there?
If each white hair is plucked out the day it comes,
When will the daily plucking ever end? [21]
Black-haired youth is not always noble;
White-haired old age need not be despised.
It's simply a matter of being a good man;
Your hair and teeth will take care of themselves.

This poem is reminiscent both in tone and in diction of Po Chü-i. Po wrote a number of poems on his hair turning white and his teeth getting loose. In one of them, *White Hairs*,[22] Po consoles his wife, who is apparently upset that Po should be getting white hairs at the early age of "forty," by telling her that his hair should actually have turned white long ago because of his excessive reading and drinking, and the sorrow caused by the deaths of friends and relatives. Both Po and Mei thus reach the philosophical conclusion that signs of incipient old age in the body are not to be feared, but accepted as part of the inevitable cycle of life, decay, and death.

Thinking of P'ei Ju-hui and Sung Chung-tao in the Moonlight,[23] probably dating from 1051, contains one of Mei's best night scenes:

No one is walking on the nine main roads;
Cold moonlight glitters like limpid water.
The mansion of the sky is washed to voidness;
The Jade Well rises southeasterly.
My horse is sleeping in the courtyard;
His head droops, his ears lie limp.
Black mane filled with crystals of frost,
He's not ready now for a thousand-mile run!
My servants are sleeping in the stable,
Back to back like a pair of *e*'s.
One of them suddenly wakes from a nightmare,
And shouts as if hit by a flying bolt.
This is the time when feelings stir in me;
I walk with my shadow in the moonlight.
Only the moonlight and my shadow
Find nothing wrong with the way I live.
P'ei and Sung, of all my friends,
Are like the moon and shadow in their hearts.
We always share both speech and silence,
And have nothing to do with the vulgar of this world.

The quiet, clear nightscape (lines one through four), the sleeping horse (lines five through eight) and servants (lines nine through twelve) are all well observed and described. Line ten, "Back to back like a pair of *e*'s," is a novel application of an image which had already been used in an entirely different context by K'ung An-kuo (c.156–c.74 B.C.). As noted by Kakehi, K'ung, in his commentary to a passage in the *I-chi* chapter of the *Book of Documents*, had written, "The *fu* decoration consists of two *chi*'s back to back." The last eight lines of the poem are subjective, and deal with the poet's thoughts and memories of his friends.

P'ei Yü (Ju-hui) reappears in the title of another 1051 poem,[24]

BORROWING RICE FROM JU-HUI

My family complain like cackling geese—
The chimney is cold, there's no fire for breakfast.

Penury must beg from poverty;
How can we help but laugh at each other?
Luckily, Mr. Yen's calligraphy is preserved
And we have the poem of Mr. T'ao as well.
They show that men of former times
Also went begging for rice, begging for food.

With characteristic humor, Mei has turned the experience of
poverty into a superb regulated verse poem. The poem displays the
technique of literary allusion at its best. Line six refers to T'ao
Ch'ien's poem, *Begging for Food;* [25] line five refers to the *Calligraphy
on Begging for Rice* by the great T'ang calligrapher Yen Chen-ch'ing
(709–784),[26] the full text of which reads, "As I am bad at making a
living, my entire family has been eating nothing but rice gruel for
several months. And now we've run out of even that!" One com-
mentator on Yen's work said, "From this we know that he was not
ashamed of poverty and low station, and could therefore hold to the
Tao," a statement which might also be applied to Mei's poem. The
expression *chü-chia,* "all the family," in the first line of the poem
also occurs in the text of Yen's calligraphy.

Eclipse of the Moon,[27] securely dated to 1058 in the *Nien-p'u,*[28]
demonstrates that Mei continued to write realistic poems of personal experience quite late in life:

Our maid comes rushing into the hall
To tell of an astonishing sight:
Heaven has turned to deep blue glass,
The moon is black obsidian in the sky.
It ought to be full now
But we only see a sliver of brightness.
My wife goes off to fry roundcakes,
My young son beats on a metal mirror:
However foolish they may seem
I respect their wanting to set things right.
Deep in the night, the cassia and the rabbit
Again lead all the stars westward.

Characteristic of Mei are the well-chosen metaphors for sky and
moon during the eclipse ("deep blue glass" and, in the original
text, "black crystal"), and the domestic details introduced in lines

seven and eight. The poet's wife and son attempt to bring back the moon, which "ought to be full at this time of year," by frying cakes which are round like the full moon, and beating on a round mirror of bronze. The latter custom is explained by a passage in the *K'ai-yüan t'ien-pao i-shih*,[29] a work compiled by Wang Jen-yü of the Five Dynasties period and dealing with events of the years 713–755: "Whenever there is an eclipse of the moon, the young ladies of Ch'ang-an face toward the moon and strike mirrors. This is done throughout the city, and is known as 'saving the eclipsed moon.' "

The fourth couplet of Mei's poem is followed by two lines of moralizing, which here seem to act as a sort of bridge between the homely intimacy of the preceding couplet and the nearly mystic awe of the final lines, as the poet watches the nightscape return to its natural cycle.

2 *POEMS OF PERSONAL EMOTION*

The poems discussed in the previous section, while various in theme, shared in common the poet's realistic approach, his closeness to the acts and objects of the everyday world. But it is not only the external world that is realistically depicted in Mei Yao-ch'en's poetry; the poet's personal emotions are also expressed with remarkable candor. There is an almost total lack of idealization or artificial romantic passion which is often extraordinarily modern in its effect. For example, in 1052, as we have seen, Mei became Inspector of the Yung-chi Granaries. Although he was already fifty-one by Chinese count, he had not been able to rise above this relatively humble post. Mei felt the full humiliation of his position when he had to spend a chilly winter night at the granary after just having recovered from an illness. The poem he wrote on this inglorious occasion,[1] quoted in the *Nien-p'u* entry for 1052,[2] is one of his most powerful:

ON THE THIRTEENTH DAY OF THE ELEVENTH MONTH I WENT
TO THE GRANARY FOR THE FIRST TIME SINCE MY ILLNESS

I am not a sparrow or a rat.
What am I doing here in this huge granary?
The warmth is gone from my tattered fox-fur robe,

Mended with patches of yellow dogskin.
Frost crystals appear as the moon descends
Weaving garlands on withered branches:
And I, a man of more than fifty,
Lie gaunt with illness as ice forms on my skin.

The stark power of the two last lines is not mitigated by the fact
that a similar idea had already been expressed in a couplet from the
thirteenth of Meng Chiao's *Autumn Thoughts* poems: [3] "Frosty
vapors enter sick bones; / Ice forms on the old man's body." In
Meng's poem, the poet is somehow idealized into the universal
"suffering poet." Mei's poem is unmistakably personal, from the
cry of indignation in the opening lines to the mention of his age in
the penultimate line. The middle couplets—a sombre evocation of
the poet's suffering in the cold, if beautiful, nightscape—act as an
effective foil to the intense emotion of the opening and closing
lines.

The event which inspired Mei to write his best poetry in this
mode was the death of his wife in 1044. The first group of poems
which he composed on this subject bears the title,

MOURNING FOR MY WIFE

Three Poems [4]

I

We came of age, and were made man and wife.
Seventeen years have gone by since then.
I still have not tired of gazing at her face
But now she has left me forever.
The white has come to my hair;
This body can't hold out much longer.
When the end comes I'll join her in the grave;
Until my death, the tears flow on and on.

II

Whenever I go out I seem to walk in a dream,
Often meeting people, forcing myself to answer . . .
Then home again to the silent loneliness;
I want to talk, but there's no one I can talk to.
A single firefly flits through the chilly window;
A solitary wild goose flies in the endless night.
There is no greater pain for a man than this:
Here my spirit is crushed, and dies.

III

There have always been long life and early death.
Who dares lay the blame on azure heaven?
I have seen many wives in this world of men,
Yet none so beautiful and wise as she.
The foolish, it seems, are granted long life:
Why was she not lent some of their years?
Can I bear to lose this jewel worth a string of cities
Sunk and buried in the Ninefold Springs?

The title of this series of regulated verse poems, *tao wang*, had been associated with the genre ever since the group (also consisting of three poems) by P'an Yüeh (d. 300).[5] (The influence of P'an's poems, and of later poems of this type, on Mei will be discussed later.) The first line of the first poem in the present group, literally, "Our hair was bound, and we became man and wife," refers to the custom of binding up the hair of a young man (or woman) when he reached the age of puberty. The seventh line of the same poem alludes to the poem *Big Chariot* in the *Airs of Wang* section of the *Book of Odes*.[6] In this poem, the poet says to his wife (in the translation of Bernhard Karlgren), "In death you shall share my grave." It will be shown later that this allusion, quite naturally, had already entered the repertoire of appropriate references for a poem on the death of one's wife. The "Ninefold Springs" of the last line of the poem are, of course, the underworld.

Immediately following these three poems is another regulated verse poem on the same subject: [7]

TEARS

Tears of blood stored life-long in my eyes
Flow all day and all night.
They spill out the bitterness of my broken heart,
Deeper than the gushing of an underground spring.
The glow of my face is washed to pallor;
My white hairs grow root to root.
This is a sorrow which from ancient times
Has been known to all—the foolish and the wise.

As if his wife's death were not enough, within less than a month after she had died, Mei also lost his second son, Shih-shih. This event is described in a poem of 1045,[8]

MOURNING FOR MY SON

His Baby Name was Shih-shih

Traveling by boat, we rested at Fu-li.
There my son, little Shih, died.
I felt only astonishment looking down at him;
Strange, but the greatest sorrows bring no tears.
Not until my feelings settled did awareness come,
And searing fires seemed to mass inside.
His mother too I lost, not long before,
And I am still grieving for her.
Now mornings are passed in weeping for my wife—
Tears drop and moisten robe and sleeves.
Then nights are passed in weeping for my son;
The doubled pain sinks into my heart.
Let me ask of heaven above:
What is the reason for all this suffering?
I only have two sons;
Why so hasty in taking one away?
It is the birds of spring alone who thrive,
Feeding the thronging young in their nests.

From this poem we learn that Shih-shih died at Fu-li in northern Anhui, just above the Pien River. This factual detail is characteristic of Mei, as is the psychological perception of lines three through six. The poet has noted that the death of a loved one is often followed by a curious emotional numbness; the full intensity of realization only comes later. Although the poem ends on a quasi-metaphoric note, the traditional ironic contrast between the poet's loneliness and the happiness of the birds seems particularly appropriate here.

Some of Mei's most powerful poems were inspired by later memories of his wife. Early in 1045, the year after her death, the contrast between the gaiety of the lantern festival, held on the night of the first full moon of the year, and his own grief, moved Mei to write the poem,

ON THE NIGHT OF THE FIFTEENTH DAY OF THE FIRST MONTH I
GO OUT AND RETURN [9]

Only depression if I stay at home:
Out to the festival to ease my pain.
But every man, rich or poor, is together with his wife;
My heart is moved only to greater grief.

Pleasures cloy so easily as old age comes;
I would go on walking but desire fades.
Home again, I see my boy and girl;
Before a word is spoken my eyes smart bitterly.
Last year their mother took them out;
They smeared on rouge, trying to be just like her.
Now their mother has gone to the Springs below;
Their faces are dirty, few of their clothes untorn.
When I reflect how young they both still are,
I can't bear to let them see my tears.
   Push the lamp aside
        lie facing the wall
A hundred sorrows clumped in me.

The poignant memory of his children imitating their mother by
smearing on make-up ("They smeared on rouge, trying to be just
like her") is also used by Mei in another poem of 1045 which has already been translated. In describing the deceased daughter of Ou-
yang Hsiu, Mei writes, "She must have been clever as she
grew, / Aping her mother, smearing on shadow and rouge." Both
passages may have been influenced by Tu Fu's *The Journey North*,[10]
in which there occurs a superb description of how the poet's
daughter attempts to make herself up like her mother: "My crazy
daughter combs her own hair, / Trying to do everything like her
mother. / She rubs on her morning make-up as best she can; / In a
moment she has smeared on rouge and shadow, / And has roughly
painted her eyebrows too far apart." The expression "imitating
mother" and the verb "apply" are common to all three passages.
Nevertheless, these correspondences do not lessen the impact of the
present poem, which is one of Mei's best.
   Also dating from 1045 is

SORROW [11]

From the time you came home as my wife
You never complained of our poverty.
Every day you sewed deep into the night;
You only ate breakfast after noon.
Nine days out of ten we dined on salted vegetables;
There might be dried meat on the tenth.
East and west we wandered for eighteen years
Sharing the bitter and the sweet.

We looked ahead to a full life of love,
But a single night was to take you from this world.
Still I remember when you were facing death,
How you caressed me, unable to speak . . .
Though this body may be alive today,
It will end as dust, mingled with your dust.

Two problems in this poem call for comment. Mei was married to his first wife from 1027 to 1044, that is, for a period of seventeen years, as he says in the first poem of the series, *Mourning For My Wife*. The "eighteen years" of line seven in the present poem must refer to calendar years. More difficult is the sense of line four. Watson takes *chao fan* to mean lunch, and translates, "Lunch ready a little past noon." The meaning would then be that Mei's wife was always diligent in preparing the noon meal at just the right time. But it is also possible that *chao fan* means breakfast rather than lunch; the line would then suggest that Mei's wife was so busy with her morning chores that she only got to eat her own breakfast after noon. Thus both the third and fourth lines, which are perfectly parallel, would describe different aspects of the "poverty" of which Mei's wife "never complained."

In a long poem written on New Year's day in 1046,[12] Mei recalls spending the New Year's of 1042 together with his wife:

NEW YEAR'S DAY

Once before there was wind and snow;
Our boat was morred at Wu Dam.
The tide hadn't reached the bay yet;
We all sat idly with nothing to do.
Sea food was found for our kitchen,
Just some salty-sour odds and ends.
But after such a long time in the north
I was delighted to eat these things again.
It was New Year's day;
I celebrated with my wife.
She improvised a New Year's meal
And hastily smeared on powder and rouge.
We made a toast with cups of wine,
Drinking to a long life with each other.
Tart oranges made our mouths tingle.
Our eyes already showed signs of age,

But how could I know that just a few years later,
Halfway through life's journey my wife would die?
Now, while others enjoy this happy day,
I must endure my tears of grief.
Past happiness has turned to sorrow;
Time is so unsure!
Looking back at that fortieth spring,
My body is all that's left of our old promise.
I'm weary of hearing about the world's affairs,
Though I can't bear to give up reading.
Things no longer seen are often forgotten,
But who can put aside his heart's long love?
When will I be able to return to Ching-k'ou
And cut away the weeds in the bamboo grove?
Then, singing as I go, I'll be happy late in life,
Gathering firewood and pulse.

The New Year's of 1042 is described in a poem written at that time, *On New Year's Day My Wife and I Wish Each Other Long Life in Our Moored Boat*.[13] This poem corroborates the accuracy of Mei's memory. "In our boat we meet the New Year; / Wind and rain blow in the lingering cold." Later in the poem, Mei relates how he and his wife celebrated: "My wife and I wish each other good fortune, / Sitting together before rows of cups and plates. / The plates hold piles of oranges; / Our mouths taste sour before we've taken a bite!" The poem goes on to describe how Mei and his wife drank wine together, and got drunk.

Ching-k'ou, or Chen-chiang in Chiangsu, was the site of the temporary grave of Mei's wife. The last four lines of the poem probably mean that Mei's only desire now is to clear the weeds from his wife's grave. Then he will be content, and will take up the life of a recluse.

In the summer of the same year, 1046, Mei dreamed of his wife, as he must often have done. This dream inspired him to write a poem, as he explains in a long prose preface: [14]

> On the twenty-second day of the fifth month of the year *ping-hsü* (June 28, 1046), I fell asleep during the day and dreamed that my deceased wife, née Hsieh, and I were traveling early on the river. Suddenly we came to the shore and approached a large mountain which we then climbed. I wrote a poem of over one hundred characters describing the things we saw there. When I awoke I could still remember two of the

lines: "Together we climbed Mica Mountain, / But could not stay in the same palace." Here I will develop these lines into a full poem to recreate the feeling of my dream.

I daydreamed that you were traveling with me;
We set out early from an islet in the river.
"Together we climbed Mica Mountain
But could not stay in the same palace."
—Why these regrets about the palace?
Maybe we had grown weary of inns!
A crow's nest dangled from the tip of a tree;
Newly hatched fledglings peered up for food.
The father and mother stood guard in the woods;
They screeched when they caught sight of a squirrel.
The startled squirrel's hair bristled in anger;
His jump released the branch like a crossbow shot.
Moments later came the roar of a windstorm;
We watched distant rains slanting against the cliffs.
A rainbow spanned south and east;
Water spurted and bubbled in ten thousand gullies.
We got lost going home,
And spoke sadly together in the twilight . . .
Suddenly I woke up; everything was gone.
The sun was high above the empty yard.

It will have been noticed that the anguished tone of the poems written immediately after the death of Mei's wife has gradually subsided, and that in this poem as in the previous one, the poet appears to be calmer and more philosophical. But another poem, also dating from 1046,[15] shatters this impression:

WRITTEN IN SORROW

Sorrow keener than any blade
Cuts and tears at me inside.
Something is left—her old things;
But only my grief can share them with me now.
Clothing sewn by her own hand—
How could I open the boxes again?
Morning and night I bow before her silent altar
And hate the portrait which has so little life.
She may be dead, but my feelings won't change;
The bond was strong when her name was changed to mine.

Soon my body too shall fade;
I chant the ode on "joining her in the grave."

The last line of this poem again refers to the *Book of Odes* poem, *Great Chariot*, as did the first poem of the series, *Mourning For My Wife*.

The poems discussed thus far in this section constitute a series which is one of the most important of its kind in Chinese literature. They belong to a tradition which began when P'an Yüeh wrote his famous three poems, and which continued to flourish in the T'ang dynasty. Two T'ang poets wrote especially fine poetic sequences on the deaths of their wives. One of these is famous—that of Yüan Chen. The entire ninth *chüan* of his collected writings [16] is devoted to poems of this kind. As a note under the title of the first poem informs the reader, "This and the following are poems on the death of my wife." In a letter to Po Chü-i, Yüan states that he had consciously taken the title *tao-wang* from P'an Yüeh.[17] Less well known is the equally important sequence by Wei Ying-wu, found in the sixth *chüan* of his works under the heading "sighs of emotion." [18] As in the Yüan Chen group, a note under the title of the first poem informs the reader that "This and the following are poems which lament the world, and mourn sorrowfully—nineteen poems in all." It is likely that these poems by Wei were still another reason for Mei Yao-ch'en's unusual interest in his work.

A number of motifs introduced by P'an Yüeh can be traced throughout the literature, and are duly employed by Mei. One of these is the sadness caused by seeing the dead wife's belongings. P'an's first poem contains these lines (in the translation of J. D. Frodsham [19]):

. . . I look at my house and think of her again,
I walk through its rooms and the past comes back to me.
No sign of her through the curtains of my bed,
Yet her brush and ink have left their traces still.
Her ambient fragrance lingers in the air,
Some things of hers are hanging on the walls.

A related idea occurs in a couplet from the second of Yüan Chen's well known *Three Poems Expressing My Sorrow*, [20] a group in which specific reference is made to the P'an Yüeh poems: "I've given away nearly all her clothes; / Her sewing needle and thread still remain, but I can't hear to open the box!" Wei Ying-wu also made use of this motif. For example, *Mourning For the Dead*,[21] the first poem in his series, contains the quatrain, "One morning I entered her chamber. / The four walls were covered with dust. / Now that she is gone forever, / Her things only cause me pain." The most extensive development of this theme occurs in Wei's magnificent poem, *Visiting Our Old Residence at Chao-kuo Hamlet*.[22] After returning to his old home and viewing the garden, the poet visits his wife's room:

Her sealed room is in the eastern chamber;
I can't bear to look at her remaining things!
The soft brush which expressed her every thought,
The headcloth still fragrant with perfume,
The scraps of handiwork, left in the box,
Some fragments of silk, cut and measured—
These things I want to take home with me
But grief stops me as I'm about to leave.
Gone forever, the joy of holding her hand!
Nothing left but a few dead things.

This motif also appears in the poem, *Chamber Music*[23] by Li Shang-yin. The poet is reminded of his dead wife by her pillow and sleeping mat, and by her "patterned lute, longer lived than she." It might finally be noted that the motif may also be used in poems of mourning for a dead friend. For example, Kao Shih (d. 765), in *Mourning for Liang the Ninth of Tan-fu, Director of the Imperial Workshops*,[24] writes, "I open the box and tears wet my breast: / Here are the books that you used to read!"

In the context of these examples, Mei Yao-ch'en's *Written in Sorrow* is seen to belong to a venerable tradition:

Something is left—her old things;
But only my grief can share them with me now.
Clothing sewn by her own hand—
How could I open the boxes again?

Another important aspect of the original P'an Yüeh poems is their remarkably subtle psychological perception. The poet, grief-stricken, attempts to divert himself from his sorrow by returning to the humdrum routine of everyday life. Directly preceding the poet's visit to his wife's rooms in the first poem, there occurs this couplet (in Frodsham's translation): "I did my best to respect the court's commands, / To busy my mind I went back to my old routine." And in the third poem (not translated by Frodsham), the poet says, "I made my heart obey the court's commands; / Wiping away my tears, I forced myself to enter the carriage. / Who says the palace of the emperor is far? / I came to the end of the road, but there was still grief to spare."

Later poets, partly inspired by these passages in P'an Yüeh, also attempted to convey the psychological effects of their bereavement. Yüan Chen's poem, *On the Empty Room—Night of the Fourteenth Day of the Tenth Month*,[25] is an excellent example:

In the morning I leave my empty room
And ride my horse to the censorate.
I spend the day there, working at trivial jobs,
Then return again to my empty room.
Bright moonlight glimmers through cracks in the dark wall.
My lamp burns down, the ashes crumble.
And I think of the road to Hsien-yang—
Her funeral hearse returning last night.

As Ch'en Yin-k'o has shown,[26] Yüan's wife, née Wei, was buried at Hsien-yang on the thirteenth day of the tenth month of the fourth year of the *Yüan-ho* period, that is, on the day before this poem was written. Yüan was then in Loyang, where his official duties at the censorate prevented him from attending his wife's funeral. As in the previously quoted lines by P'an Yüeh, here too the poet must force himself to get up in the morning and ride to work. The censorate seems "empty" (in the original text) because the poet is overwhelmed by his loss; his work seems "trivial" to him. Although it contains no explicit statements of the poet's psychological state, the poem subtly evokes understanding of his grief.

Several of Wei Ying-wu's poems also depict the feeling of loss and emptiness. *Feelings While Living in Retirement* [27] contains a number of passages of this kind:

. . . All day long I have nothing to say,
Then suddenly I shake my robe and rise with a start:
She seems to be there, behind the curtain!
But no, I remember she's gone forever.

. . . I'm indifferent to warmth and coolness alike;
Light and dark also seem meaningless.
Others have told me of loneliness, of choking inside,
And now I'm feeling it for myself.
Twilight falls on her empty chamber;
Nesting swallows come there to rest.
The summer trees are forming shade;
Who will walk now on the green moss?
How can I control these feelings when they come?
I shall always be this way, apart from the world.

The second couplet quoted is reminiscent of these lines from the second of P'an Yüeh's poems (in Frodsham's translation): "Asleep or wake, she lives before my eyes, / Her voice is ever ringing in my ears."

The second of Mei's poems, *Mourning For My Wife*, is a classic example of this type. "Whenever I go out," he writes, "I seem to walk in a dream, / Often meeting people, forcing myself to answer," just as P'an Yüeh "forced" himself to enter his carriage and drive to court. The poet then returns to the "silent loneliness," as Yüan Chen had returned to his empty room. Wei's sequence includes a poem called *Going Out and Returning*,[28] in which returning home is a painful experience for the poet. Mei's *On the Night of the Fifteenth Day of the Fifth Month I Go Out and Return* is also related to this group. In both this poem and the Wei Ying-wu poem, the poet's grief is heightened when he sees his children. Wei wrote, "My young daughter, seemingly unaware, comes out to play in the courtyard." Mei hides his tears, so that the children cannot see them.

The poems discussed here are generally free of literary allusions, but we have seen that Mei twice makes use of the expression "joining her in the grave" from the ode, *Great Chariot*—in the first poem of the group, *Mourning For My Wife* ("When the end comes I'll join her in the grave"), and in *Written in Sorrow* ("I chant the ode on 'joining her in the grave' "). Yüan Chen appears to have introduced this allusion into the repertoire. The third of his *Three Poems Expressing My Sorrow* [29] contains the line, "How can I hope to join her in the grave, when it's so far off, lost in obscurity?"

The husband's wish to join his dead wife in the grave also occurs in English poetry. The fullest expression of this idea is found in the *Exequy On His Wife* by the Bishop of Chichester, Henry King (1592–1669).[30] Toward the end of the poem, the poet addresses his wife:

My last good-night! Thou wilt not wake
Till I thy fate shall overtake:
Till age, or grief, or sickness must
Marry my body to that dust
It so much loves; and fill the room
My heart keeps empty in thy tomb.
Stay for me there: I will not fail
To meet thee in that hollow vale.

But here the similarity between King's exequy and the Chinese examples ends. The extended comparison of the poet's wife with the sun which occupies lines thirteen through twenty-six of the exequy is a most un-Chinese conceit. Mei Yao-ch'en, Wei Ying-wu, and Yüan Chen, all writing centuries before King, seem closer to us today in the directness with which they express their feelings.

Despite his grief at the death of his first wife, or perhaps because of it, Mei remarried in 1046. His poem *Second Marriage*,[31] dated to this year in the *Nien-p'u*,[32] describes Mei's emotions on this occasion:

I married a second time the other day,
Happy about the present, still grieving for the past.
Once more there is someone to take care of the household;
My shadow is no longer alone in the moonlight.
Yet from force of habit I still call my old wife's name—
My heart is just as troubled as before.
Luckily both women are kind and gentle
And I have married again the best of wives.

Not long before his second marriage, Mei had dreamt of his first wife; the poem which records this experience has already been translated. Thoughts of his first wife continued to haunt Mei after his second marriage as well. Not only did he occasionally call his first wife's name by mistake, as he relates in *Second Marriage*, but her image still appeared in his dreams. On February 12, 1048, nearly two years after he remarried, Mei dreamed of her again, and was moved to write one of his most powerful poems: [33]

THE YEAR WU-TZU, FIRST MONTH, NIGHT OF THE
TWENTY-SIXTH: A DREAM

Two years now since my second marriage;
In all that time, I've never dreamed of her.
Last night I saw her face again;
Midnight was a painful hour.
The dark lamp glowed with a feeble light,
Silently glimmering on the rafters.
And the unfeeling snow that beat against my window
Was whirled to a frenzy by the wind.

As though his feelings are too strong to be explicitly stated, the poet allows the "dark lamp . . . glimmering on the rafters" to evoke his black depression, and the snow, "whirled to a frenzy by the wind," his frustrated passion. Mei has realized here the perfect correspondence between external object and internal emotion which is perhaps the supreme achievement of Chinese poetry.

On July 7, 1048, Mei had occasion to pass by the site of his former wife's death. The poem which he wrote then [34] is quoted in the *Nien-p'u* entry for 1048: [35]

ON THE TWENTY-FOURTH DAY OF THE FIFTH MONTH I PASSED
BY SAN-KOU IN KAO-YU

On the seventh day of the seventh month of *chia-shen* [36]
We reached San-kou before the sun had risen.
My former wife, the Lady of Nan-yang,
Suddenly passed away in our journeying boat.
Her spirit went in silence, left no trace,
And I was helpless to follow in pursuit.
The grief I felt then filled earth and sky;
My mind was misted, my heart was torn.
When I stopped sobbing and no tears would come,
The wind kept soughing in the riverside grass.
She still seemed alive—I clung to her corpse
And cried aloud until my throat was in pain.
The helmsman sighed for me then,
The boat-pullers grieved.
Now in the summer of *wu-tzu* I pass by a second time
And memories of that day bring tears again.

Afraid to hurt my new wife's feelings
I make myself rub the dampness from my eyes.
The temporary coffin has still not been carried home;
This regret, this sorrow—will it ever end?

Of all Mei's poems on the death of his wife, this is probably the most original, in that, like the poems discussed in the previous section, it remains almost perfectly faithful to the actual events. Two cyclic dates appear in the text; the first line records the year, month and day of the lady's death. But the precision with which the facts are recorded, if anything, helps to intensify the impact of the passages in which the poet describes his emotions. "My mind was misted, my heart was torn"; "I clung to her corpse, and cried aloud until my throat was in pain." These lines are accepted by the reader as accurate descriptions of the poet's grief, rather than mere hyperbole. Also impressive is the psychological understanding of the penultimate couplet, and the ninth and tenth lines where, as in the previous poem, a natural phenomenon seems to echo the poet's emotion.

We have seen that Mei was moved to write poems of personal emotion not only by the death of his first wife, but by the death of his baby son Shih-shih. On May 6, 1048, Mei also lost his baby daughter Ch'eng-ch'eng, who had been born to his second wife slightly more than six months earlier on October 28, 1047. Mei wrote a group of three ancient-style poems on this occasion: [37]

ON THE TWENTY-FIRST DAY OF THE THIRD MONTH OF THE YEAR WU-TZU MY BABY DAUGHTER CH'ENG-CH'ENG DIED

I

Your father and mother joyed to give you life;
Now they must lament that you have died.
Has there been some failing in the way I've lived?
Why has your existence been so brief?
In spring, crow fledglings fill the nest;
In summer, baby bees swarm in the hive.
Thus creatures with raucous caws or poisonous stings
Give birth to young who fly happily away.
The meaning of these things cannot be known.
Weeping tears of grief I gaze at the empty sky.

II

Flowers budding on the trees—
Such was the freshness of my baby girl.
They could not withstand the winds of spring,
But were blown to the ground where they turned to dust.
This too was the fate of the child I loved;
Heaven knows nothing of sorrow!
And the tears of blood in the tender mother's eyes
Like the milk of her breasts
        have still not dried.

III

In a coffin five inches high and five inches wide
I have buried the sorrow of a thousand years.
It's hard to be torn from one loved so dearly—
My spirit has been blunted and dulled.
Tears of grief leave blotches on my robe;
I mourn for the tenderness of the severed stem.
Since Heaven allowed her to be born,
Why, once alive, did she die so soon?

The best of these poems—the second—ends with a couplet of staggering power. The use of the word "like" (*t'ung*) in the last line intimates that not only is the mother weeping and producing milk, but that these two actions are intimately related, that her tear-reddened eyes are like nipples. It is also worth noting, as Iritani Sensuke has pointed out,[38] that the second couplet is not merely metaphoric—Ch'eng-ch'eng died late in spring, when the flowers were really falling.

The third poem is remarkable in that the last character of every line ends in a nasal (*n* or *ng*—a point made by Iritani), thus echoing in sound the poet's depression, and even, perhaps, the sinking of the heavy coffin in the grave.

Series of poems on the death of a child had already been written by several T'ang poets. Yüan Chen composed a sequence of ten seven-character *chüeh-chü* poems, *Mourning for my Son*,[39] which are included, together with the poems on the death of his wife, in the ninth chapter of his collection. Of particular interest in the present context is the group entitled *Death of the Apricot Blossoms—Nine Poems* by Meng Chiao.[40] A brief preface explains the meaning of the title: "*Death of the Apricot Blossoms* refers to baby flowers. They fell when the frost cut them off. As they remind me of my grief for my dead baby, I have written these poems." The first of the series is typical:

Don't play with pearls if your hands are frozen—
They'll fly from your grip too easily!
Don't let the cruel frosts cut off spring;
They'll deprive it of its lustrous glow.
The tender flowers have scattered,
Beautiful mottling like my baby's robe.
Less than a handful, I gather them
And return at sunset with my empty grief.

The rather far-fetched metaphor of the opening couplet could only have been devised by Meng Chiao, but the extended comparison of the dead child with fallen flowers, and the poignancy of the poet's emotion in the last lines, adumbrate the second of Mei's poems.

Mei learned to live with his memories, deriving consolation from his second wife and his children. Something of this newly achieved peace is expressed in the poem,

FEELINGS ON THE SIXTEENTH DAY OF THE SEVENTH MONTH AS I GO TO THE GRANARY FOR NIGHT DUTY [41]

The glimmering sun sinks before me,
The bright moon rises behind.
Lambent moonlight, almost alive,
Hovers and glides up the willow trees—
Tall willows that face the watch house,
Wind-swept shadows dancing on the lattice.
My horse lies asleep beside the trees.
My servant, exhausted, lies propped on an arm.
The double doors are bolted—utter silence.
My thoughts turn to my wife back home.
Two little children at their mother's breast
Cry every night and question her:
"Where has father gone?" they ask,
Already they show such depth of feeling!
Alone in a traveler's bed, I shouldn't grieve,
Or feel envious when birds roost with their mates.
At home are my children to remember me,
And out there the moon is keeping watch.

I am better off by far than the long-campaigning soldier
Who listens for the alarm gong in the sand.

This poem is dated in the *Nien-p'u* to 1052,[42] when Mei was Inspector of the Yung-chi Granaries. In the poem which opened this
section, written a brief four months after the present one, Mei bitterly protests the indignity of his low official position. But *Feelings
On the Sixteenth Day . . .* is equally effective in expressing the
mood of resignation with which Mei faces his forced separation
from his family. He draws comfort from the thought that his children love him, and also from a vague sense of beneficence in nature
("out there the moon is keeping watch"). Familiar motifs are the
paired birds of line sixteen, whose happiness contrasts with the
poet's loneliness, and the expression of sympathy for the "long-
campaigning soldier" in the final couplet. Mei does not suspend his
social conscience in even the most personal of poems.

3 POEMS OF SOCIAL COMMENT

For Mei Yao-ch'en, the social function of poetry was of primary
importance. "The basic purpose of literature," he tells us, writing
around 1054,[1] "is to aid the times," a statement which is close to Po
Chü-i's famous "Literature should be written for the times." [2] In
several of the poems quoted or paraphrased in the two previous
chapters, Mei expresses his desire to revive the orthodox Confucian
tradition of poetry, which he traces back to the *Book of Odes*. In one
of these poems (dating from 1045),[3] for example, he declares that he
will not give up his effort as a poet until he has reached the level of
the two *Ya*'s, the two sections of the *Book of Odes* most closely associated with social poetry.

It is significant that Mei refers a number of times to the "Poetry
Collector," *ts'ai-shih kuan*. Toward the end of the long preface to his
poem *The Farmers' Words*, written in 1040, he says, "I have . . .
recorded the words of the farmers, and arranged them as a literary
piece to be used some day by the Poetry Collector." In a poem possibly written in 1053,[4] after recording the ideas of a friend on trans-
porting grain, Mei says, "I have written them down for the Poetry
Collector; I hope he won't be slow in visiting me!"

The *locus classicus* for the term "Poetry Collector" appears to be a passage in the *Monograph on Bibliography* of the *Han shu* which has been noted by Suzuki Torao and, more recently, Yokoyama: [5] "In ancient times there existed the office of Poetry Collector which made it possible for the sovereign to observe ways and customs, understand success and failure, and examine and correct himself." This account may have been inspired in turn by the following passage in the section *Ordinances of the Sovereign* in the *Li chi:* ". . . He commanded the Masters of Music to set before him poems by means of which to observe the ways of the people." The Poetry Collector thus came to represent poetry of social comment and protest which might influence the government's policies. It has already been shown that the term occurs in the poetry of Meng Chiao. The last poem in Po Chü-i's *New Yüeh-fu* series is devoted to the theme of the Poetry Collector; Ch'en Yin-k'o has shown that Po was interested in the idea well before writing this poem. [6] Reference has also been made to the occurrence of the term in Wang Yü-ch'eng's poem on olives; [7] in another poem, [8] he says that he wants the Poetry Collector to gather poems congratulating the emperor on the recent timely rains.

As we have seen, the Poetry Collector appears toward the end of the preface to one of Mei's most important social poems,

THE FARMERS' WORDS [9]

> In the year *keng-ch'en* (1040), an edict was issued saying that in a given family, one out of every three men who were twenty years old or more would be drafted. Non-commissioned officers were to be appointed, and the men were to be called "bow and arrow hands." Thus preparation was made for a sudden emergency. The chief officials, wanting to please their superiors by drafting as many men as possible, immediately charged the prefectural officers with the task. The prefectural officers were afraid and did not dare to carry out their orders, so they passed them on to the subprefectural magistrates. With all these officials reckoning up the number of people, neither the young nor the old could escape. Above and below, all lamented and grieved; heavy rains fell incessantly. Is this the way to aid the sovereign in his loving care for the people? I have therefore recorded the words of the farmers, and arranged them as a literary piece to be used some day by the Poetry Collector.

Who says the farmer's life is a happy one?
Spring taxes are still unpaid when autumn comes!
The village headman bangs on our gate;
Day and night he presses us for more.
In the middle of summer, the river flooded;
Turbid waters rose higher than the roofs.
Not only were our beans destroyed by the water
But our grain was eaten by locusts.
Last month an edict arrived from the capital:
The population was registered again.
Of every three men, one became a soldier
And was cruelly forced to carry bow and bowcase.
But now the Prefect's orders are even stricter;
The draft officials wield whips and clubs.
They have sought out both the youngsters and the aged,
Leaving only the blind and the lame.
Dare we vent our grief in field and village?
Father and son weep piteously by themselves.
How can we till the southern acres
When to pay for arrows we have sold our oxen and calves?
The breath of our sorrow becomes long rains;
Jar and cauldron lie empty of rice gruel.
The lame and blind are unable to plow;
Sooner or later they'll surely die.
—I hear these things and feel deeply shamed;
I enjoy my sovereign's wage in vain.
Rather should I sing *The Homecoming*
And gather firewood in some secluded valley.

While this poem is essentially a believable lamentation by the
farmers on their sad lot, Mei could not resist the temptation of introducing in line twenty an ironic allusion to the Han official Kung
Sui, under whose enlightened administration the people of Po-hai
sold their swords and knives to buy oxen and calves,[10] and pros-
pered as a result. The present farmers, however, have sold their
oxen and calves to "pay for arrows." It seems unlikely that the
farmers whose words Mei "recorded" could have negotiated such a
price of literary irony as this. Also, the eleventh line (*San ting chi i
ting*) is suspiciously similar to "Of every three men in a given family, one was drafted" from Po Chü-i's *The Broken-Armed Old Man of
Hsin-feng*,[11] with which the farmers would not have been familiar.

Still, Mei himself points out that he has arranged the farmers' words "as a literary piece." The poem remains a powerful and convincing depiction of the hardships of the common people, expressed in language which is straightforward and forceful.

It is characteristic that Mei should end this poem not with a heated condemnation of the powers that be, but with a passage of self-blame, resigned in tone, in which he expresses his wish to retire from official life, as did T'ao Ch'ien, the author of *The Homecoming*, and "gather firewood in some secluded valley." In another poem of 1040,[12] in which he speaks of his "bad administration," Mei says that he "longs to retire to a cloud-filled valley."

A group of documents written by Ssu-ma Kuang and quoted by Ch'ien Chung-shu [13] illuminate the events which inspired *The Farmers' Words*. One of these refers to the invasions of the Hsi Hsia under their ruler Chao Yüan-hao:

> In the *K'ang-ting* and *Ch'ing-li* periods (1040–1048), Chao Yüan-hao rebelled. . . . As our nation was lacking in proper soldiers, the people of Shensi were drafted at the rate of one man out of three as provincial "bow-hands." . . . The people of the villages were anxious and grieved. . . . Blood relatives were separated; the fields and gardens were in a state of complete confusion.

Another of the documents relates that the drafted men were branded on their faces or hands, and that the people were also expected to provide grain for the armies: "Thus a single family had to produce enough food for two families."

The invasions of 1040 were particularly severe, and precipitated the mass suffering which Mei Yao-ch'en describes in *The Farmers' Words*, and in another of his important social poems,

THE POOR GIRL OF THE JU RIVER BANK [14]

> Now they are again drafting "bow-hands," and both young and old are being mustered. There have been heavy rains and extreme cold; over one hundred men have died on the road. From the Jang River [another name for the Ju River] to Old Ox Slope in K'un-yang, the stiff corpses lie in an unbroken line.

> Poor girl of the Ju River Bank,
> Walking, weeping with bitter sobs.
> She says, "I only have an old father,

He alone, and not one brother of drafting age.
How cruel the clerk of the prefecture was!
My father dared not resist the magistrate—
Pressed and dispatched, not allowed to linger,
He tottered off, leaning on his staff.
Urgently I pleaded with the drafted neighbors,
Begging them to help and care for him . . .
Recently when I heard that a villager had come home,
I asked for news, thinking he might still be alive.
But now, in the midst of the chilly rains,
He lies rigid in death upon the banks of the Jang.
I, a weak girl, am left without support,
And have no way to bury his uncovered corpse.
'Better to give birth to a boy than to a girl'—
Even if I live, what will become of me?"
Striking her breast, she cries to the empty sky;
"Shall I take the way of life now, or of death?"

One of the poems in the *Chou-nan* section of the *Kuo Feng* in the *Book of Odes* bears the title *The Banks of the Ju*,[15] and also records the lamentation of a woman who "Goes along the high banks of the Ju" and "feels a pang as of morning hunger" because she "has not yet seen her lord." Kakehi suggests that Mei's poem was written in the autumn of 1040, when, after leaving his post as Magistrate of Hsiang-ch'eng, he was traveling in the Honan area. The Ju River flows south of Hsiang-ch'eng in central Honan, and K'un-yang lies still further south.

As in *The Farmers' Words*, the poet here records the words of a commoner, having presumably refined them and worked them into literary form. But while the Kung Sui allusion of the previous poem was a fairly obvious interpolation of the poet's own invention, everything said by the poor girl in the present poem is entirely consistent with her social position and emotional state. The poet refrains from any explicit statement of his own feelings, and allows the grim situation depicted in the preface and poem to speak for itself. The emotional atmosphere is highly charged, however, and the poet's anger is unmistakable.

Kakehi has stated that after the social poems of 1040, Mei no longer wrote protest poetry which was angry in tone, but limited himself to the calm, almost resigned description of scenes of poverty which bear mute testimony to the sufferings of the people.[16] As an example, he refers to a poem of 1048,

POVERTY ON THE BANK [17]

They can't plow and harvest.
They've no chickens or pigs.
Instead, they dry driftwood for roasting mussels
And strip bark from roots for making rain capes.
They weave their houses out of reeds,
Twisting green creepers into makeshift gates.
The children gather lotus leaves
To wear as short pants.

But although this poem is limited to description, another regulated verse poem written in the same year, 1048, ends on a note of indignant protest:

A LITTLE VILLAGE [18]

On the broad River Huai, dotted with islets, a village suddenly appears:
Gateways here are bramble hedges, broken and full of gaps.
Scrawny chickens cluck at their mates as they peck for food;
Old men with no robes to wear hold grandchildren in their arms.
Birds perch on the frayed hawsers of simple skiffs;
The river eats at withered mulberries, exposing the gnarled roots.
—That's how they live in this village.
How wrong to register the population in the emperor's tax-books!

The first six lines of *A Little Village* present a bleak, realistic picture of the impoverished lives led by the villagers, similar to that in *Poverty on the Bank*. But the concluding couplet is one of Mei's most explicit statements of protest against what he considers to be an example of social injustice.

Another poem which is quite explicit in its indignation was written in the spring of 1053:

CLEANING OUT THE DITCHES [19]

They've opened the spring ditches,
Flushed out the mud.
Every five paces a drain has been dug;
Earth blocks the road like a crumbled dike.
Carriage wheels have nowhere to roll, horses have nowhere to run.
Doors and gateways are obstructed, chickens and dogs are lost.

Stumbling in each direction, stepping high and low,
Straw sandals slip on moss in the chilling rains.
An old man went walking alone at night, no loving son at his side.
Eyes bedimmed, he lost his footing— nobody had pushed him . . .
Next day, who went looking for him but his careworn wife,
Holding the hand of their little daughter, weeping bitterly.
The police are out patrolling the streets, making sure that all is in order.
What do they care that a man has died or that animals are stumbling and
   crying?

Yokoyama has compared this poem with the *New Yüeh-fu* of Po
Chü-i.[20] Like many of Po's poems, it begins with two three-
character lines, expands to five-character lines in the next couplet,
and then finally to seven-character lines which are maintained until
the end of the poem. Also reminiscent of some of the *New Yüeh-fu*
is the use of narrative (lines nine through fourteen) to heighten the
emotional tone of the poem, a device also used in *The Poor Girl of
the Ju River Bank*. Lines nine and ten allude subtly to a passage in
the *Tso-chuan*, thirteenth year of Duke Chao (the translation is
Legge's): [21] "Small men know that when they are old, if they have
no sons, they will be rolled into the ditches." In the final couplet of
the poem, the wrath of the poet's righteous indignation is aimed at
the police, who are more concerned with the maintenance of order
than with the suffering of animals or even men.

The cruel indifference of the police in *Cleaning Out the Ditches* is
foreshadlowed by the cynical negligence of the military herdsmen
in a poem of 1046 entitled

MEETING THE HERDSMEN [22]

Army horses, gangs and droves,
Come to graze in the outher fields.
Larger herds of mingling hundreds;
Smaller herds of galloping tens.
Some swarm together like warring ants;
Like startled crows, some scatter quickly.
Wheat is trampled to the root.
Trees are gnawed—stripped of bark.
The soldier-herdsmen don't care,
But come to the market carrying their whips.
If they call for wine they get it;
If they want to eat, they're given food.

At sunset, drunk and full,
They lie at the road-bend, pillowed on their whips,
Oblivious: this is not their land.
They don't worry about the taxes that have to be paid.

This poem, like many of the others in Mei's collection, has a
moralizing ending. But unlike most of the other examples, this ending does not strike the reader as a gratuitous piece of didacticism; it
is developed naturally from the psychology of the herdsmen, who
actually think this way. Their swaggering manner and their indifference to the plight of the peasants are forcefully contrasted with
the ravaged pasture lands described earlier in the poem.

Mei criticized the army not only for its indifference to the suffering it sometimes caused the peasantry, but for its inefficiency as
well. The note of protest is unmistakable in

THE KAN-LING REBELLION [23]

The troops of Kan-ling have rebelled; everything is in ashes.
The fi.e roared like thunder into the sky.
It burned for three days, shattering rooftiles;
The rebels massacred everybody, even babies and children.
The officials ran away and hid in clouds of dust;
Only days later did the army come plodding along.
They circle the city walls like a mighty chain,
Ten thousand soldiers standing there in armor like glittering snow.
But who among them can act boldly?—They only think up schemes.
Yellow clay allowed to harden is not so easily crushed.

It is possible to get a fairly clear idea of the events on which this
poem is based by referring to three sections of the *Sung shih:* the
Basic Annals of Emperor Jen-tsung, the biography of Ming Hao (SS
292/16a; 989–1048), and the biography of Wen Yen-po (SS 313/10b;
1006–1097). A certain Wang Tse, originally from Cho-chou prefecture (southwest of Liang-hsiang subprefecture in Hopei), migrated
because of a famine to Pei-chou prefecture (Ch'ing-ho subprefecture in Hopei). "Kan-ling" is an old name for Pei-chou; in the *Lung-
p'ing chi,* a work attributed to Tseng Kung, the name "Kan-ling" is
also used in connection with these events.[24] After working in Pei-

chou for some time as a shepherd, Wang Tse entered the Hsüan-i Army as a minor officer. On December 18, 1047, Wang led a revolt, declaring himself to be "Prince of Tung-p'ing Commandery." He imprisoned the Prefect and had the Prefectural Vice-Administrator and other officials killed. Some officials did manage to escape, however:

> The Director-General of Weapons and Horses, and Imperial Courier of the Inner Hall, T'ien Pin and his soldiers fought with the rebels in the streets, but lost and left the city. The gates were then closed. The Judicial Intendants T'ien Ching-jen and Huang Shang, holding their official seals, left their families behind and let themselves down the city wall with ropes.

Once in control of the city, Wang Tse released all prisoners, and adopted his own reign-title. The official religion of his new state was worship of Maitreya Buddha. On December 30, Ming Hao, Auxiliary Academician of the Bureau of Military Affairs, was made Commissioner for Consolation and Inspection After a Calamity for Hopei. Ming's first attacks against the rebels' stronghold were unsuccessful. A large wall-scaling structure erected by Ming's troops was burned down by the rebels.

On January 2, 1048, an edict was issued to the effect that anyone who could lead government troops to capture the rebels would be made General of the Guards. At his own request, Wen Yen-po was appointed Commissioner-Inspector for Pacifying the Frontier for Hopei on January 26, with Ming Hao as his second in command. At midnight on February 19, Wen's best soldiers entered the city through an underground tunnel and finally defeated the rebels. Wang Tse was taken to the capital, where he was dismembered and his corpse displayed in public. As Giles has written,[25] Wen Yen-po "first distinguished himself by the energy with which he crushed the rebellion of Wang Tse, after which he was rapidly promoted and ultimately became Minister of State." Through Wen's influence, Ming Hao became Assistant Executive of the Secretariat-Chancellery, but died soon after. On February 22, a general pardon was issued for Hopei. The officers and soldiers who had helped to defeat the rebels were granted strings of cash; those who died in battle were given official burial and sacrifice. Taxes on lands which had been trampled by the soldiers were remitted. The name "Pei-chou" was changed to "En-chou."

Mei Yao-ch'en's poem appears to have been written while Ming Hao was unsuccessfully besieging the rebels. A group of poems on New Year's day follows *The Kan-ling Rebellion* in Mei's collection,[26] suggesting that the poem was written at the very end of 1047, or very early in 1048. Ming Hao had been appointed Commissioner for Consolation and Inspection After a Calamity for Hopei on the eleventh day of the twelfth month (December 30, 1047), and Wen Yen-po became Commissioner-Inspector for Pacifying the Frontier for Hopei on the ninth day of the first month (January 26, 1048), i.e., well after New Year's. Mei's sixth line, "Only days later did the army come plodding along," might refer to the relatively long period between the outbreak of the rebellion (December 18) and Ming Hao's arrival (sometime after December 30). The final couplet of the poem complains of Ming's procrastinating inefficiency, and warns that the longer the rebels are allowed to hold the fort, the more time they will have to strengthen their position. Mei was even aware that some of the city officials had escaped, and he expresses his contempt for them in the fifth line. The poem as a whole is a criticism of the army's failure to act promptly in response to an outrageous rebellion.

Mei's most intense anger was reserved for the members of his own scholar-official class who failed to live up to its high standards. Perhaps his angriest poem is

ON HEARING THAT HOLDERS OF THE CHIN-SHIH DEGREE
ARE DEALING IN TEA [27]

The fourth and fifth months are when the tea is best
    in mountain groves;
Then southern traders like wolves and jackals
    sell it secretly.
Foolish youths risk crossing the dangerous peaks
And work at night in teams, like soldiers
    with swords or spears.

The vagrant students also lust for profit;
Their book bags are turned into smugglers' sacks!
Officers may apprehend them at the fords,
But the judges let them off, out of pity for their
    scholars' robes.
And then they come to the cities, where they prate
    of Confucius and Mencius,
Not hesitating to criticize Yao and T'ang in their
    speeches.
If there are three days of summer rain,
    they rant about drowning in floods;
After five days of hot weather,
    they complain of a drought.
They make money in a hundred ways,
    dining on roast meat and wine,
While their hungry wives at home lack even dry
    provisions.
—If you end up in a ditch, you're only getting your
    deserts:
The *chin-shih* degree of Generals and Ministers
    is not for the likes of you!

Kakehi suggests that this poem may have been written sometime during Mei's period of mourning for his father, i.e., from 1049 to 1051. At this time, Mei was not himself a *chin-shih*; he had failed the examinations in 1038, and was only granted the *chin-shih* degree after returning to the capital in 1051. But, perhaps precisely because the degree was still a yearned-for goal, Mei was extremely indignant that holders of this, the highest honor to which a Confucian scholar might aspire, were disgracing themselves by engaging in trade. And what was worse, they were dealing illegally in tea, which was a government monopoly. True, it was not unheard of for officials to engage personally in commerce. As Kracke has written,[28]

> Long and persistent governmental efforts to regulate trade and control prices were matched by equally persistent and largely successful evasion on the part of the merchants. Attempts of the state to monopolize certain profitable industries had been costly and only partly successful. . . . By the eleventh century, even important officials had discovered the attractions of commerce, and many augmented their income by combining business operations with their official journeys. Merchants were socially

accepted in élite circles. Through such connections, or through their wealth, some of them secured government office, and served in positions of some importance.

Kracke refers to the case of Ma Chi-liang "of a family of tea merchants, who married into the imperial circle and had reached high office when his instinct for profit brought misfortune." But, Kracke continues, "the professional trader . . . still lacked the approval of more conservative scholars . . . in fact, specific complaints of the growing influence that merchants exercised over officials are not lacking." Mei Yao-ch'en must be numbered among these "conservative scholars." His contempt for the merchants, and especially for the scholars who emulate them, is forcefully expressed in the present poem.

Mei also dwells on the self-righteous, revivalist nature of these would-be Confucians, who are always ready to criticize the government on the slightest pretext, while their own wives starve at home. The poem ends on a note of pure contempt which is unusual for Mei.

In many of his poems, Mei describes the hardships which are endured by the common people in the course of their daily work. One of the best of these, written in 1047 or 1048, is entitled

EATING SHEPHERD'S-PURSE [29]

Men are ashamed to eat shepherd's-purse,
But I'm happy enough to eat it.
I've seen the gatherer of shepherd's-purse
Walk out along from the capital's south gate:
Brittle iron knife eroded by the earth;
Green bamboo basket mottled with frost.
He carried these to a frozen pond
Where he plucked out the purse, roots, and leaves.
His hands were chapped; he was hungry.
He'd have been thankful to eat even this plant!
Let others be greedy for such meats
As lamb and red-tail fish.

This poem invites comparison with the poems on jade quarriers by Li Ho and Wei Ying-wu which have already been discussed.

Mention should also be made of Po Chü-i's famous poem on the old charcoal-seller,[30] and Chang Chi's poem, *The Song of the Old Farmer*, translated in chapter 3. Related to this group is Yüan Chen's *Song of the Pearl Gatherers*.[31] All poems of this type can probably be traced back to such works of Tu Fu as *The Stone Caves*,[32] written in 759. In this ancient-style poem, the poet, after a harrowing journey through the mountains, encounters a bamboo gatherer who is collecting bamboo to be used for the army's arrow-shafts. The man complains that all the straight pieces have been used up, and he cannot fill his quota. "Alas!" concludes the poet, "that the cavalry of Yü-yang (i.e., the troops of the rebels An Lu-shan and Shih Ssu-ming) are sweeping so violently over the common folk!" But the semi-fantastic atmosphere established early in Tu's poem ("Behind me spirits whistle out loud") and the broad historical perspective introduced by the mention of the Yü-yang cavalry, suggest the exalted tone of the Po Chü-i and Li Ho poems more obviously than they do the intimate tone of the poems by Chang Chi and, especially, Wei Ying-wu, and it is the poems by Chang Chi and Wei Ying-wu, relatively brief and understated, that seem to lead directly to *Eating Shepherd's-Purse*.

Mei has been particularly successful in conjuring up the old purse-gatherer. The "brittle iron knife eroded by the earth," and "green bamboo basket mottled with frost" are sensitively observed details which seem to embody the man's loneliness and endurance. The use of shepherd's-purse to represent an impoverished diet occurs in a quatrain by Li Ao (d. c.844) describing Meng Chiao: [33] "Your stomach suffers from eating shepherd's-purse. / Your forced songs sound unhappy. / When you go out the door, you seem to be obstructed. / Who says heaven and earth are broad?" The irony of Mei's poem lies partly in the fact that the purse-gatherer cannot eat even the inferior vegetable he is gathering, as he must sell it in the market.

Written soon after *Eating Shepherd's-Purse*, sometime in 1048, *The Boat-Pullers* [34] uses an entirely different technique to describe the hardships endured by the men who pulled boats down the canals of China, trudging along the muddy banks with cables weighing heavily on their shoulders:

Wild goose, broken-legged on the sand bank:
He limps like a man, dragging spread wings.
The sun is setting: how can he bear the rains,
And the chilly winds now starting to blow?
There are splashes of mud on his damp feathers;
Head drawn in, he doesn't cackle.
—Boat-pullers, this is how you live,
And yet it's better than shouldering the tools of war.

Were it not for the title, the first six lines of this eight-line regulated verse poem would seem to be no more than a description of a lame goose. As such, the lines are indeed superbly graphic and again bear witness to Mei's powers of observation. But in the seventh line there is an abrupt change of mood, and the reader is forced to reread the poem as a description of a boat-puller, bent under the weight of his rope. The eighth line then takes still another leap: the boat-puller's life may be a hard one, but it's still superior to the life of a soldier. The development of the thought in this poem is unusual; it is to Mei's credit that he could encompass so much in eight brief lines.

Many Confucian polemicists, like Han Yü and Mei's contemporary Shih Chieh, launched bitter public attacks against Buddhism and Taoism which they conceived of as "aberrations" (Shih Chieh's term) from the orthodox Confucian way. While Mei does not appear to have written any explicitly anti-Buddhist or anti-Taoist protest poems, two of his poems do reveal, however subtly, his disdain for these ways of thought in their more popular manifestations. One of these, an early work, was probably written around 1036: [35]

THE TAOIST LI OF THE TEMPLE OF THE CULTIVATION OF TRUTH,
BEING OLD, POOR, AND HUNGRY, WITHOUT SUPPORT,
SUDDENLY HANGED HIMSELF TO DEATH—
I HAVE WRITTEN THIS POEM TO MOURN HIM

Descendant of the princes of the house of T'ang,
With your yellow cap, devoted to seclusion:
Your belly, fed on mists, was never full;
Your body, clothed in clouds, always exposed.
At eighty, you had still not died,
So you hanged yourself with your turban.

At first enamored of the arts of Lao and Chuang;
In the end disgusted with the poverty of the Way.
Busily striving for immortality,
Thwarted by the dust in your storage jar.

Instead of a broadside attack on popular Taoism in the manner of
Po Chü-i's *New Yüeh-fu* poem, *The Sea is Wide* [36] (which inspired
Mei's friend Liu Ch'ang to write a similar poem called *Boats Over
the Sea* [37]), Mei has characteristically chosen to deal with an actual
case. The experience of the Taoist Li, who was so frustrated by the
excruciating poverty and hardship which a Taoist priest had to endure that he committed suicide, exposes the ultimate sordidness
and inhumanity of this way of life. Unlike virtually every other
poem on Taoist recluses, this one ends, not with the subject's tri-
umphant apotheosis as an immortal astride a crane, but with the
dust that has accumulated in his storage jar. For this reason alone,
the poem is one of Mei's most original, and most modern, works.

The second of the two poems referred to above was probably
written some thirteen years later, in 1049.[38] The circumstances of
the poem's composition are explained in a long prose preface:

> Some say that when T'an-ying, the Ch'an Master of Penetrating In-
> sight, came to live at the Temple of Hidden Tranquillity, all the macaque
> monkeys scampered away and did not return. T'an-ying scoffed at this
> and said, "It happens that this mountain has many loquat trees. When I
> first arrived here they had still not borne fruit, so the monkeys went
> away. When the trees are about to bear fruit, the monkeys will surely
> come in flocks." And this, indeed, was what happened.
> T'an-ying despises the love of vulgar people for prodigies, and he
> fears that the transmission of this story will only cause delusion. At his
> request, I have written a poem to make known the truth about this mat-
> ter.

Hidden Tranquillity, temple in the mountains:
The macaque monkeys often visit there.
They left when the Buddhist teacher came,
And returned in flocks when the loquats were ripe.
Are prodigies sought for in the precincts of Ch'an? [39]
Make no mistake, dwellers, about this affair!
There has never been hatred for these creatures;
Let them hang from the branches of the old pines.

Some light is thrown on the meaning of this poem by a passage in the *Ch'uan-fa pao-chi,* a Ch'an hagiographical compilation written in the early eighth century and recently recovered from the caves of Tun-huang.[40] The famous Ch'an master Seng-ts'an, we are told, "lived in seclusion in Huan-kung Mountain. This mountain was formerly the habitat of many wild beasts which would often harm the local people. But after [Seng-] ts'an came to the mountain, most of these animals left the area." In other words, it was traditionally believed that a great monk's spiritual influence somehow drove away dangerous wild animals. It was this superstition which must have been responsible for the rumor that the macaque monkeys were so frightened or awed by T'an-ying that they left the temple where he was staying.

T'an-ying, who died sometime in the *Chia-yu* period (1056–1063) at the age of seventy-one, was one of the most famous monks of his time, known also for his scholarship in the classics and for his poetry. Even such Confucian notables as Ou-yang Hsiu, Wang Shu (who had considered Mei Yao-ch'en's poetry to be superior to anything written in the last two centuries), and Hsia Sung (984–1050), held him in the highest respect.[41] The frequency with which his name occurs in Mei's collection indicates that T'an-ying and Mei were close friends. To both of them, apparently, the superstitious aspects of popular Buddhism were anathema, and we thus have in the present poem the strange spectacle of a Ch'an monk and a Confucian scholar collaborating to deflate a Buddhist superstition.

4 MORALIZING POEMS ON LIVING CREATURES

Among Mei Yao-ch'en's strangest works are several long, quasi-allegorical poems on animals, fish, and insects. In these poems, the poet's obvious concern for drawing morals probably derives from the didactic conception of literature which prevailed among some of the scholars of the Han Yü circle. But Mei has not allowed this moralizing tendency to stifle his natural brilliance as a poet, and the poems consequently contain some startling descriptive passages. Mei carefully observes and describes the physical appearances and habits of a remarkable variety of living creatures.

The critic attempting to learn about Mei Yao-ch'en's poetry by reading the *shih-hua* literature would soon discover that one of his most famous poems dealt with the blow-fish, or "river-pig" in Chinese, a delicacy which may be fatal to the eater if not properly prepared. The circumstances under which this poem was composed are explained by Ou-yang Hsiu: [1]

> Mei Sheng-yü once wrote a poem on the river-pig fish during a gathering at the home of Fan Hsi-wen [Fan Chung-yen]. . . . The river-pig usually appears late in spring, swimming in schools on the surface of the water. He grows fat from eating willow catkins. The men of the south often make a soup of this fish and reed shoots, and claim that it is extremely delicious. Thus those who know poetry consider that the two opening lines [of Mei's poem] alone fully express the river-pig's good points. Sheng-yü has worked hard at poetry all his life, writing with feeling that is calm and detached, ancient and bland. For this reason his thought is extremely well structured. This poem was written among the cups and platters of a banquet, and yet the poet's brush is powerful and rich. It was finished in a few moments, but has become a unique work of its time.

To this should be added a brief colophon to the poem, also by Ou-yang: [2]

> My friend Mei Sheng-yü wrote this poem on the river-pig fish during a gathering at the home of Fan Jao-chou. Whenever I feel physically out of sorts, I just recite the poem several times and immediately get better. I have also copied it out a number of times for friends as an unusual gift —Written in the eastern chamber of the Han-lin Academy.

Mei's *Nien-p'u* dates the poem to 1037,[3] and adds the information that Mei wrote it while Fan Chung-yen was at Ch'ih-yang, another name for Ch'ih-chou. Fan stopped there on his way from Jao-chou in Chiang-hsi to Chen-chiang, on the Yangtze east of Nanking. As Mei was then Magistrate of Chien-te, southwest of Ch'ih-chou on the southern bank of the Yangtze, it would have been quite easy for the two men to meet.

Here is the poem, possibly Mei's most famous work: [4]

ON HEARING SOME GUESTS AT THE HOME OF FAN JAO-CHOU
SPEAK OF EATING THE RIVER-PIG FISH

When reed shoots on spring islets grow
And willow catkins on spring banks fly

This is the time when the river-pig
Is prized more highly than shrimp or other fish.
Yet not only is he weird in form,
In venom too he's unsurpassed:
Bristling belly like a bloated hog,
Glaring eyes like a frog of Wu.
Make one mistake in cooking him
And down your throat, he's dangerous as a sword.
If eating him you risk your life,
Why take even a single bite?
—Thus I questioned the southerners,
But, partisan, they continued to boast:
"He's too delicious for words," they said,
"Who says his eaters die like flies?"
Since my words did not persuade them,
Sadly sighing I recalled to myself:
When Han T'ui-chih first came to Ch'ao-yang
He recoiled from eating a caged snake.
But when Tzu-hou was living at Liu-chou
He ate a toad quite willingly.
While both these creatures may be hateful,
At least they bring no fear of death.
But in this fish, though so delicious,
Unlimited danger lies concealed.
"The most beautiful will be found the most evil";
These words indeed are worthy of praise.

Several allusions in this poem require elucidation. The "frog of Wu" in line eight refers to a passage in the *Han Fei Tzu:*[5]

King Kou-chien of Yüeh saw an angry frog and bowed before it. His charioteer asked, "Why are you bowing?" The king replied, "This frog has such spirit! How can I help but bow?" When certain knights heard of this, they said, "This king even bows before a frog with spirit. Imagine how respectful he would be toward brave knights!"

That year there was a man who cut off his own head to present to the king.

As the king was presumably in Wu when he saw the frog, Mei speaks of a "frog of Wu." Lines nineteen through twenty-two introduce material based on poems by Han Yü. In one of these,[6] Han relates how he released a snake from its cage rather than eat it as was the custom in the south. In another poem,[7] Han expresses his amazement at the fact that Liu Tsung-yüan ("Tzu-hou") willingly ate a toad. These four lines might thus be paraphrased, "Han Yü, a wiseman of the past, was disgusted at the thought of eating a snake or a toad, but even these creatures are preferable to the blow-fish." The quotation in the penultimate line derives from a passage in the Tso-chuan, twenty-eighth year of Duke Chao.[8] When Shu Hsiang of Chin was about to marry a beautiful girl, his mother, who opposed the marriage, warned him that "where there is extreme beauty, there is sure to be extreme wickedness."

As the quotations from Ou-yang Hsiu given above suggest, Mei's poem became famous almost immediately. His friend Liu Ch'ang even proposed that Mei henceforth be known as "River-pig Mei."[9] Oddly enough, the frequent references to the poem in the shih-hua literature have mostly to do with a rather trivial controversy. Yeh Meng-te (1077–1148) appears to have fired the first volley: [10]

> Ou-yang Wen-chung Kung has recorded Mei Sheng-yü's poem on the river-pig fish, "When reed shoots on spring islets grow, / And willow catkins on spring banks fly," considering that the two opening lines alone fully express the river-pig's good points. He says that the river-pig appears late in spring and grows fat from eating willow catkins. But in fact this is not the case. The people of the Che region start eating the fish before the fifteenth day of the first month; Ch'ang-chou and Chiang-yin [both in Chiang-hsi, on the Grand Canal south of the Yangtze] are the first places to get them. When they first appear, a single fish may cost as much as one thousand cash, and not many of them are to be had. Only rich people and members of important families who have bribed the fishermen beforehand can obtain them with any ease. But once the second month is past, the fish increase every day, and a single fish is only worth a hundred cash. By the time the willow catkins come out, people have already stopped eating them, calling them "mottled ones." Some say that a bug grows in their stomachs, and the people therefore dislike them at this time. And yet this is when the Chiang-hsi folk first get to eat them. For the river-pig comes from the sea, following the tides up the river. It is only late in spring that numbers of them reach the Chiang-hsi area. His Excellency [Ou-yang Hsiu] was a Chi-chou man [Chi-chou corresponds to Chi-hsien in Chiang-hsi, near Ou-yang's birthplace of Lu-ling], and so knew only about Chiang-hsi.

In the T'iao-ch'i yü-yin ts'ung-hua, Hu Tzu quotes a passage from a work entitled K'ung I-fu tsa-chi [11] which makes the same point.

After relating how Ou-yang had praised Mei's poem, the author comments, "These are merely words of praise by Yung-shu. In fact it is not so. This fish thrives in the second month. By the time of willow catkins it is past its prime." A related objection is raised by another Sung critic: [12] "In general, any fish grows fat from eating willow catkins, not just the river-pig!" Hu Tzu was inspired by the river-pig controversy to include in his book a long entry on the fish, in the course of which he debates the question of whether the fish is actually poisonous (he concludes that it is), records his conversation with a fisherman about the proper method of catching it, quotes Mei Yao-ch'en's poem and presents a *chüeh-chü* poem of his own on the subject.

The ghost of the river-pig controversy was effectively laid by the Ch'ing scholar Wu Ching-hsü. [13] After commenting on some of the allusions in Mei's poem, Wu points out that the actual facts of the matter are not really that important, as this is a poem of "small scenes," that is, an imaginative work of literature which creates its own "scenes," its own truth. It is also refreshing to find that other Sung critics besides Ou-yang Hsiu were able to appreciate the literary merits of the poem. Ch'en Yen-hsiao (c. 1147), for example, quotes more of the actual poem than any of the other critics,[14] explains clearly how the fish moves up the river from the ocean, and then continues, "Many of Sheng-yü's poems are ancient and bland, but this poem is particularly powerful and rich. For this reason, people give it special praise." The expression "powerful and rich" is borrowed from Ou-yang's commentary on the poem. Ch'en Shan (c. 1147) quotes lines fifteen and sixteen,[15]

"He's too delicious for words," they said,
"Who says his eaters die like flies?"

(The original text actually says "die like hemp," the Chinese equivalent of the English expression "die like flies.") He then compares these lines with a couplet from a poem by Ou-yang Hsiu, *On First Eating Carriage Clams*,[16] written in 1056, the penultimate couplet of the poem:

We only enjoy the flavor, never tiring of it;
Do we stop to think that they have come from far away?

[How ashamed I am before the old men of the sea
Who suffer, digging clams in the mud.]

"I feel that these lines are forced," says Ch'en, "and not as relevant to the subject as the lines from Mei's poem."

Although a number of the critics quoted above took Mei and Ou-yang to task for what was considered to be their misunderstanding of the habits of the blow-fish, none of them were as outspoken in their condemnation of Mei's poem as Chu Hsi (1130–1200). One of his disciples, Lin Yung-chung (*tzu* Tse-chih) once said to him,[17] "Mr. Ou [-yang Hsiu] liked the poetry of Mei Sheng-yü, but in Sheng-yü's poetry there are many unaccomplished passages." To this the Master replied,

> Many of Sheng-yü's poems are not good. Take, for example, his poem on the river-pig fish. At that time all the gentlemen said it was outstanding, but in my opinion that poem is like going into a man's house and cursing him to his face, just like throwing off one's clothes, going into a man's house and cursing his grandfather, cursing his father. From first to last, it is utterly lacking in deep and detached thought.

It is not easy to understand precisely what inspired this outburst. Chu Hsi also expresses his contempt for Mei's poetry in another passage: [18]

> Someone said, "Sheng-yü excelled at poetry."
> The Master said, "He cannot be said to have been good at poetry either." (Chu had just stated that Mei's annotations to the Sun Tzu were inferior to those of Tu Mu.)
> The person said, "But his poems are even and bland."
> The Master said, "They're not even and bland; they're dry and withered."

Despite the abuse heaped on Mei's blow-fish poem by Chu Hsi and others, the poem continued to be admired by those who appreciated Mei's work. It was this poem that was remembered by several of the poets who visited his grave. Describing such a visit in 1197, the poet T'eng K'o wrote, "Whenever I see the river-pig rise by spring banks, / I think with longing of Mei's noble spirit and softly chant his poem." [19]

It has been suggested by James T. C. Liu that the blow-fish poem is a polemic against factionalism: [20] "This poem intimates that forming a faction is like eating the blow-fish: it's simply not worth the danger." Kakehi, referring to this theory, admits that it is not unreasonable to regard the poem as a warning to Ou-yang Hsiu and Yin Shu against supporting men like Fan Chung-yen who engage in political factionalism.[21] Indeed, one line of the poem, "But, partisan, they continued to boast," contains the word for faction, *tang.* But Kakehi comes to the conclusion that the poem may indeed have been intended as a kind of political allegory, nothing in the actual text allows us to identify the person or persons to whom it may refer. The poem can be considered successful in that it skillfully describes the blow-fish, and expresses a general moral applicable to various problems in human society. Such a moralizing conclusion, as we shall see, was often used by Mei in poems of this kind.

It happens that Mei was not the first poet to write a poem on the blow-fish. That honor, it seems, must go to Wang Yü-ch'eng, whose collection includes a *Song of the River-Pig.*[22] (Wang uses the character *chiang* for "river" here, while Mei uses *ho.*) The poem is worth translating in full:

River-pig, river-pig
        what manner of thing are you?
With your lumpy body,
        blowing waves and spitting wavelets.
Relying on wind and water,
        you flaunt your swinish valor,
Gobbling down fish and shrimp,
        getting round and plump.
Your flesh smells, your bones are rough:
        hardly a palatable dish!
When fishermen catch you in their nets and traps
        they always throw you back.
The river clouds roll in,
        river rain starts to fall—
If heaven decides to send a rainstorm
        it doesn't bother you!

Wang appears to have been unaware that the blow-fish was considered a delicacy in certain quarters, but his evocation of the creature's strange, bloated form foreshadows Mei's treatment of the theme. This poem was known to poets of Mei's generation. Liu Pin (1022–1088) considered the poem to be a political satire: [23]

> When Wang Yüan-chih [Wang Yü-ch'eng] . . . was in the court, he wasn't able to get along with the men in power. He wrote a poem on the river-pig fish to satirize them, saying, 'The river clouds roll in, river rain starts to fall; / If heaven decides to send a rainstorm, it doesn't bother you!' [24] It is a popular belief that when the river-pig appears there will be wind and rain. Wang also says, 'Gobbling down fish and shrimp, getting round and plump.' [25] This satirizes the men in power for their bloated prosperity.

Thus, already at this early date, the river-pig theme was associated with the expression of political opinion, a fact which makes it seem less unlikely that Mei might have intended something of the kind in his own poem.

Long poems on animals, birds or fish which conclude on a moralizing note form an unusually important part of Mei's work. His *Elegy For a White Cock,*[26] tentatively assigned by Kakehi to 1032,[27] is a very early work which indicates that Mei was writing this kind of poetry even at the start of his literary career:

White cock in my courtyard,
Feathers white as white lard:
Wild dogs were my daily fear;
Malicious foxes never worried me.
Evenings, he'd roost in a nook in the eaves;
Mornings, he'd peck by the foot of the stairs.
He crowed before all the other birds,
Even in wind and rain.
My granaries were running low
But I always gave him rice to eat.
Last night when the sky turned black,
A creature of darkness prowled and spied.
Stealthily he seized the cock—
I only heard the squawks of pain.
When I came to the rescue through the gate,
He was already past the eastern wall.
At the sound of my shouts, not daring to eat,
He dropped the cock and made his escape.
Throat covered with gushing blood,
The cock gasped for air on the brink of death.

Brilliant white breast stained deep vermilion,
Frosty pinions broken and torn.
Compassionate, I wished him to live,
But his head was crushed and could not be healed.
I'll accept his fate and bury him;
Who could bear to use cinnamon and ginger on him now?
Still I see his scattered feathers
Floating, dancing with the breath of the wind.
I remember when he came to this place,
How many favors he received:
He never had to fear the block,
And never passed his days in hunger.
Why did he meet this vicious beast?
Who ever thought he'd be destroyed!
Though this may be a trifling matter,
A deeper meaning may be discerned:
Mr. Teng could coin a mountain of cash,
But starved to death in the end.
Such too, then, is the way of man—
I bow my head, full of sorrow.

Here Mei establishes a pattern which was to be repeated in the blow-fish poem some five years later. Most of the poem is given over to superb descriptions of the cock and his daily life, and to the cock's violent death. Then the poem draws to a close with an appropriate literary allusion, and a moral is pointed. Few passages in Chinese poetry can match the power of lines nineteen through twenty-two: "Throat covered with gushing blood, / The cock gasped for air on the brink of death. / Brilliant white breast stained deep vermilion, / Frosty pinions broken and torn." And then the main narrative portion of the poem is brought to a close, a perfect period of emotion, with the poet's tender memory of the dead cock's feathers: "Still I see his scattered feathers, / Floating, dancing with the breath of the wind."

We are next taken still further back in time to the start of the cock's residence in Mei's courtyard. Finally, we are told in no uncertain terms that the story has been related with a specific moral purpose: "Though this may be a trifling matter, / A deeper meaning may be discerned." This meaning is explained in the form of an allusion to the story of Teng T'ung, related in the *Biographies of Sycophantic Courtiers* in the *Shih chi*.[28] Teng was a favorite of Emperor Wen of the Han dynasty. When it was predicted that Teng would starve to death in poverty, the emperor made him a gift of Bronze Mountain in Szechwan, together with the authority to coin money from this mountain. When Emperor Wen died, however, and Emperor Ching came to the throne, Teng lost both the mountain and the right to coin money, and eventually died a pauper. "Such too, then, is the way of man." Just as the cock had enjoyed a pleasant existence for a while, but encountered a violent end, so Teng T'ung had experienced a cruel reversal of fortune.

Hsia Ching-kuan has suggested that the *Elegy For a White Cock* may be a veiled criticism of the official Chang Yao-tso who obtained the favor of Emperor Jen-tsung through the good offices of his niece, a concubine of the emperor.[29] But when the censor T'ang Chieh (1010–1069) memorialized against him, Chang was banished. The moral would thus be that those who reach high position through favoritism or sycophancy are bound to fall. A very long poem attributed to Mei, entitled *Shu ts'uan* and dated 1051, also deals with these events and goes on to relate that T'ang Chieh, for whom the poet expresses sympathy, was ultimately banished himself. According to the *Tung-hsien pi-lu*,[30] the work by Wei T'ai (c. 1082) which records this poem, Mei did not dare to show it to anyone and so it was not included in his collected writings and is little known. The fragmentary Sung edition of Mei's poetry does include the poem,[31] but a note interpolated on the wood block suggests that it is actually a forgery by Wei T'ai, whose forgery of the *Pi-yün hsia*, a book of political gossip also attributed to Mei,[32] was a well-established fact. Even if the poem *Shu ts'uan* is not a forgery, however, the political events in question do not seem relevant to the *Elegy For a White Cock*. The cock can hardly be accused of receiving favoritism, much less of being a sycophant! On the other hand, Mei's own allusion to Teng T'ung, whose story is recorded among the biographies of sycophantic courtiers, also seems somewhat irrelevant, and for the same reason. The modern reader, in fact, cannot help wondering why Mei felt it necessary to tack on a moralizing ending at all, and did not simply end his poem with the cock's "scattered feathers, floating, dancing with the breath of the wind."

It is possible that Mei himself sensed the weakness of the explicitly drawn moral, and sometimes tried to allow the events of the poem to speak for themselves. Although the explicit moral reappears in the blow-fish poem and elsewhere, the poem *Swarming Mosquitoes*,[33] probably written in 1034, already indicates that Mei was interested in a more subtle approach:

The sun has set, the moon is in darkness;
Now the mosquitoes fly forth from cracked walls.
They swarm in the void with a thunderous hum,
Dance in the courtyard like a veil of mist.
The spider's web is uselessly spread;
The mantis can't slash them with his axe.
The vicious scorpion helps them in their mischief
And freely stings with his belly's poison.
Because he has no wings to use,
He patters and scratches up the darkened wall.
Noblemen reside in lordly mansions,
Mermaid silks encircling their beds.
Would that in such homes as these
The mosquitoes flaunted their lance-like beaks!
Instead they frequent the poor and humble
With no compassion for their gauntness,
Suckers sharp, they race to the attack;
Drinking blood, they seek self-increase.
The bat flits back and forth in vain;
He cannot kill or capture them.
The chirping cicada, sated with wind and dew,
Shamelessly goes on sipping more.
—This hum and buzz can't last much longer:
The east will soon be bright.

Like the dimly perceived monsters of a painting by Hieronymus Bosch, mosquitoes, spiders, mantises, scorpions, bats and cicadas flit and creep around the poet's room. And yet, as skillfully as this vision is conjured up, it is evident that here again the poet desires to point a moral. The mosquitoes, "seeking self-increase," avoid the rich noblemen who are protected by mosquito netting of fine silk, and attack the poor instead, "with no compassion for their gauntness." It is not too difficult to see in these cruel mosquitoes the corrupt officials who tax the poor and protect the rich. Kakehi suggests that the bat which "flits back and forth in vain" may represent "ineffectual inspector-officials," and the cicada which "shamelessly" sips dew in apparent indifference to the misdeeds of the mosquitoes may represent the weak literati.[34] For Hsia Ching-kuan, both cicada and bat suggest corrupt censors.[35] In another poem,[36] probably dating from 1045, in the course of an elaborate political allegory which describes how the crow brought all his evil friends into the government, there occurs this couplet: "The bats have entered within the curtains; / How busy at night, capturing mosquitoes!" The lines may mean that along with all his other cohorts, the crow has also installed mosquitoes, and the bats must constantly keep them under control. Thus the bats are ordinarily good creatures, if rather ineffectual. The spider and mantis of *Swarming Mosquitoes* would also represent well intentioned officials who are powerless to check their corrupt colleagues. The poem with the bird allegory contains a list of the crow's friends: swallows, magpies, mynahs, quails, and others. Similarly, in *Swarming Mosquitoes*, the mosquitoes are helped by the "vicious scorpion."

Not all the imagery in Mei's poem is original. The comparison of the mosquitoes' buzzing with thunder in the third line is a convention that originated in a *Han shu* passage. In the biography of Prince Ching of Chung-shan there occurs the line, "The swarming mosquitoes create a thunderous sound." The title of Mei's poem can also be traced back to this passage. The *Song of the Swarming Mosquitoes* by the T'ang poet Liu Yü-hsi (772–842) [37] contains the line, "The flying mosquitoes await the dark, then buzz like thunder." And in *Mosquitoes* by P'i Jih-hsiu (d. c.881),[38] there occurs the line, "Hum hum, they swarm like thunder." These examples also serve to show that Mei was far from being the first poet to write on the subject of mosquitoes. Besides the poems by Liu Yü-hsi and P'i Jih-hsiu, there exist several others by T'ang poets. Po Chü-i wrote a poem entitled *Mosquitoes* [39] which ends, "Is this petty insect worth speaking about? / I have used it as a hidden symbol to alert human feelings," indicating that Po too wished to draw a moral in his poem. "When the mosquito bite grows," he warns the reader, "there is nothing you can do about it. It's best not to let the mosquito bite you in the first place!" Meng Chiao also wrote a poem called *Mosquitoes* [40] which is moralistic in tone: "All they do is seek rich blood, . . . drinking from people to steal life! I wish I could make a mosquito netting to cover the entire world, completely purifying the night air." These lines recall Tu Fu's "I wish I had a great mansion of a hundred thousand bays / To shelter all the cold scholars of the world and make them glad!" [41] One couplet from an apparently lost poem by Han Yü entitled *On Mosquitoes and Flies* is quoted by the Sung critic Huang Ch'e (c. 1140): [42] "When the cool winds come in the ninth month, / They are swept away; not a trace of them is left." Huang Ch'e also quotes a number of other poetic passages on mosquitoes, including the final couplet of Mei's poem.

The description of the scorpion in *Swarming Mosquitoes* may derive from an earlier poem. The passage in question reads:

The vicious scorpion helps them in their mischief
And freely strings with his belly's poison.
Because he has no wings to use,
He patters and scratches up the darkened wall.

This may be compared with the first five lines of the *Prosepoem on the Scorpion* by Li Shang-yin: [43]

The night wind whistles;
Scorpions crawl through the cracks and along the walls.
Without a cry, without a chirp,
But with a poisonous sting concealed within.
Like the tiger, they have no wings.

Among the several parallels between these two passages, the occurrence in both of the doublet *so-so*, descriptive of the wind in Li and of the scorpion in Mei, is particularly significant.

While not lacking in precedent, Mei's poem on mosquitoes is remarkable for its macabre eleboration of the subject, as well as for the extensive development of the social commentary in lines eleven through sixteen. Kakehi considers Mei unique in that he has evolved a criticism of contemporary society from the mosquito theme, unlike earlier writers such as Liu Yü-hsi.[44] But even this aspect of Mei's poem is adumbrated by the poem of P'i Jih-hsiu, unnoticed by Kakehi, which contains the lines, "Poor scholars have no fine silks or gauze, / But lie suffering in their thatched huts," [45] lines which are recalled by Mei's "Noblemen reside in lordly mansions, / Mermaid silks encircling their beds."

Although Mei's poem is moralistic in tone, the final couplet returns to the poet's personal experience and ends the poem on a surprisingly undidactic note.

Ou-yang Hsiu was inspired by Mei's poem to write *Echoing Sheng-yü's Swarming Mosquitoes*.[46] He apparently took it upon himself to outdo Mei. Mei's poem of twenty-four lines is quite long, but Ou-yang's has forty-four lines. And over ten years later in 1046, as though dissatisfied with this effort, Ou-yang produced another poem of seventy-seven lines entitled *Hateful Mosquitoes*.[47]

The poems dealt with in this section are of interest because they bring together three of the most characteristic aspects of Mei's poetry: the didactic tendency, the ability to observe and depict with great precision, and the interest in unusual or even "low" subject matter. That the third of these features was a conscious concern for him is clearly indicated by the title of one of his poems, a work probably written in 1045: [48]

SHIH-HOU SAID THAT FROM ANCIENT TIMES NO ONE HAD
EVER DONE A POEM ABOUT LICE AND INVITED ME TO WRITE
ONE ON THE SUBJECT

Wretched clothes, tattered and easily soiled—
Easily soiled, but hard to free of lice!
They swarm together between the belt and robe,
Then climb in droves to the edge of the fur collar.
Who can find these hidden creatures,
Eating blood and living quite comfortably?
Look up, look down, and human life is past:
Your life seems hardly worth a glance!

It is significant that Mei uses the word *shih* for "poem" in the title, because in fact at least three *fu* or prosepoems had been written on lice by earlier poets. Credit for the first of these goes to Pien Pin (d. c.500), the preface to whose *Prosepoem on Fleas and Lice* is still extant.[49] This preface begins with the lament, "I have lived for ten years in a wretched cotton robe," a sentence which may have contributed the phrase "wretched clothes" to Mei's poem. Pien Pin's *fu* was followed in the late T'ang dynasty by Li Shang-yin's brief *Prosepoem on Lice*.[50] Li duly records that lice are born from eggs, and then mocks them for eating in dirty places, but avoiding the fragrant scent which was used to keep them away from books and scrolls. We have seen that Li also wrote a *Prosepoem on the Scorpion* which probably influenced Mei's *Swarming Mosquitoes*. If Mei was, as seems likely, familiar with this work, he was probably also familiar with Li's *Prosepoem on Lice*. Finally, Lu Kuei-meng (d. c.881) wrote a *Supplement to the Prosepoem on Lice*,[51] in which he corrects what he considers to be an error in Li Shang-yin's original poem.

But the *fu* was a literary form which by its very nature encouraged unusual subject matter. By the end of the Six Dynasties, a *fu* had been composed on nearly every living creature. Mei's originality lies in the fact that he introduced such subjects as lice into the repertoire of the *shih* poet.

A single poem on lice was not enough to satisfy Mei. In 1046, the year after he wrote the previous poem, Mei produced *Hsiu-shu Has Lice in His Hair*.[52] Hsiu-shu was the poet's eldest son, Tseng.

My boy lost his mother a long time ago;
Since his hair was bound in mourning it has rarely been combed.
There's no one now to prepare his hot bath,
And so he's afflicted with a tribe of lice
They've grown all black and live in his hair;
Tattered wadding is no fine home for them! [53]
They crawl about like widly swarming ants,
And press together like newly hatched silkworms.
His hair is harder to comb than tumbleweed;
When does he have time to hanker for pears and nuts?
Giving him a haircut would be easy enough,
But I'd hate to harm that natural growth of his!

Mei here demonstrates his virtuosity at literary allusion; Kakehi identifies no less than four allusions in the poem, two of them dealing with lice. Mei's fourth and fifth lines, "There's no one now to prepare his hot bath, / And so he's afflicted with a tribe of lice," is based on this passage in the *Shuo lin hsün* chapter of the *Huai-nan Tzu:* [54] "When a hot bath is prepared, the lice condole with each other. When a great mansion is built, the swallows and sparrows congratulate each other." Mei's sixth line, "Tattered wadding is no fine home for them!" is based on this passage from Juan Chi's *Biography of the Great Man:* [55] "And have you alone not seen how lice live in one's trousers? They escape into the ample seams, and hide in the tattered wadding, considering this to be a fine home!" Mei's ninth line, "His hair is harder to comb than tumbleweed," is based on this passage from the biography of Liu Tan, Prince of Yen-tz'u, in the *Han shu:* "At that time, his hair was like tumbleweed; his suffering was extreme." And finally, Mei's tenth line, "When does he have time to hanker for pears and nuts?" is based on a couplet from T'ao Ch'ien's *Blaming My Sons* [56] (in the translation of Chang and Sinclair [57]), "T'ung is almost nine years old, / And seeks only pears and nuts to eat." It seems almost miraculous that despite the weight of scholarship it bears, the poem manages to be relaxed and good-humored in tone.

Lice figure importantly in still a third poem by Mei Yao-ch'en, written in 1047,

PICKING FOR LICE I GET FLEAS INSTEAD [58]

This is a day of satisfaction:
I was picking for lice and got some fleas instead!
But both are pests to be gotten rid of,
And happily I have found a little peace.
Who can be sure about the deaths of creatures
When the foolish grow old and the clever die young?
Ants live in hills and never bite people,
So their lives are perfectly secure.

As in the first poem of this series, Mei concludes here with a moral: if the lice and fleas stopped exposing themselves to danger by devising clever stratagems for attacking people, they would probably live much longer.

Apparently inspired by Mei's example, Wang T'ao (1030–1091) wrote a poem entitled *Burning Out the Lice,* which was echoed by Wang An-shih. Wang's poem was in turn echoed by Ssu-ma Kuang.[59]

It was seven centuries later that Robert Burns (1759–1796) wrote the most famous Western poem about a louse. His *To A Louse—On Seeing One on a Lady's Bonnet at Church*,[60] written "in the Scottish dialect," delightedly describes the progress of the "ugly, creepin, blastit wonner" up the unwitting lady's voluminous bonnet. Burns feels it would be more appropriate for the louse to "squattle" "in some beggar's hauffet." Like Mei, he ends on a moralizing note:

O wad some Power the giftie gie us
To see oursels as ithers see us!
It wad frae monie a blunder free us,
                    an' foolish notion:
What airs in dress an' gait wad lea'e us,
                    an' ev'n devotion!

In France, Arthur Rimbaud (1854–1891), another searcher for unusual poetic subject matter, wrote *Les Chercheuses de Poux*.[61] In this difficult poem, Rimbaud may use the lice to represent the forbidden joys of the child, which are systematically crushed by his two harpy-like adult sisters.

While not as explicit as the title of his first poem on lice, Mei's *Chiang Lin-chi* [Chiang Hsiu-fu] *Treats Me to Mudfish*,[62] written in 1053, can be read as a metaphoric expression of the idea that it is legitimate to introduce low subject matter into poetry, even if it is without literary precedent:

Mudfish are the lowest of all fish—
One never serves them to honored guests.
And then they are so stubborn and slimy,
A terrible nuisance for the cook to prepare.
While frying they give off a wretched smell;
I've never been anxious to taste them!
Mr. Chiang has been south on official duty,
So his kitchen is expert at making this dish.
Yesterday he asked me to dine with him
And I found it more delicious than the finest sea food.
Now I know that things of the humblest kind
Depend on their spicing, bitter or sweet.

"Things of the humblest kind," like mudfish themselves, are material for the poet, who spices them with well-wrought words.

Another of the humble creatures on which Mei wrote a poem is
the earthworm. His *Earthworms* [63] dates from 1045:

The earthworms swarm in muddy holes,
Peeking out, then pulling back their heads.
Dragons coil, so they must coil too;
Dragons cry, so they must also cry.
They think they are the dragons' equals;
What a pity that they have no horns!
The mole crickets seem to help them out,
Chirping ceaselessly in the clumps of grass,
With such a racket I can't fall asleep—
Every night I wish the dawn would come.
Heaven and earth embrace such creatures as these;
They are only despised in the hearts of men.

Kakehi points out that mole crickets, which are mentioned in line
seven, are associated with earthworms in a passage from the
Monthly Ordinances of the *Li chi:* "In the first month of summer, the
mole crickets sing and the earthworms come out." The "chirping"
of line eight need not refer only to the mole crickets, however, as it
was believed that earthworms could also produce sound (cf. line
four). The poem ends on a Taoist note which is reminiscent of a
passage in Mei's poem, *On the Fantastic Rock in the Tse-chou Garden
of Liu Chung-keng* [Liu Hsi-sou (1016–1060)],[64] written in 1059 or
1060:

Ugly things are hated by the world,
But ugliness is a virtue in this rock.
Beauty and ugliness are never innate;
Their nature must be clearly understood.

The poet must attempt, like the Taoist sage, to emulate the catholicity of nature. His work should encompass not only the conven-
tionally "beautiful," but even such despised creatures as lice, mudfish, and earthworms.

The only earlier poem on the subject of earthworms which is
known to me is the *Eulogy on Earthworms* by Kuo P'u (276–324),[65]
composed entirely of the four-character lines which are typical of
this genre.

Mei's search for low subject matter culminated in a poem written
about 1050,[66]

ON THE NINTH DAY OF THE EIGHTH MONTH I GOT UP IN THE
MORNING AND WENT TO THE TOILET WHERE I FOUND
SOME CROWS EATING MAGGOTS

Winging crows, out before the sun—
Who can tell the female from the male?
Is it because they have no rotten mice to eat
That they peck at the bugs in this filthy place?
Their stomachs full, they perch high in the trees,
Cocking their heads and cawing in the western wind.
I will pay no heed to crow-predictions
   of good and bad fortune
If they foul themselves with unclean things like this.
Prescient creatures are always known
By their personal cleanliness.

The poem itself, it must be admitted, is anti-climactic after the startling title. The moralizing ending is particularly plodding: the poet refuses to believe in prognostications based on the actions of crows in accordance with popular belief. He feels that truly prescient creatures would not dirty themselves by eating the maggots in a privy. The fourth, fifth, and sixth lines are the only ones in the poem which contain realistic description of the actual scene. But Mei's originality in writing on such a subject at all cannot be denied. The only episode I know of in earlier literature which is even faintly similar occurs in the *Chronicles of Wei:* [67] "The Lady of P'eng-ch'eng went to the toilet at night. There a scorpion stung her hand." The passage goes on to relate how the lady's ailment was cured by the semi-legendary physician, Hua T'o. Mention might also be made of an extraordinary passage in one of Han Yü's poems,[68] describing the demons of pestilence: "They seek their food amidst vomit and diarrhea, / Unaware that it's wrong to eat such filthy things." But the first of these examples comes from a history, and the second seems somehow to be an exercise in the grotesque for its own sake. The remarkable thing about the title, at least, of Mei's poem is its realism in a poetic context; while drawing his subject matter from the lowest realm of his experience, the poet remains basically faithful to that experience.

The finest poem of the type discussed in this section, and one of Mei's most outstanding works, is *A Solitary Falcon Above the Buddha Hall of the Monastery of Universal Purity,*[69] written in 1044:

My newly rented home commands a view of the temple hall;
Gold and jade-green glitter before my crumbling house.
I gaze at the temple, and watch the flocks of pigeons
Bring food and drink to their nested young,
    ignorant that the year draws to a close.
Bird droppings have dirtied all the carved eaves
    and painted walls,
Have even fallen on the heads and shoulders
    of clay-sculpted buddhas.
The monastery monks would never dare to shoot the birds
    with crossbows;
But suddenly there comes a dark falcon,
    baring his dangerous claws.
Crows caw, magpies screech, mynah birds cry out;
The hawk, excited, flies close in and catches the
    scent of flesh.
Determination in his heart, outnumbered but unafraid,
In a flash he has crushed the head of a bird
    and terrified the others.
The dead bird plunges in the void,
    has not yet reached the ground
When the hawk sweeps down with whirlwind wings
    and snatches him in mid-air.
Alone on the rooftop, he freely rips and tears,
Pecks at the flesh, pulls at the liver,
    casts away the guts.
The scavengers with no skill of their own,
    crafty and cowardly,
Circle above, waiting to descend,
    staring with their hungry eyes.
Soon the hawk has eaten his fill and leisurely flies
    off;
Who can distinguish kites from crows in the struggle
    for the leavings?
All the children point and gesture, the passers-by
    laugh,
While I thoughtfully intone my poem
    by the autumnal river bank.

The last line of this poem, *Wo fang yin i ch'iu chiang pien*, presents a problem. Kakehi takes the line to mean, "While I intone my poem and remember the autumnal river bank," thus making *i* a transitive verb with "river bank" as its object. He suggests that Mei is recalling some experience he had during his tenure as an official at Wu-hsing in Chekiang. (Mei had left Wu-hsing in the fifth month.) But this seems unlikely: why should Mei refer to a purely personal memory which his reader could not possibly share with him? Kakehi's rendering also necessitates placing the caesura after the third character of the line, or doing away with the caesura altogether, procedures which, while by no means unknown in Chinese poetry, weaken the rhythm and are rarely used in the final line of a poem. My own interpretation, taking *i* as an intransitive verb, restores the caesura to its usual position after the fourth character, and assumes "autumnal river bank" to be a locative expression naming the scene of the action. This version, however, is also not flawless. Earlier in the poem, Mei spoke of the "year drawing to a close." This expression would seem to refer to late winter, as Kakehi says, while the line in question speaks of an "autumnal river bank." I have decided to retain my version of the line, however, and to assume that *ch'iung-nien* can be broad enough in meaning to encompass late autumn.

Aside from the problem of the last line, *A Solitary Falcon . . .* is a masterpiece containing some of the most powerful language in Chinese poetry. The description of how the hawk "swoops down" and "snatches" a falling bird "in mid-air" is brilliantly written (it would be hard to find a better example of "depicting a scene that is difficult to describe, in such a way that it seems to be right before the eyes of the reader"); a sense of excitement is created by the quasi-enjambment between lines thirteen and fourteen. Lines fifteen and sixteen successfully convey the falcon's brute violence and bring the poem to an emotional climax which then slowly subsides as the falcon flies off, leaving the scavengers to fight for the leavings before a group of amused on-lookers. The work ends with the poet turning experience into verse.

The imagery of the poem is always imaginative and sometimes striking. The flawed splendor of the temple is admirably depicted. Glittering gold and jade-green, carved eaves, painted walls, and clay buddhas are contrasted with the bird droppings that have dirtied them. (A line by Wei Ying-wu is of interest here: "How hateful! My chessboard among the flowers, dirty with bird droppings." [70]) When the falcon is tearing his prey apart, the occurrence in a single line of "flesh," "liver," and "guts" creates a nearly physical impression of the falcon's power.

Kakehi has stated that the poem may contain some "hidden meaning." [71] Comparison with *Swarming Mosquitoes* does suggest that the poet might have intended the birds who were dirtying the temple to represent corrupt officials. Just as the mosquitoes were aided by the scorpion, the pigeons in this poem are joined by crows, magpies, and mynah birds. It will be recalled that crows, magpies, and mynahs were among the evil birds who won temporary control of the government in Mei's allegorical poem of 1045 (the year after the composition of *A Solitary Falcon . . .*).[72] Similarly, the monks in the present poem are powerless to drive off the birds, just as the spider, mantis, bat, and cicada of *Swarming Mosquitoes* could not destroy the mosquitoes. But while the mosquitoes were able to survive unharmed, in the present poem the offending birds are completely routed by the falcon, whose power and courage are obviously admired by the poet. Just as the swooping windhover was to inspire religious feelings in Hopkins, the "dark falcon" probably moved Mei Yao-ch'en to reflect, "If only some virtuous official had the courage to drive out all the corrupt ministers who now hold power, just as this falcon has driven away the crows and magpies!" But happily for the success of the poem, whatever moralizing thoughts the poet might have had are almost completely dissolved in his admiration for the falcon. As Ezra Pound once said: [73]

> I believe that the proper and perfect symbol is the natural object, that if a man use "symbols" he must so use them that their symbolic function does not obtrude; so that *a* sense, and the poetic quality of the passage, is not lost to those who do not understand the symbol as such, to whom, for instance, a hawk is a hawk.

5 POEMS ON ANTIQUITIES AND WORKS OF ART

The realistic, descriptive tendency in Mei Yao-ch'en's poetry reaches its culmination in a series of poems on art objects of various kinds. Mei lived at a time when such figures as Ou-yang Hsiu and Liu Ch'ang, both close friends of Mei's, were collecting and cataloguing archaeological artifacts with scientific precision. Their example undoubtedly inspired Mei to write poems on these subjects, poems which are perhaps Mei's most original works.

Within his limited means, Mei was himself a collector. In a delightful poem probably written in 1045,[1] Mei tells how he succumbed to what must have been a frequently recurring temptation:

I VISIT HSIANG-KUO MONASTERY WITH TZ'U-TAO AND PURCHASE
A BLUE-GREEN JADE VASE

Beneath the venerable cedars of this ancient temple
An old man is selling a vase of blue-green jade.
Supporting animals stand upright at the base,
Their paws and bellies raised to shoulder height.
The vessel holds no more than a spoonful;
Its color is like Indigo Stream.
And when I see it, what do I do?
One look and my eyes bug out!
At home there isn't half a cup of grain
And here I'm buying a vase for a hundred cash!
The men of the capital have missed a real prize—
Even in broad daylight, they must be blind.

Hsia Ching-kuan calls attention to a passage in Ou-yang Hsiu's *Kuei-t'ien lu* [2] which reveals that the vase described in this poem was presented to Ou-yang by Mei:

> In my home there is a jade vase which in form and workmanship is very ancient and skillful. It was given to me by Mei Sheng-yü. At first I thought it was made of simple green jade. Later, when I was at Ying-chou, I showed the vase to the subordinate officials. There was present a certain Director of Soldiers and Horses, Teng Pao-chi, an old man who had been a palace official in the reign of Emperor Chen-tsung (r. 997–1022). He recognized the material of the piece, and said, "This vessel is made of a hard substance known as *'fei-ts'ui'* [a variety of green jadeite]." He further told us that all treasured objects in the palace would be stored in the I-sheng Treasury, and that he had known what my piece was made of because there had been two cups of the same substance, *fei-ts'ui* jade, in this treasury. Later, I happened to rub a gold ring against the vessel, and the gold came off in a fine powder, as when one rubs ink in an inkstone. It was then that I learned that *fei-ts'ui* jade can pulverize gold.

The fact that in the title of his poem, Mei refers to the vessel as a "*ts'ui* jade vase" may indicate that he was already aware that the vase was made of this special variety of jade.

The second couplet of Mei's poem describes the animals at the base of the vase with characteristic care. The animals probably resembled the atlantean bears that often act as legs to Han dynasty vessels of various kinds.[3] These bears usually stand in contorted positions, as if straining under the weight of the vessel they support.

Liu Ch'ang, a good friend of Mei, has been described as "one of the important early Sung collectors." [4] Other friends of Mei were also outstanding collectors, connoisseurs, or even artists. Ts'ai Hsiang, for example, was one of the great calligraphers of his time. In a lengthy poem of 1051 or 1052,[5] Mei relates how, together with Ts'ai and their mutual friend Chiang Hsiu-fu, he examined the calligraphy and paintings in the collection of Sung Chung-tao, a third friend. First they inspect original works by such famed calligraphers as Wang Hsi-chih, Chung Yu (151–c.230), Ou-yang Hsün (557–641), and Ch'u Sui-liang (596–658). Apparently inspired by these masterpieces, Ts'ai Hsiang does some calligraphy of his own. Next several paintings are viewed: a rice-planting scene, and the portraits of over twenty famous women of the past by Ku K'ai-chih (c.344–c.406).

In an even longer poem,[6] dated 1052 in the *Nien-p'u*,[7] Mei describes some of the paintings in the collection of a certain Ho Chün-pao. The poem begins with a long discursus on water-buffalo painting. Mei explains that it is much harder to paint water-buffaloes than to paint horses, as the fine hairs of a horse can be suggested by an overall, hazy treatment, while the sparse hairs of a water-buffalo must be painstakingly depicted. All of this is by way of introduction to a scroll by the famous T'ang water-buffalo painter, Tai Sung, which Mei saw at Mr.Ho's house. He proceeds to describe in detail a scene of two water-buffaloes fighting. Toward the end of the scroll is a red seal with small characters which read, "Secretary T'ao." Mei relates how the Secretary, who lived "early in the dynasty," collected many paintings, "not sparing cash or silk." But his descendants, not faring as well financially as their illustrious ancestor, were forced to sell the collection in the market place. Thus the Tai Sung work came into Mr. Ho's hands. Hsia Ching-kuan suggests that Secretary T'ao is T'ao Ku, whose *Sung shih* biography (SS 269/1a) states that he was a collector.

Mei goes on to describe a scroll of famous legendary and historical scenes by Yen Li-pen (d. 673), including such episodes as the
Dark Lady, a goddess, handing a magic military talisman to the
Yellow Emperor, the last emperor of the Shang dynasty engaging in
various perversions, and King Fu-ch'ai of Wu entertaining the great
beauty, Hsi-shih. These are all described in considerable detail.
Never before had a poet displayed such specific interest in paintings as works of art.

Toward the end of his poem on Ho Chün-pao's collection, Mei
says that the pictures of "hawks, plants, and trees" are not worth
recording. In an earlier poem, probably written in 1043 or 1044,[8]
Mei is more generous toward this branch of the art, and inciden-
tally reveals that his chief aesthetic criterion for painting is realism:

ON SEEING A PAINTING OF PLANTS AND INSECTS
BY CHÜ-NING

When the ancients painted swans and tigers
They turned out looking like ducks and dogs.
But now I see these painted insects,
Successful both in feeling and in form.
The walkers truly seem to move,
The fliers truly seem to soar,
The fighters seem to raise their limbs,
The chirpers seem to swell their chests,
The jumpers really move their legs,
The starers really fix their eyes!
And so I learn that the Creator's power
Can't match the agility of the artist's brush.
There are many painters in P'i-ling,
Drawing and scribbling, wasting scroll after scroll.
But Chü-ning is divinely endowed—
Effortlessly he brings the others to their knees.
His roots and grasses are done with meticulous care;
His drunken ink is masterfully applied.
Men of influence and power cannot summon him at will;
For virtuous conduct he stands alone in his time.

According to the *T'u-hui pao-chien*,[9] compiled by the Yüan scholar
Hsia Wen-yen,

> The monk Chü-ning was a man of P'i-ling [Ch'ang-chou in Chiangsu].
> He liked to drink wine, and when he got intoxicated, he would enjoy

doing "ink-plays." He painted plants and insects with powerful brush-work, not merely limiting himself to the outward form. It was his custom to sign his works, "Brushed while drunk by Chü-ning."

The *Hsüan-ho hua-p'u*,[10] an annotated catalogue of the collection of Emperor Hui-tsung (r. 1100–1125), refers to Mei's poem:

> When Mei Yao-ch'en saw his [Chü-ning's] work, he praised its transcendent excellence, and sent him a poem, saying "His roots and grasses are done with meticulous care; / His drunken ink is masterfully applied." With this, Chü-ning became famous, and any connoisseur who got hold of one of his pictures would treasure it. There is at present one work of his in the imperial treasury, *Plants and insects*.

The idea expressed in Mei's first four lines—that a modern painter can surpass the ancients in the field of "flower and bird" painting—seems to have been a current view. Kuo Jo-hsü, one of the chief writers on painting of the eleventh century, felt that "in landscape, forests and rocks, flowers and bamboo, and creatures and fish, the ancients are not as good as the moderns." [11] The terms in which Mei expresses this thought derive from the *Letter of Exhortation to My Nephew* by the Eastern Han scholar, Ma Yüan, quoted in Ma's *Hou Han shu* biography. Ma warns his nephew that if he attempts to imitate two men whom Ma admires, but fails to reach their level, it will be like "sculpting a swan unsuccessfully, so that it only looks like a duck," or "painting a tiger unsuccessfully, so that it looks like a dog instead."

The implication that realism is the chief criterion in painting is also typical of Mei's generation. It is true that Su Shih's famous statement, "Those who discuss painting on the basis of physical resemblance have a childish point of view" [12] is foreshadowed by Ou-yang Hsiu's "The ancients painted the feeling, and not merely the outward form." [13] But this was an advanced view; even as late as the mid-twelfth century, Ko Li-fang found it necessary to defend Ou-yang and Su against aesthetic philistines.[14] After quoting the two passages just given, Ko writes,

> Some say, "If we adopt the views of these two gentlemen, namely that painting should not be judged on the basis of physical resemblance, then will there be such a thing as a bad painting? What if someone paints a buffalo that looks like a horse?"

Ko then explains that Ou-yang and Su meant only to emphasize the classic criterion of "spirit-resonance" (ch'i-yün).

Mei's sympathy for a realistic style was thus the rule rather than the exception. Liu Ch'ang praises a portrait painter for painting "faces that look like faces," and "bodies that resemble bodies." [15] Han Ch'i, in an inscription he wrote on an album of paintings, is still more explicit: [16] "If we examine the art of painting, we find that it is exclusively a matter of being realistic."

The circle of scholars to which Mei belonged concerned itself with archaeological studies as well as with art connoisseurship. These men were, in fact, the forerunners of an extraordinary golden age of archaeological research. Richard C. Rudolph has written of the Sung scholars who worked in this field that "they . . . were engaged in intelligent research concerned with identification, etymology, dating, and interpretation. Moreover, they practiced, within the limitations imposed upon them by the advancement of science at that time, most of the critical methods and devices used in modern archaeological work." [17] Mei's friend Liu Ch'ang was praised by Wang Kuo-wei for his sophisticated analysis of the techniques that should be employed in studying early bronzes. [18]

It was Ou-yang Hsiu who compiled the first of the great Sung archaeological catalogues, the Chi-ku lu. Mei was impressed by the early drafts of this work, and wrote two poems about it. (In the preface to the Chi-ku lu, dated 1063, Ou-yang laments the fact that the work was completed after Mei's death, and Mei was unable to see it in its final form.) In the first poem, probably dating from 1048,[19] Mei praises the book somewhat hyperbolically: "You have collected by hand ancient epigraphs in a thousand chapters (there are in fact over four hundred entries arranged in ten chapters), mostly from Hopei and Kuan-hsi." Some nine years later, probably in 1057, Mei wrote a longer poem entitled On Reading the Table of Contents of Yung-shu's Chi-ku Lu.[20] Here Mei refers to the stone drum texts, and to the monumental epigraphs of the Ch'in dynasty. He points out that very little Western Han material was available (there are only three Western Han entries in Ou-yang's book), but that there is an abundance of later inscriptions, especially from the Sui and T'ang periods.

The significance of the archaeological work of Liu Ch'ang and Ou-yang Hsiu for the present study is that it inspired Mei and other poets of his circle to write poems on epigraphs and other artifacts. One such instance will be traced in detail here.

An entry in the *Chi-ku lu* deals with a seal calligraphy inscription by Li Yang-ping,[21] who was considered the greatest master of this art in the T'ang dynasty. The entry reads,

THE INSCRIPTION OF SHU-TZU SPRING
BY LI YANG-PING OF THE T'ANG DYNASTY
—SIXTH YEAR OF TA-LI (771)

> Above is *The Inscription of Shu-tzu Spring*, composed and written by Li Yang-ping. In the fifth year of the *Ch'ing-li* period (1045) I was transferred from Hopei and demoted to a position in Ch'u-yang. I often went to the place where Yang-ping had engraved his characters in the rock, and without fail I would linger there for some time. Shu-tzu Spring was formerly a stream with flowing water, but the mountain monks have filled it in and constructed some buildings on the resulting level land. When I asked about the spring, they pointed to a large well and told me that this was Shu-tzu Spring! Is this not a great pity?

Like Ou-yang Hsiu, Wang Yü-ch'eng had also been exiled to Ch'u-chou, and while there he wrote a poem entitled *The Seal Calligraphy of Yang-ping* about precisely this monument.[22] In 1045, Ou-yang wrote a longer poem with a detailed preface: [23]

THE SEAL CALLIGRAPHY IN THE ROCK

> Let me explain:
> Recently the court has been kind enough to assign me the governorship of this prefecture (Ch'u-chou). In the southwest of the prefecture there is a Lang-yeh Mountain, the one which has the Shu-tzu Spring named after Li Yu-ch'ing of the T'ang dynasty. When I was associated with the institutes and archives, an official edict was issued saying that ancient epigraphic texts were to be sought out everywhere in the empire, and collected in the central archives. It was in this way that I got to see a rubbing of *The Inscription of Shu-tzu Spring* in seal calligraphy by Li Yang-ping. According to students of seal calligraphy, although the surviving works of Yang-ping are numerous, none of them is as fine as this inscription. For ten years I have wanted to see the original work, but I have not been able to do so. Now that I have come here, however, I have finally seen it. To the right of the rock with the inscription there is another example of Yang-ping's seal calligraphy, some ten-odd characters in length, which is even more outstanding than the inscription itself! Few copies of this work have been transmitted in the world. When

Hui-chüeh, a monk of the mountain, pointed it out to me, I lingered beneath the rock for a long time, unable to leave.

The wonderful sights of Lang-yeh Mountain have been minutely recorded both in ancient times and the present, and yet this piece of calligraphy has never been mentioned. I feel this is a great pity, and would like to write a commemorative piece myself, but I am concerned that my literary talent would be inadequate for such a task. Reflecting that Mei Sheng-yü and Su Tzu-mei are two men whose writings I have always admired and considered superior to my own, I have written a poem to send to these gentlemen, together with rubbings of the calligraphy, sealed and inscribed. I am asking them to write poems on the subject to be engraved in the rock.

By a cold cliff where a waterfall tumbles on green moss
The characters are carved in stone, astonishing to behold.
The artist is dead now, his bones decayed,
But his writing, undestroyed, is hidden here in the mountain's fold.
An old monk of the mountain, afraid the rock might split,
Has made some rubbings with paper and pine soot.
He wants the work to be transmitted in the world of men,
And so has passed it on to me, a treasure the equal of ghost-stone or
                                                             jade.
I doubt that these characters were drawn by the brush
Or that they are achievable by any human skill.
When Original Chaos first divided into heaven and earth,
Primal Ether congealed and formed this towering, craggy mass.
Some wild bird then must have danced across the mountain rock,
Leaving its footprints on the verdant slope for ten thousand ages.
To hide them from the constant prying of human eyes
The Mountain Spirit spits out clouds and vapors, burying them away.
If the immortals flying in the air wish to descend and read,
The luminous beams of the ocean moon always give them light.
But alas! What do I know of calligraphy?
Only that to see this writing opens the mind's eye!
—My poem is unworthy, the phrasing sparse, the diction mean;
Signed and sealed, I'll send this off to Su and Mei.

Su and Mei were quick to respond. Here is Su Shun-ch'in's poem: [24]

ECHOING YUNG-SHU'S POEM ON THE SEAL CALLIGRAPHY
INSCRIPTION OF SHU-TZU SPRING BY LI YANG-PING
IN THE ROCK AT LANG-YEH MOUNTAIN

After Non-dual Ether scattered and dispersed, and the myriad phenomena
   arose,

Original Essence was preserved in seal writing alone.
The drums of Chou and the mountains of Ch'in had crumbled long ago; [25]
It was only with the house of T'ang that another master appeared.
This member of the imperial clan learned Heaven's subtle forms;
His characters were firm and solid, but vibrant and full of life.
Today there are ten sites or more where his writing is preserved;
Both his styles—sparse and dense—are treasured by all men.
Among these works, the rock inscription of the Lang-yeh Mountain spring
Is in a class by itself, beyond comparison with the others.
Interlocking iron chains, mighty jade hooks—
You could hang a weight of twenty tons from the brush-strokes where they
    bend!
Or possibly some dragons planted here their horns and claws,
Embedded in the blue-green cliffs, never to uncoil.
But the world's vulgar eyes no longer appreciate art;
Only the wind and moon draw near from time to time.
A banished immortal from the Purple Palace is now the prefect,
A man who has already heard of the beautiful places here.
When he is done with official duties, he leads his guests to look,
Like a daylight hawk, swooping and soaring in the verdant spring.
Horses and carriages left far behind, they walk to the bank of the stream;
Pouring wine, enjoying the calligraphy, they pass the entire day.
The Prefect swirls the flowing water, studies the dots and strokes,
Awareness comes—he asks in wonder, "Was this my former self?"
He has written a poem, enclosed a rubbing, and sent them off to me,
Sincerely urging that I write some verses of my own.
Recently at his behest my brush was laid aside, (In a recent letter, Yung-shu
    warned me against writing poetry.)
And now, overwhelmed by his majestic lines, I find it even harder to write.
The man's high style and quality impress me more every day;
How can I go to visit him, riding the westward flying clouds? [26]

Mei Yao-ch'en sent his poem from Hsü-chou in central Honan: [27]

OU-YANG YUNG-SHU HAS SENT ME EIGHTEEN CHARACTERS OF SEAL CALLIG-
RAPHY BY LI YANG-PING FROM LANG-YEH MOUNTAIN TOGETHER WITH A POEM
OF HIS OWN. HE WANTS ME TO WRITE A POEM ON THE SAME SUBJECT. I HAVE
THEREFORE COMPOSED FOURTEEN RHYMES TO MEET HIS REQUEST.

I sit here in Hsü-ch'ang's dust and dirt,
Blue-green colors and the sound of springs far from my eyes and ears.
You are in exile as the Prefect of Ch'u-yang,
Where daily duties leave you time to explore the mountains and the
    streams.
A south-easterly wind comes blowing north-west,

And suddenly I have your poem, written on a paper scroll.
The ancient seal characters of Li Yang-ping are also sent,
Characters so noble in form, coiling like dragons and serpents.
The text consists only of his surname and name,
Dated the sixth year of *Ta-li*, the end of spring.
You explain that this writing is unknown in the world,
But a connoisseur—a mountain monk—pointed it out to you.
You stayed beneath the cliff and lingered long,
Scraped away the moss and lichens, drew spring-water to wash it clean.
Although the dots and strokes were not weakened by mistakes,
They are badly cracked, bitten by frost and eroded by the wind.
You say some bird has left its footprints in the verdant slope,
Lovingly protected by the Mountain Spirit—you must be right!
Clouds have always hidden them from the prying of vulgar eyes;
The moon and spring—fresh and limpid—are their only company.
You understand this rock, although the rock is unaware of you!
Certainly the ancients are among your closest friends.
The ink-rubbing on paper sheets can be passed down and enjoyed,
Valuable as rings of jade, always to be treasured.
And how much more so, with your poem engraved below the text,
Striking lines and forceful words to startle the Mountain God!
When will I have a little leisure to wander a while with you?
Until then, it will be a joy to wield my brush at your request.

Ou-yang Hsiu, the collector, is chiefly concerned with describing the site of the monument, and the means by which the rubbings came into his hands. Once this is done, he introduces the theme of the great antiquity of the rock in which the characters are inscribed. He then suggests that the rock is divine in nature, and is specially protected by the Mountain God. The poem ends with Ou-yang's hope that his friends will agree to write poems of their own on the calligraphy.

Su Shun-ch'in's poem, thirty lines long, is the lengthiest of the three (Ou-yang's has twenty-two lines, Mei's, twenty-eight). In the first eight lines he adopts an historical approach. The first couplet takes up the theme of primeval antiquity which had been introduced by Ou-yang. The third line moves into historical antiquity, and mentions two great monuments of ancient calligraphy, the stone drums, and the inscriptions of the Ch'in dynasty (the Ch'in Grand Counsellor Li Ssu was famous as the creator of "small seal" script). Su reveals here that he was familiar with Wang Yü-ch'eng's

earlier poem on the Li Yang-ping calligraphy. Wang too had referred to the stone drums and to the eulogistic epitaph inscribed by
Ch'in Shih-huang at Mount Yi in Shantung: "Mount Yi has crumbled away, / And there's many a hiatus in the stone drum texts. / It
is only these few characters / That retain their power and vigor by
the cloudy cave."

Su next names Li Yang-ping and praises his style. In the lines
which follow, he describes the Shu-tzu Spring inscription; as far as
the description of the actual calligraphy is concerned, Su's poem
easily leads the field. Next follows a long section relating how Ou-
yang Hsiu, the "banished immortal from the Purple Palace (i.e., the
court)," inspects the calligraphy together with some of his friends.
Su complains that he cannot possibly match the excellence of Ou-
yang's own poem, and expresses the desire to visit him.

Mei's poem is the most personal in tone of the three. It opens
with the poet sitting in "Hsü-ch'ang's dust and dirt," unable to
visit the mountains like Ou-yang Hsiu. Mei then describes the calligraphy in terms which suggest that he too was familiar with Wang
Yü-ch'eng's poem: "Characters so noble in form coiling like
dragons and serpents." Wang had written, "They are like dragons
and serpents intertwining and coiling."

Mei reveals that the text of the inscription consisted only of the
writer's name and the date. It thus appears that the rubbings sent
by Ou-yang to Su and Mei only reproduced the second, lesser
known inscription, to which he refers in the preface to his poem:
"To the right of the rock with the inscription there is another example of Yang-ping's calligraphy, some ten-odd characters in
length. . . . This piece of calligraphy has never been mentioned."
Mei's poem goes on to describe how Ou-yang discovered the calligraphy, and how he inspected it. Mei agrees with Ou-yang's theory
that the characters were formed by some primeval bird dancing on
the still molten rock, and that the Mountain God protects the work.
Like Su, Mei praises Ou-yang's poem, and ends with the hope that
he will soon be able to visit him again. Mei's poem is notably more
down-to-earth than the other two, in the personal tone of the opening passage, in the description of the actual text of the inscription,
and in the absence of any mention of "Original Chaos" or "Non-

dual Ether." Even the primeval bird and Mountain God are referred
to as creations of Ou-yang Hsiu.

The new scientific spirit of Sung archaeological studies is reflected in a number of poems by Mei in which he describes with extraordinary precision various ancient artifacts. Three of these will
be examined in detail.

The first poem was written while Mei was in the capital in
1052: [28]

> I attended a drinking party at the home of Liu Yüan-fu [Liu Ch'ang].
> Yüan-fu has two ancient coins in his collection which he shows at drink-
> ing parties. One is a "Great Knife of Ch'i," measuring five and a half
> inches in length [about 17 cm.], and the other is a "gold-Inlaid Knife" of
> the Wang Mang period, measuring two and a half inches in length
> [about 7.7 cm.].

> Our host offered his guests some wine;
> No lovely maidens urged us to drink!
> He said he would show us an ancient treasure,
> But asked us first to guess the date.
> I recalled that the sandals of Confucius
> Had long turned to smoke in the warehouse fire.
> And certainly the shuttle of Mr. T'ao
> Had flown away—red dragon in the stormy sky.
> Huang-ti's mirror is no longer in the world
> And the hundred demons are running amuck.
> I also knew that the swords of Feng-ch'eng
> Had sunk long ago in the depths of Yen-p'ing Ford.
> "Well, let's make it two hundred years old!
> Maybe it's recorded in writings and pictures."
> But laughing, he said, "Just one tenth of the truth!
> Now you must drain a goblet of wine."
> From the breast of his robe he produced two treasures:
> Coins of T'ai Kung and the House of Hsin.
> The Great Knife of Ch'i, chief coin of its age,
> Shaped like a sickle with a ring at the end.
> Of the words inscribed, only "Ch'i" could be read;
> On the reverse was depicted a perfect circle.
> Next we examined the Gold-Inlaid Knife—
> "This one knife is worth five thousand." (So reads the inscription on the
>   piece.)
> The fine bronze had not rusted or decayed;

The ring and blade kept their pristine beauty.
A parting toast!—We drained our cups
And mounted our horses in the sparkling moonlight.

In the fifth through twelfth lines of this poem, Mei again displays his virtuosity at literary allusion. According to a passage in the *Monograph on the Five Elements* in the *Chin shu*, the sandals of Confucius were among a number of treasures destroyed in a warehouse fire in 295. The biography of T'ao K'an in the same work records how T'ao once pulled in a shuttle while fishing with a net. He hung the shuttle on the wall of his house, but it turned into a dragon and flew away during a thunderstorm. Huang-ti's mirror was one of fifteen cast by the mythical emperor, which were able to keep evil creatures at bay. In a famous early T'ang story, *A Record of the Ancient Mirror*,[29] Wang Tu relates how the mirror disappeared from its box. The "swords of Feng-ch'eng" were two magic swords owned by Chang Hua (232–300) and his friend Lei Huan while Lei was Magistrate of Feng-ch'eng, according to Chang's biography in the *Chin shu*. The swords became dragons, and disappeared in the Yen-p'ing Ford.

Mei finally guesses that the treasures in question are two hundred years old. Liu assures him that they are in fact ten times older than that. This statement is clarified by a line in the poem which Liu Ch'ang wrote on the same occasion: [30] "One of them is a thousand years old, the other a thousand years older than that." To this he adds a note: "From T'ai Kung to the Hsin dynasty [i.e., the dynasty of Wang Mang] was a thousand years; from the Hsin dynasty to the present is another thousand years." It was believed that the knife coin of the Ch'i state was first cast by the semi-legendary T'ai Kung around 1122 B.C.[31] According to a passage in the *Han shu Monograph on Food and Currency*, T'ai Kung had the coin made for the Chou government, and it was subsequently circulated in Ch'i. Thus Liu's figures are roughly correct. Modern scholarship, however, dates these coins anywhere from c.680 B.C. to c.222 B.C.[32]

Mei next describes the Great Knife of Ch'i in considerable detail.[33] Reference is made to the popularity of the coin. (Kakehi takes the expression *tu hsing* to mean that this was "the only coin of Chou date to survive today." But the opening couplet of Liu Ch'ang's poem stresses the popularity of the coin, which "swept the eastern regions.") Although it is now known that the three characters which appear on these coins read *Ch'i fa huo,* "official currency of Ch'i," the Sung scholars were only able to decipher the character *Ch'i.* Already in the nineteenth century, the Feng brothers had noted this point,[34] and had wondered why such a learned scholar as Liu Ch'ang was not able to go more deeply into the matter. (On the other hand, they quote Mei's poem and commend the accuracy of his description.) The next line refers to a circle inscribed on the reverse side of the coin, a feature also displayed by several of the examples in the *Chin shih so,*[35] one of which even has three circles.

Mei then goes on to describe the gold-inlaid knife coin of the Wang Mang period; [36] his twenty-fourth line, as he informs us in a note, is a precise transcription of the inscription on the coin, which by a happy coincidence fits neatly into the five-character metre of the poem. At the end of the poem, no moral is drawn. The poet and his friends simply drink a "parting toast," and ride off in the moonlight.

It is interesting to compare Mei's poem with that of Liu Ch'ang. Liu, himself no mean poet, decided to relegate the detailed description of the coins to a note under the title. He gives exhaustive measurements for the two pieces, and points out that only the first character of the Great Knife inscription can be read. He also refers to the circle on the back of the coin. As for the Wang Mang coin, he says that the two characters "one knife" are inscribed in gold inlay, followed by the three other characters. The Wang Mang coins, he continues, were obtained in great quantities by the people of I-chou prefecture in Shantung, when they happened to uncover some ancient tombs. Many of the coins were then purchased by scholars, including a friend of Liu's from whom Liu got his own specimen. The poem itself is entirely different from Mei's. The tone is philosophical and the treatment broad; Liu's chief point is that changing coinage reflects the rise and fall of rulers in history. There is no detailed description. Thus the primary significance of Mei's poem from a literary point of view is that he has successfully communicated unwieldy descriptive material in the demanding medium of five-character verse, without any appreciable loss of precision.

In another poem, probably also written in 1052,[37] Liu Ch'ang describes a drinking party at the home of the calligrapher Ts'ai Hsiang. Among others, P'ei Yü and Mei Yao-ch'en were present. One of the lines in the poem reads, "We inspected an antique, and enjoyed discussing whether it was Han or Wei." To this line, Liu appends a note: "Chün-mo [Ts'ai Hsiang] brought out a gold-inlaid, bronze crossbow trigger with precise calibrations, truly a rare object in this world!" Mei, not content with a single line of prose description, wrote an entire poem on the trigger,[38] certainly the first if not the only poem to be written on this unusual subject:

TS'AI CHÜN-MO SHOWED ME A LARGE, ANCIENT CROSSBOW TRIGGER

Yellow bronze crossbow trigger, resplendent with gold inlay;
Zigzag threading, silver-framed, like rows of glittering sand.
Graduated markings are placed above so the arrow can be sighted;
A tripartite groove to take the arrow leads straight into a slot.
The calibration is in four inches, five divisions to the inch—
Line on line of sparkling silver without the slightest fault.
When Mr. Ts'ai brought out this piece, I asked how it had been obtained.
It was given to him years ago by a visitor from Lang-yeh.
The earth was dug deep at Lang-yeh when the city wall was built;
They found the piece, rubbed it clean, and proudly passed it on.
The man who made it is not known, nor the year when it was made;
Modern craftsmen can hardly match such exquisite artistry.
When the trigger is pulled, the arrow's height is fixed by the calibration;
People today shoot blindly and often miss their mark.
I hope Mr. Ts'ai will copy this trigger and create a new crossbow;
Don't let our border troops keep dying off like flies!

"Crossbow triggers (nu chi)," writes Needham,[39] "which involved intricate bent levers and catches, were beautiful and delicate bronze castings." These triggers are well known in modern archaeology, and their mechanisms have been fully studied.[40] Most surviving examples appear to date from the Eastern Han dynasty, while some are of the Three Kingdoms period or, rarely, the Western Han. Gold or silver inlay occurs frequently, and zigzag patterns are ubiquitous. Sometimes the decorative elements are enclosed in a frame of fine silver inlay. Triggers of this kind were among the treasures of Emperor Hui-tsung's collection.[41] Also characteristic are the tripartite depressions at the point where the end of the arrow fits between the two uprights of the release mechanism, probably to allow the feathers to lie flush with the surface.

One of the intriguing features of many of these crossbow triggers is the presence of calibrated markings on the back of the upright projection on the top of the trigger (i.e., facing the shooter's eye). The great antiquarian Jung Keng has published an illustration of a trigger which he considers to be "Han or Wei" in date,[42] on which the calibrations are inlaid in silver. The markings are evenly divided—Wu Ch'eng-lo has suggested that the spacing was arbitrary, and did not correspond to contemporary systems of measurement.[43]

The function of the calibration is in doubt. Yoshida Mitsukuni tentatively suggests that it might have been used to line up the arrow and the target: the tip of the arrow, the target, and the appropriate marking would be lined up in a row.[44] The fact that the markings face the shooter's eye would tend to support this view. A similar suggestion had already been advanced by Mei's near-contemporary, Shen Kua (1030—1094).[45] Shen also saw a calibrated crossbow trigger, and it is clear from his discussion of the object that such weapons were no longer in actual use. He calls attention to a passage in the *T'ai chia* chapter of the *Book of Documents* (in the translation of James Legge): [46] "Be like the forester, who, when he has adjusted the spring, goes to examine the end of the arrow, whether it be placed according to rule, and then lets go." Shen ingeniously suggests identifying the calibrations on the trigger with the *tu* of this passage, which would then mean, ". . . he sights the end of the arrow by means of the calibrations." (If Yoshida's theory is correct, *kua* would have to mean the *tip* of the arrow here, rather than the notch, as it is usually glossed.) Mei was also familiar with the *Book of Documents* passage, and employed the characters *hsing kua* and *tu* in his third line; thus he appears to have had the same idea as Shen Kua, and I have accordingly translated, "Graduated markings are placed above so the arrow can be sighted." Once released, the arc traversed by the arrow would, of course, depend on the angle at which one held the crossbow, and this in turn would depend on the particular marking one chose for lining up the target: "When the trigger is pulled, the arrow's height is fixed by the calibration."

Mei concludes his poem on a patriotic note. He hopes that a more efficient crossbow, modeled on the antique one, will be designed and supplied to the border troops. Mei was undoubtedly aware that "the crossbow was the standard offensive projectile arm of the Chinese frontier troops during the first century B.C. and during the first few centuries A.D.," and that "it may have been this effective weapon which gave the Chinese a slight advantage over their wild, horse-riding, bow-shooting enemies on the north." [47] Some even feel that "this was the weapon which . . . allowed the famous Han generals Li Kuang and Li Kuang-li to defeat the Hsiung-nu and subdue the Ferghana region in the second and first centuries B.C." [48] The crossbow, with its "intricate bent levers and catches," and silver-inlaid calibration, must have symbolized a past age of Chinese military glory for Mei, living as he was under the constant threat of armed invasion by northern nomads.

Another of Mei's friends who was interested in archaeological matters was Lu Ching, a Collator of Books in the Chi-hsien Library. Ou-yang Hsiu also knew Lu, and already in 1040 they had written a linked-verse (lien-chü) poem and sent it to Mei.[49] Lu was famous as a calligrapher of stone inscriptions, and Ou-yang often entrusted the actual writing of his inscription texts to Lu, partly because he realized that Lu could use the money. As a result, Lu's fame as a calligrapher grew steadily.[50] Probably in 1057, Lu showed Mei one of the standardized weights that had been issued at the beginning of the Ch'in dynasty, and Mei wrote a poem about it.[51] In the long preface, Mei quotes the inscription that was cast on all these weights: [52]

> Lu Tzu-li has shown me a treasure of the Ch'in dynasty inscribed with seal calligraphy as follows: "In the twenty-sixth year (221 B.C.), the Emperor completely annexed [the territories] of all the feudal lords in the realm. The black-headed ones [i.e., the people] enjoyed great peace. The Emperor adopted [53] the title of 'August Emperor.' He then issued an edict to his Grand Counsellors Chuang and Wan, saying that the laws and rules and the weights and measures were not unified, and that those which were uncertain should be clarified and standardized."

Mei makes two errors in his reading of the inscription: he misreads *Chuang* as *Ssu*, and *Wan* as *Kuan*.

The two Grand Counsellors were in fact named Wei Chuang and Wang Wan. Already in the sixth century, Yen Chih-t'ui (529–591) had read the inscription correctly, and had corrected a different misreading of *Chuang* as *Lin* in the *Basic Annals of Ch'in Shih-huang* in the *Shih chi*.[54] What is more, Ou-yang Hsiu was familiar with Yen's discussion of the inscription, as he refers to it in an entry in his *Chi-ku lu* headed *Inscriptions from Ch'in Dynasty Weights*.[55] It is therefore surprising that Mei misreads the inscription, although it should be noted that Ou-yang's entry is dated 1063, three years after Mei's death. In the same entry, Ou-yang points out that the inscription in question was cast on objects of various shapes, an observation which is corroborated by modern archaeology. Jung Keng has published rubbings taken from a number of these weights, including flat metal slabs.[56] That the weight seen by Mei was such a slab is proved by a statement toward the end of Ou-yang's *Chi-ku lu* entry: "Later, I also saw a bronze slab at the home of the Collator of Books in the Chi-hsien Library, Lu Ching. The piece was cast with the first of the two inscriptions [i.e., the one quoted by Mei]."

Here is Mei's poem:

When Ch'in had absorbed the feudal lords,
Li Ssu unified the weights and measures.
He cast these treasures to be passed on forever
That the empire might not crumble for ten thousand ages.
The bronze is beautiful, free of rust;
"Grand Counsellor" is inscribed in small seal letters.
After Hsien-yang Palace met with destruction,
History continued for a thousand autumns.[57]
Mr. Lu lives in Loyang city
Where a guest came to him from the valley of the Wei.
The guest told how a farmer, while plowing his fields,
Opened the earth and found an ancient storehouse.
Thus the treasure was recovered,
The text without hiatus, the writing strong.
—Then he "adopted the title of August Emperor":
How bold and majestic the wording here!
The emperor probably wished to make the black-heads ignorant;

He feared that the strife of Po-lang would arise again.
Afterward, like the imperial seal of jade,
This piece did not accompany the burial at Mount Li.
Today it forms part of Mr. Lu's collection,
A mere curiosity for idle pleasure.
Things are valuable because of their function;
How futile they seem when the times have changed!

Mei's misreading of *Chuang* as *Ssu* has led him to introduce Li Ssu in the poem. But Li did not become Grand Counsellor until "sometime between 219 and 213," [58] whereas unification had taken place in 221. It was in that year, according to the *Shih chi,* that (in the translation of Derk Bodde), "the laws and rules and weights and measures were unified." [59] On the other hand, among the "crimes" to which Li Ssu confessed in a memorial submitted to the Second Emperor was "equalizing the *tou* and *mu* measures, the measures of weight and size." [60] Thus Mei may ultimately be correct in attributing to Li Ssu the chief responsibility for this important move.

Lines nine through thirteen again narrate how the object was discovered, and how it came into the possession of its present owner. Mei next comments on the intentions of the First Emperor in unifying weights and measures: "The emperor probably wished to make the black-heads ignorant." It was the First Emperor who "gave to the people the new name of 'black-headed ones,' " [61] according to the *Shih chi.* In the biography of Li Ssu in the same work, we are told that "the confiscation and destruction of the *Shih,* that *Shu,* and the discussions of the various philosophers were done for the purpose of making the people ignorant." [62] This idea had already been expressed by Chia I (201–169 B.C.) in his essay, *The Faults of Ch'in* (in the translation of Burton Watson): [63] "Thereupon he discarded the ways of the former kings and burned the writings of the hundred schools in order to make the people ignorant." Without elaborating on how the standardization of a hopelessly confused system of weights and measures was calculated to "make the black-heads ignorant," Mei refers to another possible reason for the emperor's action: "He feared that the strife of Po-lang would arise again." This is a reference to Chang Liang's thwarted attempt to have the First Emperor assassinated at Po-lang-sha.

Fortunately, the weight was not buried together with the First Emperor at Mount Li, and Mr. Lu has been able to add it to his collection. But weights and measures have changed since the Ch'in dynasty, and the piece is now nothing more than a "mere curiosity for idle pleasure," unlike the crossbow trigger owned by Ts'ai Hsiang, which might still be able to make a contribution to the strengthening of the Chinese army.

Although unique in the accurate detail of their descriptive passages, Mei's poems on antiquities are not entirely without precedent. We have seen that Han Yü wrote a long poem on the stone drum texts, as did Mei himself. Wei Ying-wu also wrote a long poem on this subject.[64] Two other poems by Wei Ying-wu are of interest in this connection. In one, *Song of the Old Sword*,[65] Wei describes the patina of the sword: "Blue backbone crusted with fish-like scales." (Both Mei and Ou-yang were to write poems on Japanese swords.[66]) In another poem, *Song of the Old Ting Vessel*,[67] Wei again describes the patina of the vessel, as well as the seal calligraphy and carved dragons which adorn it. The poem relates how the piece was accidentally discovered by a farmer while he was plowing in the fields, as was the Ch'in dynasty weight described by Mei.

CONCLUSION

Y OSHIKAWA KŌJIRŌ has written that "poetry that was so full of description, . . . so taken up with the themes of everyday life, so socially conscious as that of the Sung, had never been known before in China." [1] The poems translated and discussed in this book have demonstrated that these features played an important role in the poetry of Mei Yao-ch'en. Of course, all of the themes dealt with here had appeared in earlier poetry. Poems on everyday life had been written, for example, by Tu Fu, Po Chü-i, and, in the Sung dynasty, by Wang Yü-ch'eng. The same poets wrote poems of social comment. Mei's poems on the death of his wife form part of a long tradition extending back through Yüan Chen and Wei Ying-wu to P'an Yüeh. Most of the living creatures on which Mei wrote his moralizing poems had already been written about by earlier poets. Mei was probably most original in his extraordinarily detailed poems on works of art and archaeological objects, but even here he was anticipated by Han Yü and Wei Ying-wu.

Nevertheless, no earlier poet had written as copiously as Mei Yao-ch'en in all of these modes. Mei was a poet of the real—the activities of everyday life, the poet's actual emotions, the realities of the contemporary scene, the habits of birds, animals, and insects, the forms of art works. In his poems, the "aesthetic distance" between the poet and his object is lessened; in such a work as the poem on the crossbow trigger, the poet describes with nearly scientific precision. Mei realized that for poetry of this kind, it was necessary to develop a more natural diction and tone than had been used by the Hsi-k'un poets, and this is probably what he had in mind when he used the expression, *p'ing-tan* ("even and bland"). Because this idea was in harmony with the mood of the times, it was to become a key concept in Sung literary criticism.

Mei's work looked ahead to significant developments in later Sung poetry. He was admired by Su Shih, Wang An-shih, Huang T'ing-chien, and Lu Yu, among others. For this reason, and because of the innate quality of his poetry, Mei deserves an important place in the history of Chinese literature.

NOTES

CHAPTER ONE: LIFE

1. OYWCKC, 126/6b–7a.
2. OYWCKC, 33/7a–9b.
3. *Nien-p'u*, p. 1a.
4. WLC, appendix, p. 10b. This appears to be an error based on the fact that Mei's great-great-grandfather was named Ch'ao. Cf. Ou-yang's grave inscription for Mei Hsün (OYWCKC, 27/1a–4a). On the other hand, it is highly unusual for men in succeeding generations to have names with the same radical ("Yüan" and "Mo"). The matter requires further research.
5. OYWCKC, 31/7b–8b.
6. Hsia, *nien-p'u*, p. 6.
7. These facts are given by Ou-yang Hsiu in his grave inscription for Mei Jang, OYWCKC, 31/7b–8b.
8. *Ibid.*, 127/9b.
9. *Nien-p'u*, pp. 1b–2a.
10. Kracke (1), pp. 74–75.
11. Quoted in TCYYTH, p. 194.
12. SKTP, 2/6b.
13. OYWCKC, 51/1b–3a.
14. Ou-yang Hsiu wrote a funerary proclamation and a grave inscription for him: *ibid.*, 24/11b–13a; 62/6b–7a.
15. *Lun-yü*, XVII, 9; Waley, *The Analects of Confucius*, p. 212.
16. WLC, 1/6b–7a; *Nien-p'u*, p. 5a.
17. *Chin shu*, biography of Wang Hui-chih.
18. WLC, 2/11a–13a.
19. OYWCKC, 51/3b–5b.
20. WLC, 2/4a–b; quoted in *Nien-p'u*, p. 6b.
21. OYWCKC, 64/7a–b.

22. *Ibid.*, 73/1a–3a.
23. *Chin shu*, biography of Hsieh T'iao.
24. James T. C. Liu (1), pp. 27–28.
25. OYWCKC, 149/1a–b.
26. *Ibid.*, 53/2b–3b.
27. *Ibid.*, 56/11a–b.
28. WLC, 2/7a–b.
29. *Nien-p'u*, pp. 6b–7a.
30. WLC, 2/7b–9a.
31. Both of Hsieh's letters are preserved in the appendix to OYWCKC, 5/22a–25a; 26b–27a.
32. *Ibid.*, 149/3a–b.
33. *Ibid.*, 149/3b–4b.
34. *Nien-p'u*, p. 8a.
35. WLC, 4/9b; Hsia, pp. 194–95.
36. WLC, 4/10b.
37. SDSNP, p. 98.
38. James T. C. Liu (2).
39. OYWCKC, 150/1a–b. See also Kakehi, BGSR, p. 435.
40. WLC, 6/1z–b.
41. *Ibid.*, 6/1b–2a.
42. OYWCKC, 149/7a–b.
43. The *Nien-p'u*, p. 12a, puts this event in 1041, but Kakehi assigns it to 1040 (BGS, *nien-p'u*, p. 165).
44. Incorporated in the *Sun Tzu Annotated by Eleven Scholars* recently reprinted by the *Chung-hua shu-chü* (Peking, 1961), according to Kakehi, BGS, introduction, p. 19.
45. WLC, 7/4a–b.
46. *Ibid.*, 8/4b–5a; Kakehi, BGS, pp. 43–47. Quoted in the *Nien-p'u* entry from 1041, p. 12a.
47. Kakehi, BGSR, pp. 435–36.
48. OYWCKC, 149/6b–7a.
49. *Ibid.*, 42/9b–10b.
50. In the addenda to the appendix of the 1830 edition of Mei's works, 2/1a; also quoted in the *Nien-p'u* entry for 1040, p. 11b.
51. WLC, 7/3b–4a. The second poem also in Hsia, pp. 14–15.
52. Watson (1), p. 175: "Looking from bank to bank . . . it was impossible to distinguish a horse from a cow."
53. Hsia takes this line to refer to the "huts built in the treetops," and claims that these were constructed from boats. I prefer to read the line together with the previous one as a description of the wreckage left behind by the receding flood waters.
54. OYWCKC, 34/8b–14a.
55. WLC, 24/2b–3a.
56. Most notably *On the Twenty-fourth Day of the Fifth Month I Passed by San-kou in Kao-yu* (WLC, 33/1a–b).
57. OYWCKC, 36/1a–2b.
58. Also translated in Masuda.
59. Hsia, p. 21.
60. *Nien-p'u*, pp. 2b and 16a.

61. WLC, 25/5b–6a. Quoted in the *Nien-p'u* entry for 1045, p. 15a.
62. OYWCKC, 2/12a. Translated in Yoshikawa, pp. 66–67.
63. WLC, 25/6a–b; Hsia, pp. 150–51. Quoted in the *Nien-p'u* entry for 1045, p. 15a.
64. *Nien-p'u*, p. 15b.
65. WLC, 32/8a–9a.
66. OYWCKC, 39/14b–15b.
67. WLC, 31/9a–b.
68. YYYC, 13/8b–9a.
69. WLC, 29/11a–b.
70. OYWCKC, 2/5a–b. Partially translated in Yoshikawa, pp. 36–37.
71. OYWCKC, 9/3b–4a.
72. WLC, 11/2b, 3b–4a.
73. SSCC, pp. 32–33.
74. WLC, 11/8a–b.
75. For these events, see James T. C. Liu (2), pp. 342–43, and the references given there. Also, SSCC, *nien-p'u*, p. 293.
76. WLC, 11/5a.
77. SSCC, *nien-p'u*, p. 294.
78. See, for example, Iritani, frontispiece.
79. OYWCKC, 27/1a–4a.
80. WLC, 31/9b; Kakehi, BGS, pp. 89–90.
81. PSCCC, 19/8a–b.
82. OYWCKC, 31/7b–8b.
83. Various archives, libraries, and research institutes. The most important of these was the Han-lin Academy, which is intended here.
84. Kracke (1), pp. 95 ff.
85. 171/6a–b.
86. Quoted in SJISHP, Vol. I, p. 376.
87. OYWCKC, 127/5a.
88. WLC, 16/7a.
89. WLHSWC, 39/5a.
90. *Ibid.*, 39/8b.
91. *Nien-p'u*, pp. 23a–b.
92. Hsia, *nien-p'u*, p. 6.
93. WLC, 40/1a–b.
94. *Ibid.*, 40/2a.
95. OYWCKC, 149/13a–14a.
96. *Nien-p'u*, pp. 24b–25a.
97. WLC, 50/10b–11a.
98. TKPS, 17/30a. Some texts read *lo* for *k'o* in the second line of this couplet, but the present example suggests that Mei was familiar with the reading *k'o*.
99. *Sung hui-yao, Examinations,* section on examiners, p. 24b.
100. OYWCKC, 127/13b–14b.
101. WLC, 51/11a–b.
102. For *wang hsing*, read *wang wang*, as in *Ou-yang Wen-chung Kung ch'üan-chi* (in SPPY), 127/9a.
103. WLC, 51/10a–b; Kakehi, BGS, pp. 138–41; Hsia, pp. 175–76.
104. Quoted in Kuo Shao-yü (1), Vol. II, pp. 33–34.

105. I.e., the Department of Ministries.

106. The names of popular dance tunes, as Kakehi points out.

107. OYWCKC, 6/7b–8a.

108. *Shih-lin shih-hua* (in LTSH), *hsia*/1b–2a.

109. WLC, 52/1b; Hsia, p. 240. I have followed Hsia's reading for the first line of the couplet.

110. This statement would seem to contradict the account in the *Ts'ai K'uan-fu shih-hua*, where it is said that after Ou-yang and his colleagues, the practice of exchanging poems "became a great tradition in the examination halls."

111. *Nien-p'u*, p. 25b.

112. TPWCSL, 9/4a ff.

113. *Ibid.*, 41/3b–4b; also in WLC, appendix, pp. 5b–7b.

114. Quoted in the *Nien-p'u* entry for 1057, p. 26a. Also quoted in YYYC, 18/4a–b.

115. OYWCKC, 128/2b.

116. WLC, 16/9a, under the title *Enjoying the Snow on the Thirteenth Day of the Twelfth Month*.

117. TPTP, 3/27a.

118. WLC, 48/11a–b.

119. LFWC, *wen-chi*, 15/39–40.

120. Wang Shih-chen, *Tai-ching-t'ang shih-hua*, 1/18b; STPC, 4/76.

121. WLC, 53/1b–2a.

122. *Nien-p'u*, p. 26a.

123. WLC, 53/1a–b; Kakehi, BGS, pp. 141–45; Hsia, pp. 119–20.

124. Karlgren, #16.

125. WLC, 37/2b–3a.

126. *Ibid.*, 23/11a–b; OYWCKC, 8/8a–b, 9a–b; KSC, 18/3a; SMKWC, 3/23a–b. For the originals, see LCHSWC, 4/7b–8a.

127. WLC, 55/4b–5b.

128. Kakehi, BGSR, p. 454.

129. Karlgren, #107.

130. Kuo Shao-yü (1), Vol. I, p. 330.

131. LFWC, *wen-chi*, 15/39–40.

132. Wang's poem might be the one at LCHSWC, 5/4a; or the one at 9/5b. Mei's might be either WLHSWC, 14/8a–b; or 37/13b–14a. Pao Ting was a famous tiger painter of the northern Sung.

133. LCHSWC, 11/3b ff.

134. OYWCKC, 144/8b–9a.

135. Appended to the *Hsin T'ang shu chiu-miu* (in *Chih-pu-tsu-chai ts'ung-shu*), entry for the fourth year of the *Chia-yu* period (1059).

136. WLC, 51/11a.

137. *Ibid.*, 20/4b–5a; quoted by Yokoyama (1), pp. 59–60.

138. WLC, 57/11a–b; Kakehi, BGS, pp. 149–51; Hsia, p. 123.

139. OYWCKC, 7/9b.

140. WLC, 59/9a–b; Hsia, p. 186.

141. CLHSC, 5/2b–3b.

142. LTC, p. 6.

143. Mentioned in Mei's SS biography; no longer extant.

144. See the *Table of Historians* ... referred to in note 135.

145. WLC, 19 / table of contents begins with a similar title, but the poem itself is missing, replaced by one with a similar title but addressed to a Mr. P'ei. The poem here quoted is recorded in the *Nien-p'u*, p. 27a.

146. OYWCKC, 127/9a.

147. Quoted in the *Nien-p'u*, pp. 27a–b.

148. OYWCKC, 128/3a–b.

149. The text quoted in the appendix to WLC, pp. 8b–11a, reads, "Shuang-yang Mountain in Hsüan-ch'eng."

150. KSC, 50/10b–11a.

151. Ou-yang Hsiu's *Grave Inscription for Chiang Lin-chi* (OYWCKC, 33/9b–11b) dates Chiang's death to May 20, 1060, i.e., eight days before Mei's.

152. *Wen Kung hsü-shih-hua* (in LTSH), pp. 1b–2a.

153. Tzu-ts'ai must be an error for Chih-ts'ai.

154. *Ching-wen chi* (in WYT), 21/9b.

155. LCHSWC, 9/7b–8a.

156. SMKWC, 3/17b. In WLC, appendix, p. 13b, these poems are wrongly attributed to Wang An-shih.

157. See the *Yüan-yu tang-jen chuan* (in *Ch'ien-yüan tsung-chi*), 2/21a.

158. *Sun Kung t'an-p'u* (in *Pai-ch'uan hsüeh-hai*), hsia/6b.

159. Unidentified, according to Kakehi, BGS, p. 133, and Hsia, p. 114.

160. WLC, 46/9b.

161. STPC, ch. 11, p. 7; quoted in *Nien-p'u*, p. 2a.

CHAPTER TWO: BACKGROUND

1. TLSH, pp. 4a–b.

2. *Ibid.*, p. 6a.

3. *Ibid.*, pp. 8a–b. The application of the term Hsi-k'un to Li Shang-yin himself is "anachronistic"; see James J. Y. Liu, p. 249.

4. TCHC, 32/13a ff.

5. The Four Lings—Hsü Chao (d. 1211), Hsü Chi (1162–1214), Weng Ch'üan (fl. 1183–1211), Chao Shih-hsiu (d. 1219)—revived the practice of writing regulated verse in the Late T'ang manner.

6. Ku Ssu-li (1669–1722) quotes this passage in his *Han-t'ing shih-hua* (in CSH), p. 82. He identifies all the poets mentioned, except for Wang Han-mou and Lu San-chiao.

7. See the previous note.

8. Chu Tung-jun (1), pp. 123–24.

9. Quoted in Kuo Shao-yü (1), Vol. II, pp. 37–38.

10. *Sheng-an shih-hua* (in LTSH, HP), 11/2a–b. The text here incorrectly reads "Chang Po" for "Chang Chi."

11. A couplet by Hsü Hun (c.844), one of the Late T'ang poets.

12. Preface to *Hsiang Tzu-ch'ien shih*, in *Hsien-chü ts'ung-shu ti-i-chi*.

13. CCCC, 4/3b.

14. Quoted in SJYH, p. 256.

15. HYC, p. 3a.

16. *Ibid.*, p. 13a.

17. *Ibid.*, p. 5a.
18. *Ibid.*, pp. 6a–b. Translated in Yoshikawa, p. 53.
19. HYC, pp. 3a–b.
20. WLC, 30/10b.
21. *Ibid.*, 31/6b–7a; *Nien-p'u*, p. 7a.
22. LHCSC, 1/5b–6a.
23. Cf. *Tz'u Hai* under *san ching*.
24. *Hou Han shu*, biography of Hua T'o.
25. LHCSC, 1/1b.
26. *Yen-chou shih-hua* (in LTSH), p. 18b.
27. WLC, 60/1b–2b. For the dated version, see LHCSC, pp. 16a–b before ch. 1. Lin Ta-nien appears in the biography of Lin Pu in SS, ch. 457.
28. LHCSC, pp. 34a–b.
29. *Ibid.*, p. 12a; PSCCC, 16/27b.
30. In addition to the Lin Pu couplet already quoted, see *Yen-chou shih-hua* (in LTSH), p. 15b.
31. HCC, pp. 61, 85, 105, 122, 152, 165, 436, 439.
32. *Ibid.*, p. 436.
33. *Ibid.*, pp. 122, 127, 153.
134. *Ibid.*, pp. 246 and 267.
35. *Ibid.*, p. 50; Yoshikawa, p. 57. This story is retold in TCYYTH, p. 167.
36. HCC, p. 189.
37. *Ibid.*, pp. 102–3.
38. *Ibid.*, pp. 39–40; and Ch'ien Chung-shu (1), pp. 6–7.
39. TKPS, 11/1a–4a, 12/18b–22a.
40. HCC, p. 185.
41. TKPS, 23/16a–b.
42. WLC, 28/14a; Kakehi, BGS, pp. 83–84.
43. HCC, p. 37.
44. *Ibid.*, p. 142.
45. *Ibid.*, p. 130.
46. OYWCKC, 11/7b; STPC, ch. 4, p. 121. See also Kung Ming-chih, *Chung-wu chi-wen* (in *T'ai-ts'ang chiu-chih wu-chung*, 4/3b; and HCLY, 34/3a.
47. HCC, pp. 80, 140, 145, 246, 267, etc.
48. Ch'ien Chung-shu (1), introduction, p. 28.
49. James J. Y. Liu, p. 249.
50. *Ibid.*, pp. 249–50.
51. HKCCC, p. 37.
52. *Ibid.*, p. 43.
53. *Ibid.*, p. 12.
54. WIHC, 4/1a.
55. *Ibid.*, 4/12a.
56. Yoshikawa, p. 56. For the poems, see WIHC, *i shih wen*, 1/1a–b.
57. *Lun-yü*, XII, 12. Translated in Waley, *The Analects of Confucius*, p. 166.
58. *Chung-shan shih-hua* (in LTSH), p. 6a. See also Yoshikawa, pp. 56–57.

CHAPTER THREE: RESPONSE

1. TCHC, 32/13b.
2. Ibid., 33/1a.
3. Chiang-hsi shih-p'ai hsiao hsü (in LTSH, HP), p. 1a.
4. The reference is to a story told in YYYC, 2/11b–12b. An actor playing the role of Li Shang-yin appeared on stage in tattered clothes. When asked what had happened to his clothes, he replied, "They've been torn off by the scholars of the institutes [i.e., the Hsi-k'un poets]."
5. Hou-ts'un Hsien-sheng ta-ch'üan-chi (in SPTK), 174/2b–3a.
6. This is a Buddhist term meaning the founder of a sect.
7. An allusion frequently used for frivolous music. See the Yüeh-chi in the Li-chi.
8. For Yin Shu's importance as a ku-wen stylist, see James T. C. Liu (1), pp. 27, 106, 144–46.
9. T'ing-chai shih-hua (in LTSH, HP), p. 10a.
10. See James T. C. Liu (1), p. 142.
11. TLHSC, 5/1a ff.
12. CLHSC, 11/1a–3b.
13. STLC, hsia/36a; and TLSC, p. 12a.
14. Kung Ming-chih, Chung-wu chi-wen, 2/2b.
15. See, for example, WIHC, 1/7b, 3/10a, 4/10b.
16. WLC, 25/4b, 27/2a.
17. TLSC, pp. 5b–6a.
18. See James T. C. Liu (1), p. 142.
19. Ch'ien Chung-shu (1), p. 1.
20. OYWCKC, 34/3b–6b.
21. Ibid., 2/2b–3a.
22. Ibid., 3/2a–b, 3/4b–5b.
23. Ibid., 66/7b–9b. Translated in James T. C. Liu (1), p. 89.
24. STLC, shang/39b.
25. OYWCKC, 66/9b–11b.
26. Ibid., 126/7b, 18a, 19a.
27. Ibid., 128/8b–9a.
28 HKCCC, p. 8.
29. Source uncertain.
30. The reference to Hsü Tung will be explained later.
31 OYWCKC, 128/3b–4a.
32. Chiang-chai shih-hua (in CSH), p. 15.
33. OYWCKC, 128/9a–b.
34. Ibid., 128/4a–b.
35. Sheng Sung chiu-seng shih (in Li Chih-ting, ed., Sung-jen chi, p. 20b).
36. Ibid., p. 1a.
37. See note 35.
38. OYWCKC, 130/5b.
39. Ibid., 128/4b–5a.
40. CTS, 26/1a.
41. Ibid., 25/25b.

42. *Lin-han yin-chü shih-hua* (in LTSH), p. 6a. *Men-se hsin-hua* (in CTMS), 7/6a.
43. OYWCKC, 128/1b.
44. *Ibid.*, 128/6b–7a.
45. *Ibid.*, 128/3b–4a.
46. *Ibid.*, 11/7b.
47. As shall be suggested in the following chapter, the *Hsü chin-chen shih-ko*, a one-volume book on poetic theory and practice attributed to Mei, is probably a forgery.
48. WLC, 25/4b. Partially paraphrased in Yoshikawa, pp. 46 and 75; and in Kakehi, BGSR, p. 449.
49. WLC, 27/2a–b. Partially paraphrased in Kakehi, BGSR, pp. 449–50.
50. PSCCC, 28/9a.
51. OYWCKC, 2/10b–11b; WLC, 24/1a–2a.
52. CTS, 12/88a.
53. WLC, 24/12b–13a.
54. *Ibid.*, 46/1b–2b.
55. *Ibid.*, 33/10a–b.
56. *Ibid.*, 35/7a–8a.
57. James T. C. Liu (1), pp. 26, 143–44.
58. *Tung-kuan chi* (in *Ch'iao-fan-lou ts'ung-shu*), 3/7a. HCC, p. 153, and Yoshikawa, p. 57.
59. OYWCKC, 128/11b–12a.
60. WLC, 36/15a.
61. *Ibid.*, 30/3b.
62. CLHSC, 7/9b.
63. WLC, 3/9b–10a; Kakehi, BGS, pp. 9–12.
64. OYWCKC, 9/2b–3b.
65. WLC, 12/7a.
66. CLHSC, 5/20a–b.
67. WLC, 59/6a–7a.
68. CLHSC, 5/6a–7b.
69. KSC, 17/6a.
70. YYYC, 14/11b–12a.
71. WLC, 33/10b.
72. MTYSC, p. 149.
73. PSCCC, 28/1b–13a.
74. *Ibid.*, 65/3b.
75. HCC, pp. 42 and 183.
76. OYWCKC, 128/4b; and see 130/a–b for a slightly different version.
77. *Ibid.*, 42/10b–12a.
78. WLC, 7/13b.
79. MTYSC, pp. 161–62.
80. *Wen-hsin tiao-lung*, Chapter 28.
81. MTYSC, p. 99.
82. HCC, p. 142.
83. MTYSC, p. 45.
84. *Ibid.*, p. 88.
85. *Ibid.*

86. Quoted by Yang Shen in *Sheng-an shih-hua,* (in LTSH, HP), 8/3a.
87. WLC, 28/12a.
88. *Ibid.,* 36/8b–9a; Kakehi, BGS, pp. 105–7.
89. OYWCKC, 3/10b–11a.
90. WLC, 30/13b–14a; Hsia, pp. 78–79.
91. MTYSC, pp. 58–62.
92. See OYWCKC, 5/3b; 5/5a, 5/9a, etc.
93. Graham, p. 68.
94. *Ibid.*
95. *Ibid.*
96. *Ibid.*
97. OYWCKC, 6/11a.
98. WLC, 52/1a; Hsia, pp. 116–17.
99. Ch'ien Chung-shu (2), pp. 195–96.
100. WLC, 35/7b.
101. WLC, 25/8b–9b.
102. LTC, pp. 1–4. Partially translated in Graham, pp. 83–88.
103. WLC, 59/9a–b; Hsia, p. 186.
104. See note 56.
105. WLC, 55/5b–6a.
106. See note 56.
107. See note 56.
108. See note 55.
109. See note 71.
110. *Chung-shan shih-hua,* p. 7a.
111. *Chang Chi shih-chi,* pp. 16–17.
112. PSCCC, 1/2a–3a.
113. *Chang Chi shih-chi,* p. 93.
114. PSCCC, 3/6a–b.
115. *Chang Chi shih-chi,* p. 92.
116. *Ibid.,* p. 3.
117. See his letter to Han, *ibid.,* pp. 107–8.
118. See note 55.
119. OYWCKC, 52/2a.
120. *Ibid.,* 54/11b–12a.
121. *Ibid.,* 4/1b–2a.
122. See note 50.
123. WLC, 15/15a–b.
124. *Ibid.,* 39/9b.
125. PSCCC, 18/11a–b.
126. WLC, 54/3b–4a.
127. *Ibid.,* 41/2a–b.
128. *Po Hsiang-shan shih-chi* (in SPPY), *pieh-chi* /4a–b.
129. WLC, 10/9a–10a.
130. PSCCC, 12/12b–20b; 22a–24b.
131. See note 45.
132. OYWCKC, 1/3a.
133. *Ibid.,* 56/6a. Translated in Yoshikawa, p. 65.

134. PSCCC, 28/11a.

135. *Ibid.*, 6/11a.

136. SJYH, p. 256.

137. TLSH, p. 4b.

138. HCC, p. 168.

139. Quoted by Ch'ien Chung-shu (1), p. 13.

140. Liang K'un, p. 42.

141. *Feng-yüeh-t'ang shih-hua* (in *I-ching-t'ang ch'i chung*), *shang* /16a.

142. WLC, 3/11a.

143. *Ibid.*, 26/10a–11a. This poem probably dates from 1046, the year after Ou-yang's banishment.

144. Quoted in TCYYTH, p. 98.

145. OYWCKC, 73/4b–5a. For the poem by Wei, see WSCC, p. 355.

146. WLC, 12/6a.

147. WSCC, p. 346.

148. WLC, 40/4b–5a.

149. WSCC, p. 158.

150. *Ibid.*, p. 298.

151. *Ibid.*, p. 104.

152. The actual poem written by Mei is not outstanding and will not be translated.

153. WSCC, pp. 239–40.

154. *Ibid.*, pp. 396–97.

155. *Li Chang-chi ko shih* (in SPPY), 2/8b–9a.

156. *Ibid.*, 2/9a.

157. *I-yüan chih-yen* (in LTSH, HP), 4/6a.

158. *T'ing-chai shih-hua* (in LTSH, HP), p. 7a.

159. *Ou-pei shih-hua* (Taipei, 1962), 11/1b.

160. WLC, 51/1a–b.

161. The character *chen* should read *Juan*, as in WLHSWC, 51/1b.

162. WLC, 46/9b.

163. *Ibid.*, 54/1b.

164. *Ibid.*, 41/3a.

165. *Ibid.*, 12/5b–6a.

166. TKPS, 6/1a–b.

167. WLC, 33/14a.

168. TKPS, 9/1a–2b.

169. OYWCKC, 129/3a–b.

170. E.g., Liu Pin, *Chung-shan shih-hua*, p. 6b.

171. *Keng-ch'i shih-hua* (in LTSH, HP), *shang*/5a.

172. OYWCKC, 128/3b–4a.

173. TKPS, 21/12a–13a.

174. See note 39.

175. OYWCKC, 134/17b.

176. *Ibid.*, 54/2a.

177. *Ibid.*, 5/8b–9a.

178. *Ibid.*, 5/6a–7a.

179. TCYYTH, p. 197.

180. WLC, 52/4a.

181. LTPS, 12/15a–b.
182. WLC, 44/11b.
183. LTPS, 20/13b–14a.
184. WLC, 10/6a–b; Kakehi, BGS, pp. 48–51. Also translated in Watson (2).
185. WLC, 26/12b–13a, Kakehi, BGS, pp. 76–78.
186. See notes 160 and 161.
187. Yokoyama (1), pp. 60 ff.
188. WLC, 36/11b.
189. *Ibid.*, 17/2a.
190. *Ibid.*, 43/13a–b.
191. JSTC, pp. 63b ff.
192. WLC, 25/12b.
193. *Ibid.*, 36/9a.
194. Yokoyama (1), pp. 61–62.
195. WLC, 41/11a–b.
196. WLHSWC, 39/10a.
197. WLC, 40/8b–9a.
198. JSTC, p. 73a.
199. WLC, 11/10a–b.
200. *Huai-nan hung-lieh chi-chieh* (Shanghai, Commercial Press, 1923), 16/4a–b.
201. WLC, 9/8b–9a.
202. *Ibid.*, 23/14a.
203. *Ibid.*, 60/2a.
204. See note 87.
205. *Ibid.*, 37/1b–2a.
206. HCC, pp. 102–3.
207. WLC, 24/16a–b.
208. *Ibid.*, 25/8a–b.
209. *Ibid.*, 12/5b.
210. TYMC, 3/22a–b.
211. WLC, 24/10b–11a.
212. TYMC, 2/1a–2b.
213. Yokoyama (1), p. 62.
214. WLC, 52/3a.
215. TYMC, 5/1a–2b.
216. WLC, 3/3b–4b.
217. *Ibid.*, 50/1a–2a.

CHAPTER FOUR: THEORY

1. Appended to the 1830 edition of Mei's works.
2. Kakehi, BGS, introduction, p. 19.
3. CTS, 26/9b.
4. OYWCKC, 128/5a–b.
5. In Yoshikawa, p. 78. Also partially translated in James T. C. Liu (1), pp. 135–36.
6. For this interpretation of *shuai-i* see Kakehi, BGSR, p. 455.
7. CCCC, 3/1b.

8. CTS, 18/91a.

9. *Ibid.*, 10/2b.

10. *Wen Fei-ch'ing chi chien-chu* (in SPPY), 7/5a.

11. CCCC, 8/2a.

12. *Chung-shan shih-hua*, p. 3a.

13. The *P'ei-wen yün-fu* quotes the present passage twice, under *ma-ku* and under *huai-ken ch'u*, simply naming *Liu-i shih-hua* as the source. Elsewhere (OYWCKC, 130/6b), Ou-yang writes, "Once when I was in Lo [yang], I heard Hsieh Hsi-shen [Hsieh Chiang (995–1039)] recite, 'The district is ancient; locust roots protrude. / The official is virtuous; the horse's bones jut out.' . . . He said, 'The feeling of virtuous hardship exists beyond the words themselves, and yet is perceived within the words." This is very close to the second part of Mei's statement on poetry. It is, of course, possible that the precise wording of Hsieh's comment here is attributable to Ou-yang himself, writing years later under the influence of Mei's dictum.

14. LHCSC, p. 21b.

15. Fang, p. 11.

16. For the *Chuang Tzu* quotation, see Watson (1), p. 302. For the Chung Hung quotation, see *Shih-p'in* (in LTSH), preface, p. 2b.

17. Chu Tung-jun (2), pp. 287–88.

18. *Wen Kung hsü-shih-hua*, p.6b.

19. TKPS, 2/4a–b.

20. YYYC, 1/4a–b.

21. For the poems quoted, see WLC, 3/12a, 3/11b, 3/9a, 5/15a.

22. WLC, 60/2a.

23. *Ibid.*, 28/11b–12a.

24. *Ibid.*, 46/9b.

25. Shao was known for his seal and "clerk style" calligraphy, and participated, as did Mei, in the compilation of the *New T'ang History.*

26. OYWCKC, 33/7a–9b.

27. Kakehi, BGSR, p. 444.

28. WLC, 5/7b–8b.

29. Tu wrote, for example, a poem entitled *Climbing the Heights at Ch'i Mountain on the Ninth Day, Fan-ch'uan wen-chi chu* (in SPPY), 3/11b.

30. WLC, 24/16a–b.

31. *Ibid.*, 27/8b.

32. *Nan-yang chi* (in SSC), p. 18b.

33. Kakehi, BGSR, pp. 445–46; Yokoyama (2), p. 33.

34. *Shih p'in* (in LTSH), chung/3a.

35. *Ibid.*, preface, p. 2a.

36. Kakehi, BGSR, pp. 446–47.

37. WLC, 17/2a.

38. *Ibid.*, 18/4a–b.

39. *Ibid.*, 57/5b–7b.

40. *Lao Tzu*, ch. 35.

41. Watson (1), p. 94.

42. WLC, 60/2a.

43. Watson (1), p. 143. To this may be added the following passage from the *Shan-mu* chapter of Chuang Tzu: "The friendship of a gentleman, they say, is insipid as

water (*tan jo shui*); that of a petty man, sweet as rich wine. But the insipidity of the gentleman leads to affection, while the sweetness of the petty man leads to revulsion. Those with no particular reason for joining together will for no particular reason part." (Watson, p. 215.)

44. Liu Shao, *Jen-wu chih* (in SPTK), 1/1b–2a.
45. Kakehi, BGSR, p. 446.
46. *Ibid.*
47. Quoted in *P'ei-wen yün-fu* under *p'ing-tan hsien*.
48. Kakehi, BGSR, p. 446.
49. JSTC, p. 22a.
50. Kakehi, BGSR, p. 446.
51. Yokoyama (2), p. 34 and n.2 on p. 40. See *Erh-shih-ssu shih-p'in* (in LTSH), p. 1a.
52. *Chinese Literature* (Peking), No. 7 (1963), pp. 65–66.
53. Chu Tung-jun (2), p. 279.
54. *Erh-shih-ssu shih-p'in*, pp. 2a, 3a, 4b. *Chinese Literature*, No. 7 (1963), pp. 68, 69, 73.
55. See note 136 to chapter 3.
56. CLHSC, 5/5a–6a; Kakehi, BGSR, p. 447.
57. CLHSC, 2/4a–5a.
58. OYWCKC, 128/2a.
59. Kakehi, BGSR, pp. 447–48.
60. PSCCC, 28/11a.
61. *Ibid.*, 6/10b–11a.
62. *Ibid.*, 1/6b–7a.
63. SSCC, p. 60.
64. *T'ang Fu-li Hsien-sheng wen-chi* (in SPYK), 16/9b.
65. *Ts'ang-hai shih-hua* (in LTSH, HP), p. 1a.
66. *Ibid.*, p. 3a.
67. Yokoyama (2), p. 36.
68. Chu Tung-jun (3), pp. 84–85.
69. CTS, 23/1b.
70. *Ibid.*, 22/91b.
71. *Shih-shih* (in LTSH), p. 8b.
72. As Ho Wen-huan points out in his notes to this passage in the *k'ao-so* appended to LTSH (p. 1b), Ssu-ma Hsiang-ju's wife Cho Wen-chün is probably intended here.
73. HCC, p. 23.
74. *Ibid.*, pp. 283–84.
75. WLC, 24/16a–b.
76. *Ibid.*, 28/11b–12a.
77. See note 56.
78. WLC, 5/8a.
79. WLC, 25/4b–5a. Paraphrased in Yoshikawa, p. 75, and Kakehi, BGSR, p. 449.
80. TPSH, pp. 4a–b.
81. SJYH, pp. 218–19.
82. WLC, 37/1b–2a.
83. *Ibid.*, 45/9b–10a.

84. *Ibid.*, 45/8a–b.
85. OYWCKC, 2/5a–b.
86. Yoshikawa, pp. 36–37.
87. HCC, p. 62.
88. OYWCKC, 4/8b.
89. WLC, 45/11a.
90. OYWCKC, 128/6b–7a.
91. *Sui-han-t'ang shih-hua* (in LTSH, HP), *shang*/4a.
92. WLC, 11/10a; Hsia, pp. 24–25.
93. Chu Tung-jun (3), p. 94.
94. Quoted in W. K. Wimsatt, *Hateful Contraries* (Lexington, Kentucky, 1966), p. 157.
95. YYYC, 1/9b.
96. WLC, 45/7a–b, 9b, 9b–10a, 11a; 46/9b. Some errors in Ko's text have been corrected. In some cases, the original title begins "Responding to" rather than "Reading."
97. Hsia, pp. 165–66.
98. *Ibid.*, pp. 166–67.
99. In his book, *The Chinese Knight Errant* (University of Chicago, 1967), p. 50, James J. Y. Liu refers to a general named Ts'ao Hsieh "who studied poetry under the famous poet Mei Yao-ch'en." Mei "praised his works."
100. *Nan-yang chi*, pp. 20a–b.
101. Holly Stevens, ed., *The Palm at the End of the Mind: Selected Poems and a Play by Wallace Stevens* (New York, Alfred A. Knopf, 1971), p. 158. Reprinted with permission of the publisher.

CHAPTER FIVE: PRACTICE

1   *Poems Describing Everyday Life*

1. *Nien-p'u*, p. 8b.
2. WLC, 4/3b–4a; Hsia, pp. 5–6. Hsia, pp. 5–6.
3. Hsia suggests that *p'o* ("broke") is a mistake for *pi* ("their").
4. The expression *yin chin chui* is explained by a passage in the biography of Chia Shan in the *Han shu*: "Ch'in Shih-huang-ti built highways throughout the world. . . . The roads were fifty paces broad, and were planted with trees every thirty feet. Thick earthen walls were built on either side, pounded with metal mallets." A gloss on this passage says that *yin* here means "to pound."
5. WLC, 7/12a–13a; Kakehi, BGS, pp. 37–42; Hsia pp. 126–27.
6. TKPS 6/25a–27b.
7. CLHSC, 3/1a–b.
8. WLC, 11/9b; Kakehi, BGS, pp. 57–59; Hsia, p. 24. Also translated in Watson (2).
9. WLC, 26/12b–13a; Kakehi, BGS, pp. 76–78. Also translated in Rexroth, p. 48.
10. WLC, 13/2b–3a.
11. *Ibid.*, 27/4a–b.
12. *Ibid.*, 27/12b.
13. *Shih-hu chü-shih shih-chi* (in SPTK), 27/4b.

14. WLC, 28/14a; Kakehi, BGS, pp. 83–84. Also translated in Watson (2).
15. See chapter 2, notes 40 and 41.
16. WLC, 30/3b–4a; Kakehi, BGS, pp. 86–87; Hsia, p. 76.
17. WLC, 33/10b–11a.
18. HCC, p. 152.
19. *Tung-kuan chi*, 2/5a.
20. WLC, 35/12b; Hsia, p. 91.
21. For *po jih*, "in bright daylight," which makes little sense here, Hsia suggests reading *jih po*, "getting white every day."
22. PSCCC, 9/11b–12a.
23. WLC, 13/6b–7a; Kakehi, BGS, pp. 109–12; Hsia, pp. 29–30.
24. WLC, 38/4b.
25. TYMC, 2/9a–b.
26. *Yen Lu Kung chi* (in SPPY), 24/10b ff.
27. WLC, 19/1b; Kakehi, BGS, pp. 154–55; Hsia, p. 44. Also translated in Watson (2).
28. *Nien-p'u*, p. 27a.
29. Quoted in the *T'ai-p'ing yü-lan*, ch. 4, under "lunar eclipse."

2   Poems of Personal Emotion

1. WLC, 16/7a–b; Hsia, p. 36.
2. *Nien-p'u*, pp. 22a–b.
3. MTYSC, p. 61.
4. WLC, 10/6a–b; Kakehi, BGS, pp. 51–55. First poem also translated in Rexroth, p. 45; third poem in Watson (2).
5. *Wen hsüan*, ch. 23.
6. Karlgren,#73; Waley, #58.
7. WLC, 10/16b.
8. *Ibid.*, 24/11b–12a.
9. *Ibid.*, 11/14a–b; Kakehi, BGS, pp. 62–64; Hsia, pp. 26–27. Also translated in Watson (2).
10. TKPS, 11/3a.
11. WLC, 24/12a–b; Kakehi, BGS, pp. 64–66; Hsia, p. 62. Also translated in Watson (2).
12. WLC, 26/7a–b; Kakehi, BGS, pp. 71–75.
13. WLC, 8/11a–b.
14. *Ibid.*, 27/12b–13a.
15. *Ibid.*, 27/14a.
16. YSCCC, ch. 9. For a discussion of these poems, see Ch'en Yin-k'o, pp. 94 ff.
17. YSCCC, 30/2b.
18. WSCC, pp. 261 ff.
19. Frodsham, p. 86.
20. YSCCC, 9/2b.
21. WSCC, p. 261.
22. *Ibid.*, pp. 267–68.
23. *Yü-ch'i-sheng shih chien-chu* (in SPPY), 4/12b–13a. Translated in James J. Y. Liu, p. 158.
24. *Kao Ch'ang-shih shih chiao-chu* (Taipei, 1965), ch. 1, p. 12.

25. YSCCC, 9/2a.
26. Ch'en Yin-k'o, pp. 95–96.
27. WSCC, pp. 268–69.
28. WSCC, p. 263.
29. YSCCC, 9/2b.
30. Sir Arthur Quiller-Couch, ed., *The Oxford Book of English Verse, 1250–1918* (New York, 1942), pp. 296–98.
31. WLC, 28/8b–9a; Kakehi, BGS, pp. 80–81; Hsia, p. 72. Also translated in Watson (2).
32. *Nien-p'u*, p. 15b.
33. WLC, 31/9b; Kakehi, BGS, pp. 88–89.
34. WLC 33/1a–b; Kakehi, BGS, pp. 91–93.
35. *Nien-p'u*, p. 17b.
36. I.e., August 2, 1044.
37. WLC, 32/7b–8a; Hsia, p. 83 (first two only). The second poem is also translated in Rexroth, p. 41.
38. Iritani, pp. 48–54.
39. YSCCC, 9/7a–b.
40. MTYSC, pp. 187–89.
41. WLC, 15/13b; Kakehi, BGS, pp. 112–14.
42. *Nien-p'u*, p. 22b.

3   Poems of Social Comment

1. WLC, 42/7a.
2. PSCCC, 28/6b.
3. WLC, 25/4b–5a.
4. *Ibid.*, 40/4a–b.
5. Suzuki Torao, p. 4, and Yokoyama (1), p. 55.
6. Ch'en Yin-k'o, pp. 281–83.
7. HCC, p. 62.
8. *Ibid.*, p. 53.
9. WLC, 7/7a–8a; Kakehi, BGS, pp. 27–32; Hsia, pp. 15–16; Ch'ien Chung-shu (1), pp. 19–21.
10. *Han shu*, ch. 89.
11. PSCCC, 3/9b–11a.
12. WLC, 7/3b–4a.
13. Ch'ien Chung-shu (1), p. 22.
14. WLC, 7/8b–9a; Kakehi, BGS, pp. 32–35; Hsia, pp. 16–17; Ch'ien Chung-shu (1), pp. 21–22.
15. Karlgren, #10; Waley, *The Book of Songs*, #147.
16. Kakehi, BGSR, pp. 439–40.
17. WLC, 33/12a; Kakehi, BGS, pp. 95–96.
18. WLC, 34/2a; Kakehi, BGS, pp. 96–97; Hsia, p. 230.
19. WLC, 17/8b–9a; Kakehi, BGS, pp. 121–23; Hsia, pp. 141–42.
20. Yokoyama (1), p. 56.
21. Legge, *The Chinese Classics*, Vol. V, p. 648.
22. WLC, 26/10a; Hsia, p. 69.
23. WLC, 31/5b–6a.

24. *Lung-p'ing chi* (edition of 1708), 8/14b.
25. Herbert A. Giles, *A Chinese Biographical Dictionary* (London and Shanghai, 1898), p. 876.
26. WLC, 31/7a–8b.
27. *Ibid.*, 34/15a; Kakehi, BGS, pp. 97–100.
28. Kracke (2), pp. 484–85.
29. WLC, 31/5b; Hsia, p. 80.
30. PSCCC, 4/8b–9a.
31. YSCCC, 23/5a.
32. TKPS, 11/10b–11b.
33. Quoted in *Chung-shan shih-hua*, p. 6b.
34. WLC, 34/10a; Hsia, p. 89.
35. WLC, 4/12b–13a.
36. PSCCC, 3/6a–b.
37. KSC, 17/2a.
38. WLC, 36/11a–b.
39. The character *hsi* ("grieve") in SPTK is a misprint for *i* ("prodigy") (see the 1830 edition, 36/9a).
40. Philip B. Yampolsky, *The Platform Sutra of the Sixth Patriarch* (New York and London, 1967), pp. 5 ff., and p. 12.
41. *Sōden haiun* (in *Dai Nihon Bukkyō zensho*), ch. 51, p. 433.

4 Moralizing Poems on Living Creatures

1. OYWCKC, 128/2a–b.
2. *Ibid.*, 73/8a.
3. *Nien-p'u*, p. 9a.
4. WLC, 5/8b–9a; Kakehi, BGS, pp. 17–21; Hsia, pp. 11–12.
5. *Han Fei Tzu* (in SPPY), *Nei-ch'u shuo shang*, 9/12a.
6. CLHSC, 6/7a–b.
7. *Ibid.*, 6/7b–8a.
8. Legge, *The Chinese Classics*, Vol. 5, p. 726.
9. Kua Shao-yü (1), Vol. I, p. 122, #10.
10. *Shih-lin shih-hua, shang*/2b–3a.
11. TCYYTH, p. 209.
12. Kuo Shao-yü (1), Vol. II, p. 97, #82.
13. Wu Ching-hsü, *Li-tai shih-hua* (Chung-hua shu-chü ed.), Vol. II, pp. 833–35.
14. *Keng-ch'i shih-hua, hsia*/6b.
15. *Men-se hsin-hua*, 8/3b.
16. OYWCKC, 6/6a–b.
17. *Chu Tzu yü-lei* (printing of 1872), 140/10a–b. Quoted in Kakehi, BGSR, pp. 433–34.
18. *Ibid.*, 139/16b.
19. WLC, appendix, p. 14a. This poem is one of a pair dated 1197 in Mei's *Nien-p'u*, pp. 28b–29a.
20. James T. C. Liu (2), p. 342, bottom.
21. Kakehi, BGSR, p. 432.
22. HCC, p. 194.
23. *Chung-shan shih-hua*, p. 2b.

24. Liu reads *kan* for *wu*.
25. Liu reads *ts'an* for *t'un*.
26. WLC, 1/3a–b; Kakehi, BGS, pp. 3–8; Hsia, pp. 1–2.
27. See Kakehi, BGS, p. 164, *nien-p'u*, under 1032.
28. *Shih chi*, ch. 125.
29. Hsia, p. 2.
30. Quoted in TCYYTH, p. 210.
31. WLHSWC, 13/3b.
32. See James T. C. Liu (2).
33. WLC, 3/7a–b; Kakehi, BGS, pp. 13–16; Hsia, p. 4.
34. Kakehi, BGS, p. 16.
35. Hsia, p. 4.
36. WLC, 24/15a–b.
37. *Liu Pin-k'o chi* (in SPPY), 21/4a.
38. *P'i Tzu wen-sou* (*Chung-hua shu-chü*, 1959), p. 121.
39. PSCCC, 11/13a.
40. MTYSC, p. 160.
41. TKPS, 6/26b.
42. *Kung-ch'i shih-hua* (in LTSH, HP), 7/2b.
43. *Li I-shan wen-chi ch'ien-chu* (published by Hua-ch'i ts'ao-t'ang, 1708), 10/15b–16a.
44. Kakehi, BGSR, pp. 430–31.
45. See note 38.
46. OYWCKC, 52/4a–b.
47. *Ibid.*, 3/4a–b.
48. WLC, 24/10a. Also translated in Watson (2).
49. Yen K'o-chün, ed., *Ch'üan Ch'i wen*, 21/10a–b.
50. *Li I-shan wen-chi ch'ien-chu*, 10/14b.
51. *Ibid.*, 10/15a–b, and *T'ang Fu-li Hsien-sheng wen-chi*, 14/33a.
52. WLC, 27/12a; Kakehi, pp. 78–80.
53. As Kakehi points out, *huai* "feelings," is an error for *huai*, "spoiled."
54. *Huai-nan hung-lieh chi-chieh*, 17/10b.
55. JSTC, p. 47a.
56. TYMC, 3/26a.
57. Lily Pao-hu Chang and Marjorie Sinclair, trans., *The Poems of T'ao Ch'ien* (Honolulu, 1953), p. 72.
58. WLC, 30/5a; Hsia, pp. 76–77.
59. LCHSWC, 11/3a–b; SMKWC, 3/25a–b.
60. *The Complete Poetical Works of Robert Burns* (Cambridge edition, 1897), pp. 43–44.
61. Oliver Bernard, ed., *Rimbaud* (Harmondsworth, Penguin Books, 1962), pp. 142–43.
62. WLC, 17/8b, Kakehi, BGS, pp. 120–21.
63. WLC, 25/13a; Kakehi, BGS, pp. 66–67.
64. WLC, 23/6b; Kakehi, BGS, pp. 157–58; Hsia, pp. 59–60.
65. *T'ai-p'ing yü-lan*, 947/2b.
66. WLC, 36/8b–9a; Kakehi, BGS, pp. 105–7.
67. Quoted in the *T'ai-p'ing yü-lan*, 947/3b.

68. CLHSC, 7/8a–b.
69. WLC, 11/12b–13a; Kakehi, BGS, pp. 59–62; Hsia, pp. 132–33.
70. WSCC, p. 200.
71. Kakehi, BGS, p. 61.
72. WLC, 24/15a–b.
73. Quoted in William Pratt, *The Imagist Poem* (New York, 1963), p. 34.

5 Poems on Antiquities and Works of Art

1. WLC, 11/14b; Hsia, pp. 27–28.
2. OYWCKC, 127/16a.
3. See, for example, René-Yvon Lefebvre d'Argencé, *Chinese Treasures from the Avery Brundage Collection* (The Asia Society, 1968), #30 and #21.
4. Rudolph, p. 175.
5. WLC, 13/7b–8b; Hsia, pp. 134–35.
6. WLC, 15/1a–2a; Hsia, pp. 137–39.
7. *Nien-p'u*, p. 22b.
8. WLC, 10/13a; Hsia, p. 20.
9. *T'u-hui pao-chien* (in *Mei-shu ts'ung-k'an*, Vol. II, Taipei, 1964), p. 105.
10. *Hsüan-ho hua-p'u* (in *Hua-shih ts'ung-shu*, Shanghai, 1963), p. 258.
11. *T'u-hua chien-wen chih* (in *Mei-shu ts'ung-k'an*, Vol. II), p. 56.
12. STPC, 4/63.
13. OYWCKC, 6/7a.
14. YYYC, 14/7b–8a.
15. KSC, 17/10b–11a.
16. *An-yang chi* (in SSC), quoted in introductory essay, p. 1a.
17. Rudolph, p. 169.
18. *Ibid.*, p. 175.
19. WLC, 33/9a.
20. *Ibid.*, 54/9a.
21. OYWCKC, 140/15b.
22. HCC, p. 46.
23. OYWCKC, 53/12b–13b.
24. SSCC, pp. 47–48.
25. I.e., the stone drum texts and the monumental inscriptions carved in the Ch'in dynasty.
26. At this time, Su was in Su-chou in southern Chiangsu, i.e., to the southeast of Ch'u-chou.
27. WLC, 26/11b–12b.
28. WLC, 16/1a–b; Kakehi, BGS, pp. 115–19; Hsia, pp. 34–36.
29. In the *T'ai-p'ing kuang-chi, ch.* 230.
30. KSC, 18/9a.
31. See Giles, *A Chinese Biographical Dictionary,* #1862.
32. See Arthur Braddan Coole *et al, An Encyclopedia of Chinese Coins,* Vol. I (Denver, 1967), p. 430; and Max Loehr, *Relics of Ancient China* (New York, 1965), p. 161.
33. For pictures of the coins, see Kakehi, BGS, frontispiece, and Loehr, p. 145.
34. *Chin shih so,* section on knife coins (not paginated).
35. *Ibid.*
36. For the bibliography on this coin, see Coole (note 32), p. 476.

37. KSC, 5/9b.
38. WLC, 16/3a–b.
39. Joseph Needham, *Science and Civilization in China*, Vol. 4, Part II (Cambridge, 1965), p. 69.
40. See Schuyler Van R. Cammann, "Archaeological Evidence for Chinese Contacts with India During the Han Dynasty," *Sinologica*, Vol. 5 (1956), figures 2 and 3 on p. 18; Yoshida Mitsukuni, "Yumi to ōyumi", *Tōyōshi kenkyū*, Vol. 12, #3 (1953); and the article by Kao Chih-hsi in *Wen Wu*, 1964, #6, pp. 33–45.
41. *Hsüan-ho po-ku t'u-lu (I-cheng-t'ang* ed. of 1752), 27/9a–11b.
42. Jung Keng, *Sung-chai chi chin t'u-lu* (Peking, 1933), plate 37 and pp. 23a–24a.
43. Wu Ch'eng-lo, *A History of Chinese Weights and Measures* (Commercial Press, 1937), pp. 213–15.
44. Yoshida Mitsukuni (note 40), pp. 88–89.
45. Hu Tao-ching, ed., *Meng-ch'i pi-t'an* (Shanghai, 1956), ch. 19, p. 635.
46. Legge, *The Shoo King*, p. 202.
47. C. Martin Wilbur, "The History of the Crossbow. . . ," *Annual Report of the Smithsonian Institution*, 1936, pp. 429–30.
48. Richard C. Rudolph, in his review of Cheng Te-k'un, *Archaeology in China, Vol. 3, Chou China* (Toronto, 1963), in *Journal of the American Oriental Society*, Vol. 87 (1967), p. 331.
49. OYWCKC, 54/11b–12a.
50. SJISHP, Vol. I, pp. 391–92.
51. WLC, 53/10b–11a; Hsia, pp. 121–22.
52. Also translated in Edouard Chavannes, *Les Mémoires Historiques de Se-ma Ts'ien*, Vol. II (Paris, 1897), p. 550.
53. Mei has omitted the character *li*, which should appear between *an* and *hao.*
54. *Yen-shih chia-hsün* (in SPPY), 6/10b–11a.
55. OYWCKC, 134/14b–15b.
56. Jung Keng, *Ch'in chin-wen lu* (Peking, 1931), ch. 1, *passim.*
57. Taking *wang*, "King," in the sense of *wang*, "continue, go by," with Hsia.
58. Derk Bodde, *China's First Unifier* (Leiden, 1938), p. 80.
59. *Ibid.*, p. 79.
60. *Ibid.*, p. 51.
61. *Ibid.*, p. 79.
62. *Ibid.*, p. 79.
63. *Wen hsüan*, ch. 51. Translated by Burton Watson in Birch, p. 47.
64. WSCC, p. 379.
65. *Ibid.*, p. 371.
66. WLC, 55/11b–12a; OYWCKC, 54/7a. Ou-yang's poem is translated in Yoshikawa, pp. 10 ff.
67. WSCC, p. 393.

CONCLUSION

1. Yoshikawa, p. 42.

GLOSSARY OF CHINESE NAMES AND TERMS

Ao T'ao-sun 敖陶孫
"bitter and hard" 苦硬
"bland and common" 淡俗
"calm and bland" 閒澹
Chang Chi (c.765–c.830) 張籍
Chang Chi (933–996) 張洎
Chang Chi, *tzu* Yü-kung 張績，禹功
Chang Hsien 張先
Chang Pi 張碧
Chang Shih-tseng 張師曾
Chang Yao-tso 張堯佐
Chang Yung 張詠
Chao Kai 趙槩
Chao Pien 趙抃
ch'en chi 晨蹲
Ch'en Shan 陳善
Ch'en Shih-tao 陳師道
ch'en teng 晨登
Ch'en Ts'ung-i 陳從易
Ch'en Yen-hsiao 陳嚴肖
Cheng Ku 鄭谷

Ch'i fa huo 齊法貨
Chia Tao 賈島
Chiang Hsiu-fu 江休復
Chiao-jan 皎然
Ch'ien Wei-yen 錢惟演
Chou P'u 周朴
Chu Hsi 朱熹
Chu Pien 朱弁
Chü-ning 居寧
Ch'ung Fang 种放
Chung Hung 鍾嶸
ch'ung-tan 沖淡
Discourse on Aberrations 怪說
"even and bland": see *p'ing-tan*
Fan Chen 范鎮
Fan Ch'eng-ta 范成大
Fan Chung-yen 范仲淹
Fang Hui 方回
Fang Kan 方干
Han Ch'i 韓琦
Han Chiang 韓絳

Han Chü 韓駒

Han Wei 韓維

Han Yü 韓愈

Ho Chün-pao 何君寶

Hsi Chien 郤鑒

Hsiang Ssu 項斯

Hsieh Chiang 謝絳

Hsieh Ching-ch'u, *tzu* Shih-hou
謝景初，師厚

Hsieh Ching-wen, *tzu* Shih-chih
謝景溫，師直

Hsieh Ling-yün 謝靈運

Hsieh T'ao 謝濤

Hsü chin-chen shih-ko 續金針詩格

Hsü Hsüan 徐鉉

Hsü Hun 許渾

Hsü I 許顗

Hsü K'ai 徐鍇

Hsü Tung 許洞

Hsü Yen 胥偃

Hu Yüan 胡瑗

Huang Ch'e 黃徹

Huang T'ing-chien 黃庭堅

Juan Chi 阮籍

Ko Li-fang 葛立方

K'ou Chun 寇準

kua, "arrow tip" 括

Kuo Jo-hsü 郭若虛

Kuo P'u 郭璞

Li Ao 李翱

Li Fang 李昉

Li Ho 李賀

Li Kuan 李觀

Li Po 李白

Li Shang-yin 李商隱

Li Ting 李定

Li Tsung-o 李宗鶚

Li Yang-ping 李陽冰

Lin Pu 林逋

Lin Yung-chung, *tzu* Tse-chih
林用中，擇之

Liu Ch'ang 劉敞

Liu K'ai 柳開

Liu K'o-chuang 劉克莊

Liu Pin 劉攽

Liu Shao 劉邵，劭

Liu Tsung-yüan 柳宗元

Liu Yü-hsi 劉禹錫

Liu Yün 劉筠

Lu Ching 陸經

Lu Kuei-meng 陸龜蒙

Lü Pen-chung 呂本中

Lu San-chiao 魯三交

Lu T'ung 盧仝

Lu Yu 陸游

Mei Chih 梅摯

Mei Hsün 梅詢

Mei Jang 梅讓

Mei Mo 梅邈

Mei Ting-ch'en 梅鼎臣

Mei Yao-ch'en 梅堯臣

Mei Yüan 梅遠

Meng Chiao 孟郊

Meng Hao-jan 孟浩然

Meng Pin-yü 孟賓宇

Ming Hao 明鎬

Mu Hsiu 穆修

Ou-yang Hsiu 歐陽修

P'an Lang 潘閬

P'an Yüeh 潘岳

P'ei Yü 裴煜

P'i Jih-hsiu 皮日休

Pi-yün hsia 碧雲騢

Pien Pin 卞彬

p'ing-tan 平淡，澹

Po Chü-i 白居易

"poetry collector" 采詩官

"refined and bland style" 雅澹之體

"river pig" 河豚

Shao Pi 邵必

Shao Po 邵博

Shen Kua 沈括

Sheng Tu 盛度

Shih Chieh 石介

Shih Yen-nien, *tzu* Man-ch'ing
石延年，曼卿

Shu ts'uan 書竄

shun-wu tzu-jan 順物自然

"sparse and bland" 疏澹
Ssu-k'ung T'u 司空圖
Ssu-ma Kuang 司馬光
Su Ch'e 蘇轍
Su Shih 蘇軾
Su Shun-ch'in 蘇舜欽
Sun Chin 孫僅
Sun Ho 孫何
Sun Sheng 孫升
Sung Ch'i 宋祁
Sung Chung-tao 宋中道
Sung Hsiang 宋庠
Sung Min-ch'iu 宋敏求
Tai Sung 戴嵩
T'an-ying 曇穎
T'ang Chieh 唐介
T'ao Ch'ien 陶潛
T'ao Ku 陶穀
tao wang 悼亡
T'eng K'o 滕珂
"thought bland and diction unusual"
思澹而詞迂
Tiao Chan 刁湛
Tiao Wei 刁渭
Tiao Yüeh 刁約
t'ien-tan 恬淡
Ting Wei 丁謂
Ts'ai Hsiang 蔡襄
Tseng Chi-li 曾季貍
Tseng Kung 曾鞏
tu, "calibration" 度
Tu Fu 杜甫
Tu Hsün-ho 杜荀鶴
Tu Mu 杜牧
Wang An-shih 王安石

Wang Chien 王建
Wang Ch'in-ch'en 王欽臣
Wang Ch'ou 王疇
Wang Han-mou 王漢謀
Wang Kuei 王珪
Wang Shu (997–1057) 王洙
Wang T'ao 王陶
Wang Tse 王則
Wang T'ung 王通
Wang Wei 王維
Wang Yü-ch'eng 王禹偁
Wei Ch'ing-chih 魏慶之
Wei Hsien 魏閑
Wei T'ai 魏泰
Wei Yeh 魏野
Wei Ying-wu 韋應物
Wen T'ing-yün 溫庭筠
Wen Yen-po 文彥博
"withered and bland" 枯澹
Wu Ch'u-hou 吳處厚
Wu K'o 吳可
Wu-k'o 無可
Yang I 楊億
Yang Shen 楊慎
Yao Ho 姚合
Yeh Meng-te 葉夢德
Yen Chen-ch'ing 顏眞卿
Yen Chih-t'ui 顏之推
Yen Li-pen 閻立本
Yen Shu 晏殊
Yen Wei 嚴維
Yen Yü 嚴羽
yin chin chui 隱金鎚
Yin Shu 尹洙
Yüan Chen 元稹

BIBLIOGRAPHY with ABBREVIATIONS

NOTE: Abbreviations and shortened forms as used in notes appear below in boldface.

1 COLLECTANEA

CSH. Ting Fu-pao 丁福保, ed. *Ch'ing shih-hua* 清詩話. Chung-hua shu-chü edition, 1963.
CTMS. *Chin-tai mi-shu* 津逮祕書.
LTSH. Ho Wen-huan 何文煥, ed. *Li-tai shih-hua* 歷代詩話.
LTSH, HP. Ting Fu-pao, ed. *Li-tai shih-hua, hsü-pien* 續編.
SPPY. *Ssu-pu pei-yao* 四部備要.
SPTK. *Ssu-pu ts'ung-k'an* 四部叢刊.
SSC. *Sung-shih ch'ao* 宋詩鈔.
TSCC. *Ts'ung-shu chi-ch'eng* 叢書集成.
WYT. *Wu-ying-tien chü-chen-pan ts'ung-shu* 武英殿聚珍版叢書.

2 TEXTS

1830 edition. *Yeh-yin-lou* 夜吟樓 edition of the tenth year of the Tao-kuang 道光 period (1830).
WLC. *Wan-ling chi* 宛陵集, in SPTK.
WLHSWC. *Wan-ling Hsien-sheng wen-chi* 宛陵先生文集. Commercial Press reprint, 1940, of the fragmentary Sung edition of 1224.

3 PRIMARY SOURCES

CCCC. Chia Tao 賈島 (c.793–c.865). *Chia Ch'ang-chiang chi* 賈長江集, in SPPY.

Chang Chi 張籍 (c.765–c.830). *Chang Chi shih-chi* 詩集. Chung-hua shu-chü edition, 1959.

CLHSC. Han Yü 韓愈 (768–824). *Chu Wen-kung chiao Ch'ang-li Hsien-sheng chi* 朱文公校昌黎先生集, in SPTK.

CTS. *Ch'üan T'ang shih* 全唐詩. 32-chapter edition of 1887.

HCC. Wang Yü-ch'eng 王禹偁 (954–1001). *Hsiao-ch'u chi* 小畜集, in *Basic Sinological Series.*

HCLY. Chiang Shao-yü 江少虞 (c.1131). *Huang-ch'ao lei-yüan* 皇朝類苑, in *Sung-fen-shih ts'ung-k'an* 誦芬室叢刊.

HKCCC. *Hsi-k'un ch'ou-ch'ang chi* 西崑酬唱集, in TSCC.

HYC. P'an Lang 潘閬 (c.1000). *Hsiao-yao chi* 逍遙集, in *Chih-pu-tsu-chai ts'ung-shu* 知不足齋叢書.

JSTC. Juan Chi 阮籍 (210–263). *Juan Ssu-tsung chi* 阮嗣宗集, in *Han Wei Liu-ch'ao chu-chia wen-chi* 漢魏六朝諸家大集.

KSC. Liu Ch'ang 劉敞 (1019–1068). *Kung-shih chi* 公是集, in WYT.

Kung Ming-chih 龔明之. *Chung-wu chi-wen* 中吳紀聞, in *T'ai-ts'ang chiu-chih wu-chung* 太倉舊志五種.

LCHSWC. Wang An-shih 王安石 (1021–1086). *Lin-ch'uan Hsien-sheng wen-chi* 臨川先生文集, in SPTK.

LFWC. Lu Yu 陸游 (1125–1209). *Lu Fang-weng chi* 陸放翁集. Reprinted in *Wan-yu wen-k'u* 萬有文庫, Taipei.

LHCSC. Lin Pu 林逋 (967–1028). *Lin Ho-ching Hsien-sheng shih-chi* 林和靖先生詩集. Edited by Shao P'ei-tzu 邵裴子. 1935.

LTC. Lu T'ung 盧仝 (d. 835). *Lu T'ung chi* 集, in TSCC.

LTPS. Li Po 李白 (701–762). *Fen-lei pu-chu Li T'ai-po shih* 分類補註李太白詩, in SPTK.

MTYSC. Meng Chiao 孟郊 (751–814). *Meng Tung-yeh shih-chi* 孟東野詩集. Edited by Hua Ch'en-chih 華忱之. Peking, 1959.

Nien-p'u. Chang Shih-tseng 張師曾, compiled, Nien-p'u 年譜 of Mei's life, dated 1336. Printed in 1830 edition of Mei's works.

OYWCKC. Ou-yang Hsiu 歐陽修 (1007–1072). *Ou-yang Wen-chung Kung chi* 歐陽文忠公集, in SPTK.

PSCCC. Po Chü-i 白居易 (772–846). *Po-shih ch'ang-ch'ing chi* 白氏長慶集, in SPTK.

SJYH. Wei Ch'ing-chih 魏慶之 (c.1240). *Shih-jen yü-hsieh* 詩人玉屑. Chung-hua shu-chü edition.

SKTP. Huang T'ing-chien 黃庭堅 (1045–1105). *Shan-ku t'i-pa* 山谷題跋, in CTMS.

SMKWC. Ssu-ma Kuang 司馬光 (1019–1086). *Wen-kuo Wen-cheng Ssu-ma Kung wen-chi* 溫國文正司馬公文集, in SPTK.

SS. *Sung shih* 宋史, *Wu-chou t'ung-wen shu-chü* 五洲同文書局. Edition of 1903.

SSCC. Su Shun-ch'in 蘇舜欽 (1008–1048). *Su Shun-ch'in chi* 集. Chung-hua shu-chü edition, 1961.

STLC. Shih Chieh 石介 (1005–1045). *Shih Tsu-lai chi* 石祖徠集, in *Cheng-i-t'ang ch'üan-shu* 正誼堂全書.

STPC. Su Shih 蘇軾 (1037–1101). *Su Tung-p'o chi* 蘇東坡集, in *Basic Sinological Series*.

TCHC. Fang Hui 方回 (1227–1306). *T'ung-chiang hsü-chi* 桐江續集, in *Ssu-k'u ch'üan-shu chen-pen* 四庫全書珍本.

TCYYTH. Hu Tzu 胡仔 (c. 1147). *T'iao-ch'i yü-yin ts'ung-hua* 苕溪漁隱叢話, in TSCC.

TKPS. Tu Fu 杜甫 (712–770). *Fen-men chi-chu Tu Kung-pu shih* 分門 集註杜工部詩, in SPTK.

TLHSC. Shih Chieh. *Tsu-lai Shih Hsien-sheng wen-chi* 祖徠石先生文集. Edition of 1883.

TLSC. Shih Chieh. *Tsu-lai shih-ch'ao* 祖徠詩鈔, in SSC.

TLSH. Yen Yü 嚴羽 (c. 1200). *Ts'ang-lang shih-hua* 滄浪詩話, in LTSH.

TPSH. Su Shih. *Tung-p'o shih-hua* 東坡詩話, in *Shuo-fu* 說郛.

TPTP. Su Shih. *Tung-p'o t'i-pa* 東坡題跋, in CTMS.

TPWCSL. Su Shih. *Ching-chin Tung-p'o wen-chi shih-lüeh* 經進東坡文集事略.

TYMC. T'ao Ch'ien 陶潛 (372–427). *T'ao Yüan-ming chi* 陶淵明集, in SPTK.

Wei Yeh 魏野 (960–1019). *Tung-kuan chi* 東觀集, in *Ch'iao-fan-lou ts'ung-shu* 峭帆樓叢書.

WIHC. Yang I 楊億 (974–1020). *Wu-i hsin-chi* 武夷新集, in *P'u-ch'eng Sung Yüan Ming ju i-shu* 浦城宋元明儒遺書.

WSCC. Wei Ying-wu 韋應物 (736–c. 790). *Wei Su-chou chi* 韋蘇州集. Reprinted in *Wan-yu wen-k'u*, Taipei.

YKLS. Fang Hui. *Ying-k'uei lü-sui* 瀛奎律髓.

YSCCC. Yüan Chen 元稹 (779–831). *Yüan-shih ch'ang-ch'ing chi* 元氏長慶集, in SPTK.

YYYC. Ko Li-fang 葛立方 (d. 1164). *Yün-yü yang-ch'iu* 韻語陽秋, in LTSH.

4 SECONDARY SOURCES IN CHINESE AND JAPANESE

Ch'en Yin-k'o 陳寅恪. *Yüan Po shih chien-cheng kao* 元白詩箋證稿. Reprinted Hong Kong, 1962.

Ch'ien Chung-shu (1). Ch'ien Chung-shu 錢鍾書. *Sung-shih hsüan-chu* 宋詩選註. Peking, 1958.

Ch'ien Chung-shu (2). Ch'ien Chung-shu. *T'an-i lu* 談藝錄. Shanghai, 1948.

Chu Tung-jun (1). Chu Tung-jun 朱東潤. "Shu Fang Hui shih-p'ing" 述方回詩評. *Wen-che chi-k'an* 文哲季刊, Wuhan University 武漢大學, Vol. 2, No. 1 (1931).

Chu Tung-jun (2). Chu Tung-jun. "Ssu-k'ung T'u shih-lun tsung-shu" 司空圖詩論綜述. *Wen-che chi-k'an*, Vol. 3, No. 2 (1934).

Chu Tung-jun (3). Chu Tung-jun. *Lu Yu yen-chiu* 陸游研究. Chung-hua shu-chü, 1961.

Hsia. Hsia Ching-kuan 夏敬觀. *Mei Yao-ch'en shih* 梅堯臣詩. 1940.

Hu Yün-i 胡雲翼. *Sung-shih yen-chiu* 宋詩研究. 1930.

Iritani. Iritani Sensuke 入谷仙介. *Sōshi sen* 宋詩選. Tokyo, 1967.

Kakehi, BGS. Kakehi Fumio 筧文生. "Bai Gyō-shin" 梅堯臣, in *Chūgoku shijin senshū* 中國詩人選集. Tokyo, 1962.

Kakehi, BGSR. Kakehi Fumio. "Bai Gyō-shin ron" 梅堯臣論. *Tōhō Gakuhō* 東方學報, Kyoto, No. 36, 1964.

K'o Tun-po 柯敦伯. *Sung wen-hsüeh shih* 宋文學史. 1934.

Kuo Shao-yü (1). Kuo Shao-yü 郭紹虞, ed. *Sung shih-hua chi-i* 宋詩話輯佚. Harvard-Yenching Monographs, 1937.

Kuo Shao-yü (2). Kuo Shao-yü. *Chung-kuo wen-hsüeh-p'i-p'ing shih* 中國文學批評史. Reprinted by *Hung-chih shu-tien* 宏智書店. Hong Kong, n.d.

Liang K'un 梁崑. *Sung-shih p'ai-pieh lun* 宋詩派別論. 1938.

James T. C. Liu (1). See Western Language Sources.

James T. C. Liu (2). James T. C. Liu 劉子健. "Mei Yao-ch'en *Pi-yün hsia* yü ch'ing-li cheng-cheng-chung ti shih feng" 梅堯臣碧雲騢與慶曆政爭中的士風. *Ta-lu tsa-chih* 大陸雜志, Vol. 17, No. 11 (1958).

SDSNP. *Sōdai shi nempyō* (hokusō) 宋代史年表(北宋). Compiled by the Japanese Committee for the Sung Project 宋史提要編纂協力委員會. Tokyo, 1967.

SJDK. *Sōjin denki sakuin* 宋人傳記索引. Compiled by the Japanese Committee for the Sung Project. Tokyo, 1968.

SJISHP. Ting Ch'uan-ching 丁傳靖, ed. *Sung-jen i-shih hui-pien* 宋人軼事彙編. Reprinted Taipei, 1966.

STCC. *Combined Indices to Forty-seven Collections of Sung Dynasty Biographies* 四十七種宋代傳記綜合引得. Harvard-Yenching Institute.

Suzuki Torao 鈴木虎雄. *Shina shiron shi* 支那詩論史. Tokyo, 1927; reprinted 1967.

Yokoyama (1). Yokoyama Iseo 橫山伊勢雄. "Bai Gyō-shin no shiron" 梅堯臣の詩論. Tōkyō Kyōiku Daigaku Kambun Gakkai 東京教育大學漢文學會, *Kambun gakkai kaihō* 漢文學會會報, No. 24 (1965).

Yokoyama (2). Yokoyama Iseo. "Sō shiron ni miru 'heitan no tai' ni tsuite" 宋詩論にみる平淡の體について. Tōkyō Kyōiku Daigaku Kambun Gakkai, *Kambun gakkai kaihō*, No. 20 (1961).

5 WESTERN LANGUAGE SOURCES

Birch, Cyril, ed. *Anthology of Chinese Literature from Early Times to the Fourteenth Century.* New York, 1965.

Debon, Günther. *Ts'ang-lang's Gespräche über die Dichtung.* Wiesbaden, 1962.

Fang, Achilles, trans. "Rhymeprose on Literature—the Wen-fu of Lu Chi," in John L. Bishop, ed., *Studies in Chinese Literature.* Cambridge, Mass., 1965.

Frodsham, J. D., and **Ch'eng Hsi.** *An Anthology of Chinese Verse—Han Wei Chin and the Northern and Southern Dynasties.* Oxford, 1967.

Graham, A. C. *Poems of the Late T'ang.* Harmondsworth, Penguin Books, 1965.

Karlgren, Bernhard. *The Book of Odes.* Stockholm, 1950.

Kracke (1). E. A. Kracke, Jr. *Civil Service in Early Sung China, 960–1067.* Cambridge, Mass., 1953.

Kracke (2). E. A. Kracke, Jr. "Sung Society: Change Within Tradition." *Far Eastern Quarterly,* Vol. 14, No. 4 (1955).

Liu, James J. Y. *The Poetry of Li Shang-yin.* Chicago, 1969.

James T. C. Liu (1). James T. C. Liu. *Ou-yang Hsiu—An Eleventh Century Neo-Confucianist.* Stanford, 1967.

James T. C. Liu (2). See Secondary Sources in Chinese and Japanese.

Masuda, Norman T. *Poems of Mei Yao-ch'en.* M.A. Thesis, Stanford University, 1966.

Rexroth, Kenneth. *One Hundred Poems From the Chinese.* New York, 1965.

Rudolph, Richard C. "Preliminary Notes on Sung Archaeology." *Journal of Asian Studies,* Vol. 22, No. 2 (February 1963).

Waley, Arthur, trans. *The Analects of Confucius.* Paperback edition. New York, Vintage, n.d.

Waley, Arthur, trans. *The Book of Songs.* Paperback edition. New York, 1960.

Watson (1). Burton Watson, trans. *The Complete Works of Chuang Tzu.* New York, 1968.

Watson (2). Burton Watson. *Chinese Lyricism.* New York, 1970.

Yoshikawa. Kōjirō Yoshikawa, *An Introduction to Sung Poetry.* Trans. by Burton Watson. Cambridge, Mass., 1967.

INDEX

TRANSLATIONS FROM THE ORIENTAL CLASSICS

The Complete Works of Chuang Tzu, tr. Burton Watson   1968

The Romance of the Western Chamber (Hsi Hsiang chi) tr. S. I. Hsiung   1968

The Manyōshū, Nippon Gakujutsu Shinkōkai edition. Paperback text edition.   1969

Records of the Historian: Chapters from the Shih chi of Ssu-ma Ch'ien. Paperback
   text edition, tr. Burton Watson   1969

Cold Mountain: 100 Poems by the T'ang Poet Han-shan, tr. Burton Watson. Also
   in paperback ed.   1970

Twenty Plays of the Nō Theatre, ed. Donald Keene. Also in paperback ed.   1970

Chūshingura: The Treasury of Loyal Retainers, tr. Donald Keene   1971

The Zen Master Hakuin: Selected Writings, tr. Philip B. Yampolsky   1971

Chinese Rhyme-Prose, tr. Burton Watson   1971

Kūkai: Major Works, tr. Yoshito S. Hakeda   1972

*The Old Man Who Does as He Pleases: Selections from the Poetry and Prose of Lu
   Yu*, tr. Burton Watson   1973

The Lion's Roar of Queen Śrīmālā, tr. Alex & Hideko Wayman   1974

*Courtier and Commoner in Ancient China: Selections from the History of The
   Former Han by Pan Ku*, tr. Burton Watson   1974

*Japanese Literature in Chinese. Vol. I: Poetry and Prose in Chinese by Japanese
   Writers of the Early Period*, by Burton Watson   1975

STUDIES IN ORIENTAL CULTURE

COMPANIONS TO
ASIAN STUDIES

INTRODUCTION TO
ORIENTAL
CIVILIZATIONS

Wm. Theodore de Bary, *Editor*

Sources of Japanese Tradition	1958	Paperback ed., 2 vols.	1964
Sources of Indian Tradition	1958	Paperback ed., 2 vols.	1964
Sources of Chinese Tradition	1960	Paperback ed., 2 vols.	1964